The Kitchen in Washington's Headquarters at Morristown, New Jersey.

From a Photograph by Parker, Morristown.

Old Roads from the Heart of New York

Journeys Today by Ways of Yesterday

Within Thirty Miles Around the Battery

By

Sarah Comstock

With 100 Illustrations by the Author and Others

G. P. Putnam's Sons
New York and London
The Knickerbocker Press
1915

The Knickerbocker Press, New York

To

L. S. C.

THE SEARCHLIGHT

PICTURE a searchlight installed at the Battery, revolving, swinging its rays forth from the heart of New York, and flinging them upon historic spots for thirty miles around. Like the circuit of rays from that central light, so ferries and roads, old and new, darted and still dart in all directions.

These chapters have attempted to follow approximately some of the most familiar of the old ferries and roads, although the new courses, for the most part, but roughly correspond to the ways of yesterday. Changes develop in the course of every road. No attempt has been made to trace the old routes of land- and water-travel precisely. But we may follow their general direction, and arrive at the same villages and other historic spots at which they arrived.

To the *New York Times* I am indebted for permission to reprint those chapters which first appeared in that publication, having since been expanded and rearranged. Chapters I, XXII, and XXIII have never before been published.

If I could name all the persons to whom I am

indebted for assistance in collecting material and locating landmarks, my thanks would describe a circle of thirty miles around New York. Among them I wish to acknowledge especial indebtedness to the Rev. Andrew M. Sherman of Morristown; Col. J. C. L. Hamilton of Elmsford; Dr. Frank Bergen Kelley of the City History Club of New York; librarians of the New York City Public Library, Departments of Genealogy, American History, and Maps, and of the Jackson Square Branch; of the New York Society Library and the New York Historical Society; of the New Jersey Historical Society (in Newark) and of the Long Island Historical Society (in Brooklyn); curators of the Staten Island Association of Arts and Sciences; and librarians in the public libraries of Jamaica, Flushing, Elizabeth, Plainfield, Bound Brook, Morristown, Passaic, Paterson, Tarrytown, White Plains, and New Rochelle.

The many reference works used are named in the Bibliography. For much of the study of Long Island, Thompson's history has furnished a basis, as has Clute's for that of Staten Island and Bolton's for that of Westchester County. Lossing's *Pictorial Field-Book of the Revolution* has supplied countless minor details which other volumes omit. The story of André's capture, traced on both sides of the Hudson River, follows in the main the account given by Fiske in his *American Revolution.*[1] Among the books which have been of especial assistance in detailed study where history is either meager or confused, are: *The Greatest Street in the World*, *The Old Boston Post Road*, and *The Story of the Bronx*, by Stephen Jenkins; *Historical Guide to the City of New York*, compiled by Frank Bergen Kelley; *Historic Houses of New Jersey*, by W. Jay Mills; *New York: Old and New*, by Rufus Rockwell Wilson; *Half-Moon Papers*, Second Series; *Israel Putnam*, by William Farrand Livingston; *Memorial History of Staten Island*, by Ira K. Morris; also, *The Country Thirty Miles around the City of New York*, a map by I. H. Eddy, 1828, in the New York City Public Library.

S. C.

NEW YORK, April, 1915.

[1] The extracts on pages 75, 76, and 245–248 are reprinted by permission of Houghton, Mifflin & Co.

CONTENTS

INTRODUCTORY

WESTWARD INTO NEW JERSEY

NORTH—FROM THE SHORES OF THE HUDSON TO LONG ISLAND SOUND AND EAST RIVER

BACK TO THE HEART OF NEW YORK

ITINERARIES

LONG ISLAND

NEW YORK HARBOR AND SANDY HOOK REGION

STATEN ISLAND AND BEYOND

NEW JERSEY

MANHATTAN

ILLUSTRATIONS

Old Roads from the Heart of New York

INTRODUCTORY

CHAPTER I

HOW THE NEW YORKER OF YESTERDAY SET FORTH ON HIS JOURNEY

WHEN the early New Yorker, with a hogshead of molasses for fellow-passenger, entrusted himself to the mercies of a dugout canoe and let the old ferryman transport him all the way to Flushing, he was proving a universal law; namely, that humanity won't stay at home. The dugout was both uncomfortable and dangerous, and the hogshead of molasses could hardly be called companionable; nevertheless the Manhattanite accepted the conditions of travel, for travel he would

Smug in the thought of our Twentieth Century tubes and ferries, our trolleys and subways and express trains and automobiles, we hardly realize how much traveling he did. Manhattan then, as now, was the hub from which darted forth innumerable paths, roads, and waterways.

The small size and unique situation of the island have always led to exploration beyond. Water on all sides—and just beyond the water, piquing the curiosity at every turn, lies enticing land. The first impulse was to investigate.

The Indian trail has been, throughout our country, the beginning of the road. In his turn the Indian often followed the trail of the beast. Such beginnings are indiscernible for the most part, in the dusk of history; but we still trace many an old path that once knew the tread of moccasined feet.

The Indian dweller upon Manhattan Island set forth upon his journey in his simple canoe, dug out from a tree-trunk. Arrived upon the farther shore, he followed a winding path through the wilderness. It yielded to the law of least resistance, and added many miles unto itself by its zigzag course. The white people gradually straightened these paths, so that the present highways form a finished product of which the trail was a rough sketch.

At first the trails around Manhattan were widened to little more than bridle paths, as the New Yorker rarely traveled except on horseback. As travel increased, both for pleasure and commerce, the paths were widened to wagon roads. These, for many years, adhered to the original windings, and showed a submissive habit of turning out to permit a tree to stay where it wished, and of ducking here and there into a gully which was only occasionally filled in with a pile of branches upon which loose earth was thrown. These conditions hardly made for comfortable traveling; nevertheless the New Yorker traveled, even though his vehicle had to be pulled out as often as it became stuck in the mud.

At last, in the early eighteen-hundreds, entered the era of the turnpike, and one such road followed fast upon another, until New York was the center of many roads, leading off from the ferry landings in all directions, themselves intersected by other roads, a mesh of highways all about Manhattan Island. Stages as well as private vehicles carried the traveler in many directions; bridges were built; public ferries grew in number and capacity; the merry journeying went on apace.

Toward the north, means of exit developed as early as the middle of the Seventeenth Century. In *The Story of the Bronx* Stephen Jenkins states that in 1658 the director-general of New Netherland "authorized the maintenance of a ferry with a suitable scow between Harlem and Broncksland. Nothing was done, however, until 1666, when Governor Nicolls granted a charter to the Harlemites, in which, among other things, he allowed them 'a ferry to and from the main which may redound to their particular benefit,' and to construct one or more suitable boats or scows for the transportation of men, horses and cattle at reasonable charges. In January of the following year (1667) the authorities of Harlem, in carrying out the provisions of the charter, determined to establish a good ferry, and that a suitable ordinary, or tavern, should be built for the accommodation of those who used the ferry. Mayor Delaval promised to furnish the nails for the making of a scow, provided their value should be paid to him by the ferryman."

And so a ferry, under the charge of Johannes Verveelen, was established. Previous to this the communication had been by means of canoes and dugouts. The new ferry was a little west of First Avenue as we know it, at East 123d Street. Here Verveelen entered into competition with Nature, who had already made what was called the "wading place"—a natural ford through Spuyten Duyvil Creek. Those of an economical turn of mind still preferred the free ford, and Verveelen was much annoyed at the loss of their fees.

The earliest ferries in the vicinity of New York were maintained in a large dugout called a periauger. These plied the Hudson River as well as the waters toward the northeast. Next came the large scow, that established at the Harlem ferry being an example, capable of transporting wagons and animals.

As travel increased, it was deemed expedient to build a bridge to assist communication with the mainland toward the north. In January,

1693, Frederick Philipse offered to build one at his own expense, since the city authorities had been deterred by the cost. It was built the same year, about where the Broadway bridge of to-day crosses, and was constructed with a draw that boats might pass. Other bridges followed as the years advanced, one at last replacing the old ferry at the eastern end of the river. Roads grew, leading from these bridges into Westchester County, from the Albany Post Road along the Hudson, to the Boston Post Road near the Sound. Indian trails were broadened and new ways were laid out. The Westchester Path was famous among them.

In the other directions the history of exit from Manhattan is much the same story. First the dugout or canoe, followed by a larger ferryboat; at its landing, the trail, developing into the road. Across the East and North rivers, the ferryboat still plies in paths not far from the original. The first public ferry to Long Island, established about the middle of the Seventeenth Century, was a flatboat summoned by the blowing of a horn. The crossing of the rivers was difficult, even dangerous, before the day of the large ferryboat. In his *History of New York City* William M. Stone quotes a letter from Isaac Rushmore of Long Island, an early-day traveler:

"When a boy of fifteen I first visited New

York City, in 1801. Then we crossed from Brooklyn in small sail-boats—two cents ferriage. With ice in the river, it was sometimes extremely perilous. To get a gig across, of course, the wheels must be taken off, and the horse jumped."

The "horse-boats" were an innovation and solved many problems of crossing the East and North rivers, clumsy as they appear to us to-day. The paddle-wheels which propelled them were turned by four horses, which walked around a shaft on board the boat. The fare charged was four cents. Up to 1812, when Fulton revolutionized the water travel, these were "modern" ferryboats. It was in this year that Fulton bridged the North River with his twin steamboats, and soon after the East River was crossed in the same manner. These first boats are described by Cadwallader D. Colden as being two complete hulls united by a deck or bridge, sharp at both ends and so moving either backward or forward with equal ease, and able to retrace their course without turning. The floating or movable dock was instituted, and the method by which boats were brought to them without shock. As James Grant Wilson comments, except in the increased power of its engine the modern ferryboat shows little improvement.

Early in the Eighteenth Century developed the system of "working the roads." According to Jenkins, "The Act of October 30, 1708, establishes not more than six days' work on the roads by the inhabitants each year, or a payment of three shillings for each day neglected." The Provincial Assembly of New York was endeavoring to bind the parts of the Province together and, in turn, bind it close to the other colonies.

But still the roads remained difficult, and it is no wonder that the turnpike era caused a new impetus such as travel had never known hereabouts. The first turnpike road in the United States was laid out in Virginia in 1785. The Lancaster Turnpike followed, and by the early years of the Nineteenth Century, these toll-gate roads were appearing everywhere. Previously, the New Yorker had much preferred travel by water, but now the roads offered comfort for both man and beast. It was to the interest of the private companies who collected the toll to keep them in good condition; no longer did the wagon wait, stuck in a mud-hole, until the mud should dry up and free it.

Everywhere this road system at first met with opposition. Americans claimed that the toll system was un-American. Farmers protested against paying for what had been free to them. Congressman Beeson is said to have made a speech in which he defended the National Pike, ordered laid out in 1806 by Congress, saying that the smithies of the country would ring with the horseshoes it would wear out, and no man need be out of employment, by virtue of the increased demand for horseshoe nails. It did not take the citizens of New York and the surrounding country long to discover that the well-kept road with its toll was economy in the end.

As has been stated, the first road-travel which was not afoot was ahorseback. A pack slung upon his shoulder carried the first pedestrian's merchandise or luggage; the pack-horse soon entered, followed by the cart for heavy freight. The Indian trail broadened to make room for its lumbering and clumsy figure. Post-riders carried the mails. They served as guide to other travelers, who followed them on horseback through devious ways. The famous journal of Madame Sarah Knight describes a trip of this sort, between Boston and New York. She says:

"About four in the morning we set out . . . with a french Doctor in our company. Hee and ye Post put on very furiously, so that I could not keep up with them, only as now and then they'd stop till they see mee."

Madame Knight's trip indicated great "advancement" on her part. Travelers of the gentler sex usually rode seated on a cushion behind the gentleman. Chairs, gigs, and chaises, light vehicles of two wheels, were used on the crude roads in colonial days.

In the Eighteenth Century the stagecoach

developed, and it ruled travel at a later period. In *The Old Boston Post Road*, Jenkins thus describes the early type:

"The stage wagons were boxes mounted on springs, usually containing four seats, which accommodated eleven passengers and the driver. Protection from the weather was furnished by a canvas or leather-covered top with side curtains which were let down in inclement and cold weather. There were no backs to the seats, and the rear seat of all was the one usually preferred on account of the passengers being able to lean against the back of the wagon. If there were women passengers, they were usually allowed to occupy this seat. There were no side entrances to the vehicle, so that any one getting in late had to climb over the passengers who had pre-empted the front seats. Fourteen pounds of baggage were all that were allowed to the passenger to be carried free; all over that had to pay the same price per mile as a traveller. The baggage was placed under the seats, and was generally left unguarded when the stage stopped at taverns for meals or for change of horses. The roads were poor, the stage uncomfortable, and the whole journey was tiring and distressing; but we must remember that the people of those days were accustomed to inconveniences that we would not submit to now, though we have our own troubles in the way of strap-hanging in street cars and crowded conditions in subway and elevated trains."

Private vehicles of many new types appeared upon the better roads of the early Nineteenth Century, in the years of happy reaction after the close of the Revolution. And so, with the great improvement in ferries and other boats, in roads and in vehicles; with the rapid growth and firm prosperity of New York; travel developed, far beyond the bounds of mere necessity, and became a common form of pleasure. To be sure, jaunts that are a mere half-hour's run by train in our day were trips to be planned for then, and to go thirty miles was to make a journey. Nevertheless the New Yorker traveled, and the visitor to New York was a sightseer then as now, not only within the island but over the surrounding country. In *The Picture of New-York; or the Traveller's Guide through the Commercial Metropolis of the United States, by a Gentleman Residing in this City*, a complete guide-book issued in 1807, we find not only directions for tours all over the city itself, but an appendix devoted to "Tours in the Neighborhood of New-York." These are six in number, and extracts from the descriptions are as follows:

"1. To NEW UTRECHT. This is the nearest place for sea-bathing and air. The best road to it is from the village of Brooklyn, through Flatbush. On the road thither, the traveller may note several things connected with the Revolution. [Here the guide describes many relics of Putnam's defense of Brooklyn Heights, most of which have since disappeared.]

"2. TOUR TO ROCKAWAY. The route is from Brooklyn through Jamaica. You may travel thither along the old road, through Bedford, and by the half-way house. But a more agreeable and instructive route is by the new road, over the Wallabogt bridge, through Bushwick and Newtown to Jamaica. The mill-pond over which this bridge passes, belongs to the national navy-yard. The road from Newtown and Flushing is shortened 2 or 2½ miles by it. . . . Newtown is famous for its pippins. . . . Hempstead-plain is a noted resort of plover, and great numbers of these savoury birds are shot every year.

"3. TOUR TO ISLIP. Instead of visiting Rockaway, you may travel strait onward to Hempstead village . . . and eastward . . . to Islip.

"4. TOUR TO PASSAICK FALLS. You are to cross the Hudson from Courtlandt street ferry, and pass over to Powles-hook. You may carry horses and carriages over with you, or you may take seats in one of the ordinary lines of stages as far as Newark. Then you may make such further arrangement as you please, in a village where there is no difficulty in procuring the means of conveyance. But a better method than either, if several are going together, is, to make an agreement with one of the stage-offices in New-York, a day or two before-hand, for a carriage to meet you from Newark, with a single or double team as you may wish it, and to be on the ground at Powles-hook, at the precise day and hour you may name; and for the stipulated price you may agree upon. . . . Some persons who are fond of active exercise, go to Newark on foot, a distance of only eight miles. . . . Formerly the passage from Powles-hook to Bergen was through a slough; but it is now a fine smooth Road. The rivers Hackinsack and Passaick were, until about fifteen years ago, passed in flats at ferries; but since that time, travellers cross them on bridges, for the payment of a toll prescribed by law. . . . Not far above the village [Paterson] is the highly picturesque cataract which the Passaick forms in descending from the top to the bottom of the precipice formed by a chasm between the rocks. There is a great deal of rare and sublime scenery hereabout. On an album at the inn you may write your name and your reflections.

"5. To King's Bridge. This may be performed by proceeding from one of the livery stables or genteel boarding houses in the lower parts of the city.

"6. Trip to Sandy-Hook and the Sea-Bass

BANKS. There are several modes of being conveyed thither. One is, to engage a passage on board the public revenue cutter. Another is, to procure accommodation in one of the pilot boats. But a third, and more easy course is, for a convenient number of gentlemen to charter a suitable coasting vessel or packet, to carry them a short trip to sea, and bring them back again."

It is apparent from this that feminism in 1807 had not advanced to a point which included ladies in pleasure excursions to the "Sea-Bass Banks."

A similar volume, published in 1828 and entitled *The Picture of New-York and Stranger's Guide to the Commercial Metropolis of the United States*, adds to the above tours similar jaunts to Long Branch and Staten Island. It also gives directions for the "Tour around Manhattan Island," by boat, which "may be conveniently made in a few hours," and calls attention to the many reminders of Revolutionary history to be seen on the trip—Fort Washington, Harlem Heights, and so on.

So, as did the traveler of a century ago, let us set out to-day from the heart of New York and read the history written all around us. We shall follow, one by one, those ferries and roads which most nearly correspond to the ferries and roads of other days. Starting toward the east, we can trace the old ways to and upon Long Island; south toward the Highlands, over Staten Island, into New Jersey—moving northward until the Palisades are reached, and Rockland County in New York State—crossing the Hudson, we enter Westchester County, move across it to the shore of the Sound and East River, and find ourselves back on Long Island once more. Thus the circle is complete.

EASTWARD INTO LONG ISLAND

CHAPTER II

THE JAMAICA AND JERICHO TURNPIKE

TURNING toward the east, the early New Yorker began his jaunt by means of a ferry to Brooklyn, or Breuckland—*broken land.* When John Areson was the lessee, the charge of ferriage for a single person was eight stivers in wampum, or a silver two-pence; for each person in company, half that amount; after sunset, double the price; and for each horse or beast, one shilling if alone, and nine pence in company.

Rip Van Dam took a lease of the ferry in 1698, for a period of seven years, to pay 165 pounds a year. During the period of the Revolution, the old ferry was run by Van Winkle and Bukett, who charged for ferriage six pence.

At present let us pass through Brooklyn, for the greatest event in her history calls for a chapter alone—the Battle of Long Island. We will follow the great artery which led directly east into the island.

One hundred and twenty-nine years ago it was declared in a town meeting of Jamaica that "no hogs shall be permitted to roam about the streets." By this act the people of that Long Island village were declaring themselves for civic improvement quite as forcibly as any present-day municipality when it demands improved traffic control and underground trolley wires. The restraint of willful hogs was an advanced thought in that day.

Jamaica was progressive. Along with Brooklyn, it had deplored the conditions of travel on the island, and when, in the early eighteen-hundreds, the turnpike became popular in the United States, the Brooklyn and Jamaica Turnpike Company was formed, and it was only a short time before these toll-gate roads were running out from Jamaica like fingers from a hand. Most famous of all was the Jamaica and Jericho Turnpike, which still leads to the old Quaker settlements.

Jamaica is a town of much historic interest. Its most distinguished building is the former home of Rufus King, or King's Mansion. It faces the highway. Its large grounds are now city property and form a fine shaded park open to the public. Far back from the street the house stands, carefully preserved, and treasuring within its walls many relics—carved furniture of ancient pattern, a quaint marriage chest, and so on. On Mondays between ten and four o'clock this museum is open.

This dignified building was erected in 1750, although it was not until 1805 that it won the distinction of being King's country seat. It was then that he had finished his arduous duties as Minister to the Court of St. James, the appointment made by Washington and endorsed by Adams and Jefferson. As Harvard student, as lawyer, as aide-de-camp to Glover in the Revolution, as delegate to the Continental Congress, and as Minister to England, he had won a series of distinctions, and whoever visits this peaceful home in Jamaica can realize what a rest it must have meant to settle down here after the strenuous career which he had followed.

Thompson says of him: "Mr. King's manner in the Senate was highly dignified, and in private life, that of a polished gentleman. His speeches, in manner and weight, gave him an exalted rank. Among his superior advantages, was an accurate knowledge of dates and facts, of most essential service in the Senate. His two finest speeches are said to have been, on the burning of Washington by the British, and on the exclusion of Mr. Gallatin from the Senate, for the reason that he had not been a citizen of the United States long enough to entitle him to a seat there."

Continuing along Fulton Street, the introduction to the old turnpike, you come to several interesting buildings reminiscent of early-day Long Island. Grace Episcopal Church, east of Church Street, is the descendant of the early Episcopal Church which the English settlers established, and it still possesses the communion service sent from England in 1702 by the Society for the Propagation of the Gospel in Foreign Lands.

On Fulton Street, too, is the Presbyterian Church, standing close to the original site. As that happened to be exactly in the middle of the street, it was found convenient to set the later building a trifle farther back. A small warfare took place here in the early Eighteenth Century: the Episcopal rector, Mr. Bartow, under the endorsement of Lord Cornbury, seized the Presbyterians' building and held services there, claiming the right of the Church of England. It was many years before a happy settlement of the difficulty was made. Even the old Burying Ground, over in the South Quarter of the town, was drawn into the unfortunate wrangle.

On the west side of Union Hall Street is the old Union Hall Academy, whose charter was signed in 1792 by Governor Clinton at the request of fifty individuals, including Eliphalet Wickes. It was the third academic building on Long Island, or rather, the original was, for the

Cannon at Hollis, near the Spot where Woodhull was Captured.

A Tablet on the School Building at Hollis, Placed by Sons of the American Revolution in Honor of Woodhull.

King's Park, Jamaica, once the Grounds of Rufus King.

building standing now was erected in 1820, to give scope for the growth of the school. The schools which preceded it were those of East Hampton and Flatbush.

The Jameco Indians, a group living near the site of the town, gave rise to the name which was finally adopted as permanent—or so it is supposed, although the origin of the word has been questioned. The Dutch settlers had previously called the place "Rusdorp." A clause in the confirmatory deed, which was afterwards obtained from the Rockaway tribe of Indians, read:

"One thing to be remembered, that noe person is to cut downe any tall trees wherein Eagles doe build theire nests."

Jamaica came to be the seat of justice for the north riding of Yorkshire, at its organization in 1665. This headquarters was not changed until 1788, when the courthouse was erected on Hempstead Plains.

Interesting town records, dating back almost to the middle of the Seventeenth Century, are preserved in Jamaica. Thompson gives an account of the arrangement made at a town meeting in the summer of 1660, that the inhabitants should mow the common meadows by squadrons, an agreement being made that lots be cast for the south meadows, "for which purpose the meadows were divided into four parts, the inhabitants into four squadrons."

Items which he quotes from other records are as follows:

April 30, 1661. "Voted to hire a person to keep the towne's cowes and calves for the year, and also to pay Mr. Coe £11.17*s.* in good passable wampum out of money lent to the towne by Nicholas Tanner."

May 12, 1661. "Whereas the towne are informed off one y[t] milkt other ffolke cowes, being catcht by some off the town, they have chosen William ffoster to prosecute y[e] cause to y[e] uttermost, either here or at the Manhattans, and the towne will satisfie him ffor what charge he shall be at about y[e] business."

January 30, 1662. "The town doe promis to give Abraham Smith 30 *s.* ffor beating y[e] drum a year."

Hollis is about a mile east of Jamaica. Here the Woodhull tradition centers. You will find, still standing, the tavern erected in 1710 and practically unchanged to-day, where General Nathaniel Woodhull was captured by the British. "Goetz's" is the name by which you may know it; Increase Carpenter owned it during the Revolution.

In August, 1776, Woodhull, having sent his men on to a point four miles east of Jamaica, set out to follow them. A storm overtook him; he sought refuge in this inn, and here the enemy surprised him and his capture ensued.

A detachment of the 17th Regiment of British dragoons and the 71st Regiment of infantry composed the party, under the guidance of certain inhabitants who had become disaffected.

Woodhull, realizing that he was discovered, immediately gave up his sword in token of surrender, but this was not enough to satisfy the officer who approached him. This is said to have been Major Baird, of the 71st Regiment. "Say, 'God save the King!' " he commanded. "God save us all," replied the American general. The British officer, enraged, fell upon Woodhull with his broadsword, and nothing saved his life at the time but the charitable interference of another officer, said to have been Major De Lancey. As it was, Woodhull sustained severe wounds in the head, and the mangling of one arm caused, finally, his death.

The British, resigning the purpose of compelling him to say "God save the King!", now carried him to Jamaica where they had his wounds dressed. The next day he was taken, along with some eighty other prisoners, to Gravesend, where he was confined on board a vessel. This vessel was not adapted for passengers; it had been used merely for the purpose of transporting live stock for the army, and the unsanitary conditions aboard it were of the worst. The suffering of the wounded general grew so serious that an officer, observing his condition, remonstrated with those in charge of the affair, and the upshot was that Woodhull was released, taken to a house in New Utrecht, and there attended by a physician.

But the case had advanced too far, and it was found necessary to amputate the injured arm. The General sent for his wife and requested that she bring with her all the money in her possession. When she arrived with it, he ordered that it be distributed among the American prisoners. The operation was then performed, but death followed, on the twentieth of September. His wife took the body seventy miles, to the Long Island farm which had been the family home.

Thompson quotes a remarkable ballad on this theme, for a copy of which he acknowledges indebtedness to Philip J. Forbes of the New York City Library. Some of its score or more of stanzas run in this wise:

Stay! Traveller, stay! And hear me tell
  A gallant soldier's fate!
'Twas on this spot brave Woodhull fell!
  Sad story to relate!

Full twenty foes about his head
  Their glittering sabres flung,
And down, on his uplifted blade,
  Swift blows descending rung!

"Who will not say 'God save the King,'
  No mercy here shall find;
These are the terms from George we bring;
  Art thou to these inclin'd?"

"I freely say '*God save us all,*'
  Those words include your King;
If more ye ask, then must I fall,
  Naught else from me ye'll wring."

Yet still he held his trusty sword
  Uprais'd above his head,
And feebly strove his life to guard
  While he profusely bled!

A more heroic, gallant end,
  No age nor clime can boast;
Yet history ne'er the tale hath penn'd,
  And but for me 'twere lost!

It is not probable that "full twenty foes" did thus fall upon the General, but his "heroic, gallant end" is to be remembered. It is commemorated on the grounds of a public school near the tavern, where stands a cannon, a monument to Woodhull. On the school building is a tablet "in memory of General Nathaniel Woodhull, President of the Provincial Congress of New York in 1775 . . . citizen, soldier, patriot of the Revolution."

Before setting out on the long road to Jericho, a side-trip, leading into the old Hempstead

Turnpike, carries you past highly developed land, spacious country residences, and hosts of modern bungalows—through a region where the real-estate agent thrives like a green bay tree and the hum of the automobile is abroad in the land—straight to a peaceful old building untouched by modernness. It is St. George's Church, that historic Hempstead house of worship whose communion service was presented by Queen Anne two centuries ago.

The building first erected here was demolished, but the site is the same. The gravestones in the green churchyard are, many of them, as quaint as those found in the Sleepy Hollow Cemetery and others of that period. Queer little distorted angels hover at their tops, and the long "s" is in evidence. Many distinguished names are to be found here, among them several of the Seaburys, the Reverend Samuel, for one, long rector of this parish. The inscription reads, "Here lieth Interr'd The Body of the Revd Samuel Seabury, A.M., Rector of the Parish of Hempstead, who with the greatest Diligence and most indefatigable Labor for 13 years at New London and 21 years in this Parish, Having Discharged every Duty of his Sacred Function Died the 15th of June An. Dom. 1764."

A near-by stone bears the name of Captain David Seabury, and the date 1750.

The town of Hempstead was settled by a group

of English from Wethersfield and Stamford, some of whom are supposed to have been natives of Hemel Hempstead, near London. It is not known why they chose to leave New England and emigrate to Long Island soil; but in 1643 they sent a committee to blaze a trail for the little colony, and purchase land from the Indians. The group followed the next spring, crossing the Sound and landing at Hempstead Harbor. They immediately began their settlement, where the town arose later, and obtained their patent or ground-brief from Kieft.

These Puritans, religious and sober-minded though they were, nevertheless permitted the sale of intoxicating liquors within their boundaries. They issued licenses for the same, ordaining that one-half of the money received from the unlicensed sale of beer, wine, or strong liquors, should be used to pay the public expenses, and the other half devoted to the education of poor children. An item in the town records of 1659 indicates, however, that trouble ensued:

"Whereas there hath formerly an ordre been made agst the Sinn of drunkennesse, and that wee finde by daylie Experience, that itt is practised in this place to ye dishonnor of God, and therefor wee doe Againe reniue ye same, and doe ordre that Any that have formerly or shall hereafter transgress shall pay for ye first fault

10 guilders, for the second 20 guilders and for the third to stand to the determinacion of ye court according to ye first ordre."

To reach the Jericho Turnpike again, you may go by way of Mineola. From this town the distance is a matter of some half-dozen miles to the old terminus of the road. The trolley line deviates a trifle from this route, going as far as Hicksville.

As you push on, you are in the midst of old Quaker associations. The land on which Jericho stands was a part of the purchase made by Robert Williams in 1650, and settled not long after by a colony of Quaker families. They built their little meeting-house in 1689, and in it the great leader, Elias Hicks, officiated from time to time.

On the trolley route between Mineola and Hicksville, the traveler passes the town of Westbury. North of this lies old Westbury, the village which was built by farming Friends. It is a short detour from the turnpike.

"Wallage" was the Indian name for this spot, and it was a center for many a thrifty family who found the soil of Long Island to their liking. The Friends established two meeting-houses here, and the old cemetery with its half-forgotten graves is to be seen in the midst of this green sweep of fine land.

In Jericho did Elias Hicks find the Quaker

St. George's Church, Hempstead, One of the Earliest Parishes on Long Island.

The Mansion once Belonging to Rufus King, Jamaica.

The Tavern at Hollis, in which Woodhull was Captured.

maiden who became his wife. Although he was born in Hempstead, it is Jericho which is most strongly associated with his remarkable life, for here he made his home for all the years after his marriage in 1771. It was the headquarters from which he started on his preaching tours, covering more than ten thousand miles on foot during the years when he traveled through the United States from Maine to Ohio, and through much of Canada, teaching the Gospel.

One thousand times Hicks spoke in public, never accepting a cent for his labors in the service of God, and subsisting by the products of his little Long Island farm. He was one of the most forceful, and one of the earliest, Abolitionists, and he waged war in his sermons against negro slavery, being the power behind the Act of 1827, which freed all the slaves in New York State. For him Hicksville was named, and from his teaching sprang the Hicksites, now one of the two great divisions of the Friends' Church.

So popular did the Jericho Turnpike become that it was not long before an extension was built to Smithtown. Until the turnpike era, Long Island had been backward in road development. This was partly the result of mail conditions. When the mail-carrier service had been first introduced, there was a generally awakened interest in the improvement of public roads; Franklin, as Postmaster-General, had established the service. But the Long Islanders apparently were not letter-writers, the mail deliveries were a week, or even a fortnight apart, and before the Revolution the service was withdrawn. Once more the "better roads" enthusiasm slumbered. Furman speaks of "a respectable old Scotchman named Dunbar" who "was in the habit of riding a voluntary post between the city of New York and Babylon, thence east, and to Brookhaven." But until almost the Nineteenth Century Long Island had not a single post office.

Furman describes an early-day stage trip from Brooklyn to Hempstead and Babylon. It was customary, he says, for the regular mail stage to leave the former town once a week, at about nine o'clock on Thursday morning—"they were not, however, particular as to a half-hour." This stage was at one time the only conveyance travelers could have through the Island, unless they took a private carriage. At Hempstead they dined; at Babylon they supped, and put up for the night. "No one was in haste to get to his journey's end, and if he was, and intended going the whole route, he soon became effectually cured of it."

At times the traveler would descend from the vehicle to observe the bright waters or the fine vegetation. "After walking for some two or three miles upon the green sward at the edge of the road, gathering and eating the berries as you strolled along, until you were tired, you would find the stage a short distance behind you, the driver very complaisant, for you have much eased his horses in their journey thro' the heavy sand."

The second night of the journey was spent "at a place called Quagg, or Quogue." Next morning breakfast was had at Southampton, later on the "Shinecoc" Hills were passed, Sag Harbor offered dinner, and Saturday evening found the weary traveler at Easthampton.

The mail was delivered on this journey somewhat as the rural carriers of to-day deliver it. If a town did not lie on the post route (sometimes one was as much as a mile away), the carrier would leave letters in a box fastened to a tree, or on a rock specified for the purpose.

For the traveler who attempted to make his way into the island without depending on the stage driver's knowledge, dire results were liable to ensue, as Prime sets forth in his account of the difficulties of Long Island roads. The three principal roads, distinguished as the North, Middle, and South, were intersected by many little roads and wood-paths which confused the stranger hopelessly. They were so worn by constant carting that they "not unfrequently appear the most direct and most used, . . . the stranger is constantly liable to go astray; and that too, where he might remain a whole day, without meeting a person to set him right."

CHAPTER III

TO ASTORIA AND FLUSHING

ANOTHER early road from Jamaica led to Flushing, that stronghold of the Quakers. In fact, for many years after the establishment of the latter town, there was no way to reach it from New York except by way of Brooklyn and Jamaica. Forests, brooks, and swamps cut off the approach from other directions. Thompson relates the story of a man who lived near the head of the bay, where he kept a country store, and, desirous of increasing his income, added three or four passengers to the hogshead of molasses which he was in the habit of carrying across in his Indian canoe. This, however, could hardly be called systematic transportation, as both molasses and passengers could make their trip only in fair weather.

The Flushing Bridge and Road Company, incorporated in 1802, improved the road from Brooklyn, shortening it by about four miles.

As ferries and roads developed, there came to be another way of reaching Flushing from New

York. This was by a more northern course. It cannot be exactly followed to-day, owing to the shiftings of land and watercourses; but it is approximated by starting from the foot of East Ninety-second Street, where the present Astoria ferry plies. The New Yorker of yesterday betook himself to the foot of East Eighty-sixth Street, where the East River Park was laid out later, including the point known as Harris Hook. There the ferryboat awaited him.

Even in the Twentieth Century there is a spirit of quaintness about this uptown ferry, so much used, and yet so unknown to many residents of Manhattan. A venerable ticket-seller counts your pennies while his great gray cat checks them off with shrewd and unwinking golden eyes. Such a ticket-seller, such a cat, seem to belong to a generation that is past.

On a map now more than half a century old one may see, jutting out from the east shore of the East River, that same squarish bump of land which is known to-day as Astoria—a promontory which seems a clumsy excrescence on a smooth shore. One may read "Hell Gate" in the water beside it; to the south is Blackwell's Island, just as now, but to the north, that great block of land on which the walls of the Inebriate Asylum and the Emigrant Hospital rise, is found marked as "Great Barn Island."

About the period of the map which I have in mind, the Ravenswood region which lay near Astoria and toward Hunter's Point was connected with New York City by a system of stages. They ran by way of Astoria and the ferry at Eighty-sixth Street, to the end of the Bowery far below. This route is fairly covered by a modern boat and an electric elevated railway to-day; yesterday, by a boat of ancient pattern and a stage drawn by horses.

As you make the crossing now, you pass from the crowded shore of Manhattan to what appears an equally crowded shore on the other side. The vivid green of the park, and of the islands to your north and your south, makes bright blotches of color in the midst of drab masses of manufacturing. A brief voyage, and you arrive at Astoria: a part of greater New York, a large, busy, crowded town, and yet a place never seen by many Manhattanites.

The northern corner of this promontory is called Hallett's Point, which name, along with that of Hallett's Cove, came from William Hallett, who emigrated to this place from Dorsetshire as early as 1652. A grant from Stuyvesant and a purchase from the Indians gave him all the land which is now covered by Astoria, and he may justly be regarded as the pioneer of this point.

It was in 1839 that the region of Hallett's

Cove was made an incorporated village, and something like a boom occurred. A female seminary was started, and John Jacob Astor, being interested in the place, promised to contribute largely to its support. The name "Astoria" was given to the new village, the ferry to Eighty-sixth Street was established, and the growth was rapid.

As you glance along the picturesque shore of this irregular portion of the East River, you can readily realize why it was a fashionable suburban district three-quarters of a century ago. The broken lines of water and land, the green islands, the heights, were quite sufficient to lure the builder of a countryseat. General Ebenezer Stevens built himself a summer home facing the bay opposite the upper end of Blackwell's Island, and there commanded a fine view of land and water from his height. Other wealthy men followed his example, and the locality soon came to be reckoned "elegant."

On the same old map one can trace a fine line leading from the shore of the Astoria promontory, running back into Long Island, moving almost due east, and bearing the mark "Toll Gate." Here ran one of the old roads which found its way eventually to Flushing. Beyond Flushing it was extended, continued eastward until it brought up at last in one of the north shore's numerous bays.

St. George's Church—the New Building—Flushing.

The Bowlder Marking the Spot where George Fox Preached.

A Fine Type of Well-Preserved Old Building, once the Flushing Institute.

A trolley running from the Astoria ferry follows a similar direction. It passes through the town of Astoria, on to Woodside, thence straight into the center of Flushing, after skirting Flushing Bay with its merry showing of summer vacation boats. This town was one of the earliest settlements on Long Island.

St. George's Church stands on Main Street. The building which rises before you, large and prosperous, is the modern house of worship erected by the old parish; but back of it, just beyond the group of old gravestones, stands the original church, gray and weather-beaten, clad in its stout shingles of early date. This building is carefully preserved at the rear of the church property, and is used as a Sunday-school room.

The first establishment of the Church of England in this vicinity placed the triplet towns, Flushing, Newtown, and Jamaica, under one clergyman's care. One of the early preachers, who held services once a month in the Flushing Guard House, wrote of the town that "most of the inhabitants thereof are Quakers, who rove through the country from one village to another, talk blasphemy, corrupt the youth, and do much mischief." Others, however, were of another mind as regards these thrifty settlers.

St. George's parish still preserves two manuscript sermons of the Reverend Thomas Poyer, that brave clergyman who lived through such grievous struggles with the Nonconformists. He had a tragic experience of American life. It was in December, 1710, that he came from Wales; he traveled for three months, crossing the Atlantic, and when he reached the coast of Long Island, only a hundred miles from his destination he was shipwrecked.

The poor man was rescued only to plunge into more trouble. He entered upon his work, and soon found himself the object of the villagers' persecutions. The shopkeepers would not sell him provisions, and he feared starvation; the miller would not grind his corn, and advised him to eat it whole, "as do the hogs." For more than twenty years he fought his battle, at last asking to be relieved of the labor; but the same year he was stricken with smallpox, and died.

The charter of this famous old church was dated June 17, 1761, which was the first year of the reign of George the Third. But a few blocks away, beyond the park, near where the public playground has been laid out, is another famous old church. This is the meeting-house of the Religious Society of Friends erected in 1694. You read, "Meetings for Worship First Days at 11 A.M. All welcome. First Day School at 10 A.M."

This is the house of worship erected by some of the earliest and most courageous settlers of the Island, and we have but to look at its sturdy old walls to conjure up a picture of the Friends of long ago wending their way along green lanes and across footpaths through the fields, all gathering here for worship.

Some of the first Quakers in Flushing came from Gravesend, where they had settled, but, persecuted by Governor Stuyvesant, they moved to a point where they thought they could have more freedom. A familiar name among the worshipers in this church was that of John Bowne.

It is in the Bowne house that you will find the most remarkable glimpses of long ago still cherished in this vicinity. But a short distance back from the meeting-house, on Bowne Avenue, it stands, surrounded by a large yard, and fairly smothered by trees and vines. It looks as homelike a spot to-day as it must have looked in struggling early days to George Fox, when he sought rest within its walls.

It was in 1672 that this preacher came to Flushing from Oyster Bay, a journey which he bravely faced in spite of the difficulties of travel. Neither miles nor hardships nor persecution daunted the valiant Fox.

John Bowne offered his house as headquarters, and the Friends assembled from far and near to hear the great speaker. "We had a very large meeting," he wrote with pardonable satisfaction, "many hundreds of people being there, some coming thirty miles. A glorious and heavenly meeting it was (praised be the Lord God!), and the people were much satisfied."

Step across the street for a moment and see the spot where he stood to address this "glorious and heavenly meeting." A large bowlder marks it now; formerly the visitor could see the oaks themselves, long known as the "Fox Oaks," under which he stood. Gabriel Furman visited the spot in 1825 and measured the trees, finding one of the splendid trunks to be thirteen feet in circumference, the other twelve feet four inches. They have long since fallen, one in 1841, the other in 1863, having lived, it is supposed, to be as much as four hundred years old.

Back in the Bowne house, you will be shown the couch on which Fox reposed when he had finished his labor. It is only one of many hoarded relics. The rooms are filled with old pieces of furniture, samplers, pictures, countless other reminders of past Quaker days. The building is kept open for the benefit of the public.

In the library you may see the secret spot where the family silver was hidden during the war. Toy cribs, a good type of spinning wheel, and a bookcase constructed in the house, are

The Friends' Meeting-House in Flushing, Erected in 1694.

The Old Home of the Prince Family, Flushing. The Grounds were once Included in the Linnæan Botanical Gardens, the First Nursery in America.

The Great Horse-Chestnut Tree at the Head of Fox Lane, beside the Bowne House, Flushing.

on display here. The samplers are of interest. One is signed "Eliza Bowne, Nine Partners Boarding School, 1800, Aged 12 years," and runs:

> Blest solitude, how sweet thy peaceful scenes!
>   Where contemplation's vot'ries love to stray;
> Where in her sapient dress religion reigns,
>   And shines more splendid than the noontide ray.

And farther on, in one of the bedrooms, to offset the solemnity of this sampler, one may read:

(Sir R. Peel)—"I am afraid, Mrs. Fry, there is too much Sugar in the Brandy."

(Elizabeth Fry)—"Thou must take it *in the spirit* in which it is given."

With "in the spirit" carefully italicized, lest the sober Quaker mind miss the point of Elizabeth Fry's demure jest.

There are, among the treasures, a rope bed, a Grannie Grace chair, a portrait of Fox, and an oak table put together with wooden pins—the last-named as old as the house itself, and formerly used at the yearly meetings held there. For a long time this was the chief meeting place of many Friends, and the old oven used to open like a giant mouth to receive the hordes of loaves which were fed into it for these conferences. Logs dragged by chains were brought in to keep up the roaring fire. Thirty or forty loaves were a mere bagatelle for the Bowne kitchen to produce. Under the stairs the logs were stored, ready for the strenuous baking days.

Preserved in one of the rooms is the gallant staff of Thomas Bowne, *émigré* 1649, with which he is said to have killed a bear.

Close to the house, at the head of Fox Lane, stands a handsome old horse-chestnut tree, characteristic of Flushing. The town is famous for its very large, very well-preserved, and very varied trees, and thereby hangs a tale. In 1732 William Prince established the Linnæan Botanic Garden, the first "modern" nursery of America, making himself thus the pioneer nurseryman of his country.

Not only did his own work, carried on under the Linnæan system, thrive marvelously, but others took it up, making Flushing the most famous town in America for the raising of trees, shrubs, and flowers. At the time of the Revolution the Prince garden was so wonderful that General Howe was moved to place a guard at either end when the British troops entered the town, that no depredations might be committed. During the war three thousand cherry trees were cut down for hoop poles because they could not be sold; this gives some idea of the extent of the nurseries. William IV. of England, then

Prince William, visited the town to see the Linnæan Garden in 1782.

William Prince has long since gone, but the old Prince home is to be seen now at No. 20 Broadway, and in the yard is still standing one of the cedars of Lebanon, several of which in old days graced the lawn.

On Main Street, not far from the railroad station, stands a large colonial building with a broad lawn before it. This was once the Flushing Institute, established in 1827, and directed by the Reverend Dr. William Augustus Muhlenburgh.

The "Hotine House," as it is familiarly known, at 189 Broadway, is a representative of early days, dating back before the Revolution, although much altered in outward appearance. Although local tradition has occasionally labeled it "Washington's Headquarters" and "Howe's Headquarters," it is doubtful whether any Revolutionary history of importance attaches to it—although the secret closet hidden within its walls is mysterious enough to lend credence to many tales. The house was erected sometime before the Revolution by Mr. Aspinwall, has passed through several hands, and is now owned by Dr. Bloodgood.

The history of the town of Flushing is difficult to trace in many details, because of the lamentable fact that its records, long ago kept in the house of John Vanderbilt, the town clerk, were burnt along with the house at the end of the Eighteenth Century by two slaves, Sarah and Nelly. The culprits were hanged in 1790, Aaron Burr being the prosecuting attorney, but this satisfaction of a primitive public vengeance did not restore the missing links of history.

The names of the town's pioneers are therefore buried forever. But it is known that a group of English, who had lived for a time in Holland, were probably the first settlers here. It is supposed that they were induced to emigrate to this region by agents of the province of New Netherlands. The civil and religious privileges of a new country were the chief inducement held out to them.

These planters had been kindly treated by a Holland community, and in gratitude for this recollection they gave their new town that other town's name—Vlishing, or Vlissengen. It was in the spring of 1645 that they arrived here; they obtained a patent or ground-brief from Kieft, and the place grew rapidly. The soil was phenomenally good, which accounts for the later development of the nurseries, although, as Thompson comments, it leaves us at a loss to know why the Dutch had not already seized upon so fertile a spot.

In very early days the public business of the town was mostly transacted in a building called

St. George's Church—the Old Building—Flushing, in which the Manuscript Sermons of the Rev. Thos. Poyer are Preserved.

A Corner of the Bowne House, Flushing.

The Bergen Homestead.

The Old Lefferts Homestead in Flatbush.

the Block House, which stood near the site of the town pond. Pond and Block House have both vanished. Here were kept the town records, where arms and ammunition were stored.

The illiberal methods of the powers that were, aroused much hard feeling among the settlers, and a state of friction arose, sometimes culminating in overt insubordination. A glimpse of this spirit is caught in a public record of 1648:

"Thomas Hall, an inhabitant of fflishingen, in New Netherlands, being accused that he prevented the sheriff of fflishengen to doe his duty, and execute his office, in apprehending Thomas Heyes, which Thomas Hall confesseth, *that he kept the door shut*, so that noe one might assist the sheriff, demands mercy, and promises *he will do it never again*, and regrets very much that he did so. The director and council doing justice condemn the said Thomas in a fine of 25 guilders, to be applied at the discretion of the council."

CHAPTER IV

DUTCH HOMESTEADS ON THE WAY TO FLATLANDS

TAP at an ancient Dutch door with its brass knocker, and the upper half will open cautiously until you, as a stranger, are appraised. If you are favored, the lower half will open and let you in.

And this depends upon your own powers of imagination. If you see before you merely a dilapidated building, then you may as well take your leave at once. But if the very rat-tat of the old knocker conjures up before you a buxom, brass-polishing Dutch matron; if the sight of twenty small panes in a window suggests to you a rosy, cap-framed Dutch face peeping forth; if you see at once a picture of sand-strewn floors and shining pewter and corded bedsteads and hairy trunks and hand-spun linen and knit worsted stockings and Bibles dangling at round belts—then the door of the past swings wide to you, and you are admitted to the Dutch days on old Long Island.

Over the yellowed surface of an old map one may trace a road which led from Brooklyn somewhat east of south, toward the beach. It passed through Flatbush and Flatlands; just below the latter it forked, and several tines of the fork all pointed toward Jamaica Bay. Along this road the old map indicates homesteads; the names "J. Lefferts," "J. Cortelyou," "G. Vandeveers," and "J. Johnson," are among the sturdy list.

In this direction the early Holland residents took up land and built themselves farmhouses. Here they planted, cultivated, prospered. They built substantially, according to the custom of their time, and many of their houses stand to-day almost as they were in days before the Revolution shook our country. Their churches, too, are standing; and in their quiet yards many of these old settlers lie sleeping.

To-day a trolley line carries the traveler along a road which, in the main, follows the direction of that of the yellowed map. Back in the Seventeenth Century, the roads on Long Island were little more than bridle paths, and the ladies who traveled over them usually rode horseback. A cushion was placed behind the saddle of the gentleman, and thereon the lady was mounted for her ride.

The lumber wagon and the sleigh, which ran upon split saplings, were the earliest vehicles used by the Dutch on Long Island. Previous to the Revolution, the one-horse chaise, mounted upon its two wheels, came into fashion, and in this the prosperous Long Islander made his jaunts.

The Dutch homes hereabouts were mostly built of wood. Now and then a dwelling of brick or stone arose. The houses were constructed with an overshot roof which formed a piazza by its projection from the front of the house; occasionally the roof was overshot at both front and rear. The houses had one low story, above which heavy oak beams formed a basis for the attic floor. These beams above the unceiled rooms are still to be seen in the best preserved dwellings.

The familiar pair of chimneys, one at each end of the house, rose from a pair of huge fireplaces. They were made so wide that the entire family—by no means small in number—could gather about the fire. Some of the fireplaces, in the better houses, were adorned with Dutch scriptural tiles of Delft blue and white. In the great chimneys, meat was hung to be roasted or cured.

The main room of the house, the "best room," was used as a dining-room on great occasions, although the enormous bedstead was the principal piece of furniture there displayed. The two feather-beds, one to rest under, one over the victim, were always in evidence.

Flatbush Avenue carries you along the path of this early Dutch life. As you pass beyond the closely-built business district of Brooklyn you will catch glimpses here and there of early types of houses, more or less altered. At last, on the left, you come upon a fine old specimen—gray, well-ordered, shaded by large trees, and surrounded by a broad lawn. Its roof has a curving sweep; at each end rises a chimney, and the low porch extends under the old overshot roof.

This, No. 563 Flatbush Avenue, is the Lefferts homestead of pre-Revolutionary period —or rather, the original house was built before the war, burned during its storm and stress, and rebuilt, on the same spot, of the same model, soon afterwards. Pieter Lefferts, that esteemed settler, was the inhabitant then, and the house has remained in the family ever since.

There is a tradition to the effect that the large barn standing behind the dwelling used to harbor slaves in slavery days.

The small eagle now to be seen above the front door is a treasured heirloom. The broad hall and spindle balusters are unchanged. A story pertaining to the modern history of the house is that a moving-picture company, aware of the building's perfection of type, decided to make a bold dash and invade it in the owner's absence. A young woman was alone there, a caretaker; when the company arrived, hoop skirts, soldierly uniforms and all, prepared to seize upon the great hall and staircase for the delightful background which they afforded, the young woman stood her ground as if she were resisting a British invasion—ghosts of the Revolution returned to invade the old residence—and the "movey" heroes and heroines retired in confusion, routed.

A short walk along the avenue from this spot brings you to that church which is the lineal descendant of the one built by the first Dutch settlers of Flatbush. The first was erected upon this site by order of Governor Peter Stuyvesant in 1654, and three churches have occupied the ground. The second was built in 1698 and the present in 1796. Its tablet states that "the emblem of the Reformed Dutch Church of America consists of the Coat of Arms of William of Orange combined with the ecclesiastical symbols, the pillars and stars."

It is recorded in early annals that the minister became inattentive to his calling, and complaint was made by the people. He was holding services but once in a fortnight, they claimed, and even then for only fifteen minutes, merely reading a prayer instead of a sermon. Great

Church of the Early Dutch Settlers in Flatbush.

Old Well, Philipse Manor.

Erasmus Hall High School To-day, Built about the Old Erasmus Hall Academy. The Original School Founded in 1787.

was the offense felt by these pious settlers. The Governor listened to the complaint and issued orders to the minister that he "should attend more diligently to his work.'

Behind the building, which replaces the ancient wooden one, you will find many crumbling old red stones of that period, half-hidden among the more pretentious gray and white monuments of recent years. The names are spelled in old lettering, and the inscriptions are in the language of the settlers. Partly obliterated, such words as "Vrou", and "Hier licht begraven," catch the eye. Several members of the Lefferts family are buried here; "Sarah Van Der Bilt," "Rem Vanderbelt," are found. One stone is "in memory of Phebe Voorhees, the affectionate wife of Peter I. Cortelyou," and her epitaph can be traced:

> Here lies a friend bereaved of life,
> A pious mother, a loving wife.

Across the street from this church, Erasmus Hall High School proudly rises, not in the least suggesting the modest Erasmus Hall Academy which was its forebear. A part of its walls is of the old building, but that is hidden in the new. This was one of those early educational institutions which distinguished Long Island. It was established in 1787, and one of its earliest principals was John Henry Livingston, the first theological professor whom the Dutch Reformed Church had in our country.

Continuing along Flatbush Avenue, you will come upon several more old homes, still in fair or even excellent preservation. For one, there is the house at the corner of Avenue J. It stands a bit back from the street, and the country around it is sufficiently open to give a suggestion of the days when this, like the other homesteads, was an isolated farm-house, surrounded by fertile acres which Dutch diligence tilled.

Other homes of this period were: the Henry S. Ditmas house at the corner of Ditmas and Flatbush avenues, known for its fine example of an old Dutch door; the Lott house (there were several Lotts) at 1084 Flatbush Avenue; and the Vanderbilt home at 610, with its Dutch oven in the cellar, now demolished.

Flatbush of now was Midwout, or Middle Woods, in ancient days. The settlement was begun about the middle of the Seventeenth Century, probably in 1651. Even earlier than this, in 1636, was that neighboring settlement started, called by the Dutch New Amersfort, now known as Flatlands. At the time of the latter settlement, there was a tobacco plantation in the town, owned by ex-Governor Van Twiller, which was commonly called Van Twiller's Bowery and was well known long after the hamlet was established.

The boundary lines of these towns are unnoticeable in the merging of modern building, and the road runs imperceptibly from Flatbush on into Flatlands. On your left you will spy a shining white tower, rising as peaked, and as cleanly snowy, as the toy church steeples of your childhood's play. Around it the little pointed lawn is so green, all the paint is so gleaming, that the whole effect suggests something rather unreal, like an imaginary Spotless Town holding aloof from this grimy, dusty, smoky world.

This is the old Reformed Dutch Church of Flatlands, a most picturesque link in this chain of Long Island tradition. It is trim and prim as one of New England's dapper meeting-houses, and the inscriptions on the churchyard stones are delightfully quaint. The church stands on the King's Highway—a road with a history of its own—at the intersection of East Fortieth Street

Here, as in the Flatbush churchyard, the oldest inscriptions are largely in the Dutch language. Some in English, however, appeal to the English-speaking observer.

"Sarah Spong, d. 1830, Aged 81," appears on a stone above the lines:

How lov'd how valu'd once avails the not
To whom related or by whom begot.
A heap of dust alone remains of thee
'Tis all thou art and all the proud shall be.

A gentler reflection on death is embodied in the epitaph of "Wilhelmina, daughter of Nicholas and Alette Schenck, 1816, 21 years."

Here Wilhelmina's ashes lay
The grave receives her precious clay
But angels waft her soul on high
All hail her Savior in the sky.

This church was organized on February 9, 1654, and was a gathering place for Dutch farmers for many miles around.

Near Bergen Beach beyond, where the merry-go-round and the ice-cream-cone vender now flourish, the trail of history is still to be traced. The ancient Schenck house standing near the beach is one of the oldest to be found anywhere about. Several houses of old Dutch architecture still stand. One of them, hardly changed in outer appearance, distinctly of the period of Holland settlers, with sloping low roof, is now equipped with hot and cold running water and all modern improvements which tend to make country life comfortable; thus are the past and present happily wedded!

Most famous of all these old homes is the

Bergen homestead on East Seventy-second Street. The charm of its detached situation, its old trees and gray shingled walls, draws many a visitor. We found the present resident sitting on its broad lawn under the shade of one of its trees.

"What do you know about the place?" we asked him, wondering if traditions hitherto unpublished were stored in his mind.

"That I can't drive a nail nur a screw into these old hand-made shingles," he responded. "I've tried it an' tried it, an' they're hard as bricks. They don't make shingles o' that kind o' wood nowadays! Nur build that way nowadays! That house was built to last, I know that much about it."

He settled down comfortably for a chat. "There isn't much telling just when the beginning of this house was," he went on. "They say that end of it—" pointing to the western portion of the building—"was a kind o' cabin belonging to a hunter in early days—some fellow that hunted and trapped hereabouts, selling skins and making his living that way. That was before farming came to be the business o' this community. Then Bergen came along, they say, and liked the situation, and he bought the land—all this land—" with a vast sweep of the hand, "cabin and all, and since it was a solid enough kind o' building, though small, he built on till there was a good-sized house. It belonged in the Bergen family till maybe twenty years ago."

The accepted date of the homestead is 1655 or 1656, and it is said that in 1791 John Bergen came into possession of this beach, and enlarged the house to meet his growing demands. Some of its treasures, such as the old Dutch knocker, have melted away, but the tiny-paned windows remain, a flawless relic of the old days.

Within sight of this place, only a few minutes' walk beyond, is the noisy whirl of fortune-tellers and peanut venders and wheels that carry shrieking pleasure-seekers into the air. It is a world far removed from the sober round of farm and household toil which the settlers of these parts followed, day in and day out, through their diligent lives. It takes a very austere form of sobriety to settle a raw country. The American of to-day has leisure and nickels for peanuts and pleasure-wheels because the settlers of this period allowed themselves no leisure whatever. But there is something which strikes one as a trifle impertinent on the part of a bumptious young pleasure-spot like Bergen Beach thus thrusting itself under the very nose of ancient sobriety.

That bold, brave, stubborn old dictator, Peter Stuyvesant, permitted no church except the Dutch Reformed to be established in his territory.

The Old Dutch Church of Flatlands, Organized 261 Years Ago.

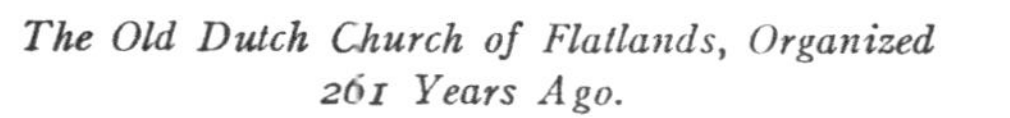

The Maryland Monument on Lookout Hill, Marking the Site of the Battle of Long Island.

Where the Prospect Park Swan Boat now Plies, the Din of Battle once was Heard.

The Battle Pass Tablet in Prospect Park, Marking the Outer Line of Defense in 1776.

Robert Hodgson, a Quaker refugee, was brought before Stuyvesant and his council, was not permitted to utter a word of defense, and was sentenced to hard labor at the wheelbarrow for two years. He was chained to the wheelbarrow and ordered to go to work, loading and wheeling it, on a hot midsummer day; when he refused to accept this punishment for no crime save that of preaching his religion, he was beaten, starved, and tortured. Not till public sympathy stirred in his behalf was he released.

This was the grim conception of government under which life moved. It created in the people a spirit of stern industry, at once forceful and narrow. Stuyvesant's employers in Holland rebuked him for over-zeal, and a gentler sway followed.

The first houses built on the Island were protected against marauding Indians by strong palisades. These girt the houses about, and disappeared as the need for them disappeared.

East of Coney Island lies another island which belonged to the town of Flatlands. In early years it was much larger than it is now, and was covered with red cedar and other trees, not in the least suggesting its later name of Barren Island. This spot of land is said to have been one of the headquarters of a band of early-day pirates the band ruled by the famous Gibbs. Here they hid away much of their booty, which was chiefly in the form of Mexican dollars, as they had suffered the misfortune of losing the rest of it when their boat upset in their attempts to land. These men were later on convicted of piracy and murder, being turned over to the law by one of their own number, and all but the tale-teller paid the penalty by being executed together on Gibbet Island in New York Harbor in the year 1831.

When the early Holland emigrants arrived at New Amersfort, they found an Indian trail leading from Jamaica Bay to East River. This the farmers, "boers" as they were then called, traced, and found that it led to Midwout. For protection, they planted their homesteads fairly near together along this path, and thus began the first road between the towns.

Ross states that not until 1704 was a real effort made to improve the roads throughout the State. The Legislature passed a law by which three commissioners were appointed in each of the counties in Long Island, to lay out a highway from Brooklyn ferry to Easthampton. The Kings County Commissioners set promptly about their task, and they laid out the road which is now a part of Fulton Street, beginning at "low water marke at the ferry." They followed the old path, and so on to New Lots. When this road was completed it constituted the King's Highway, which was the first of the famous highways of Long Island. A portion of it still retains the old name—we have come across it at the Flatlands church to-day. As the order then went forth, it was to be laid out with a uniform width of four rods, and was "to be and continue forever."

CHAPTER V

OVER THE BATTLEGROUND OF LONG ISLAND IN THE FOOTSTEPS OF PUTNAM

RETURNING from the roads which lead us out into Long Island, we are once more within the city of Brooklyn. Dutch and Quaker days and ways have been recalled; Brooklyn, with its most vivid bit of history, brings us into the period of the Revolution. There is little left to-day to mark the old sites made famous during Putnam's defense of Brooklyn Heights; we can, however, retrace the footsteps of the Americans in a general direction if not exactly. Some of the modern streets coincide with the old ones; and at least the battlegrounds are to be seen, even though the relics of the encounters have vanished forever.

In the heart of Brooklyn's busiest district, hundreds and hundreds of people come and go and pass every day in the year, and never notice a simple bronze tablet which clamps the corner of a square-shouldered business building at the intersection of Fulton Street and Flatbush Avenue. The tablet is small and unobtrusive, and people who pass are thinking about a real-estate deal, or an exploded tire, or the new styles in millinery. It bears a brief inscription—merely four names, set down for what they are worth, without comment:

"Washington. Putnam. Sullivan. Stirling."

And beneath these, a small relief of a battle scene, and the words: "Line of Defense. Battle of Long Island. August 27, 1776. From the Wallabout to the Gowanus."

It is telegraphic in its brevity, contrasted with the elaborate eulogies of the usual battle monument or tablet. But "from the Wallabout to the Gowanus" tells Brooklyn's greatest story. To-day the Wallabout is merely that bay at the crook of the East River, where the Navy Yard fronts the water; and the Gowanus, that indentation in our Upper Bay overlooked by Greenwood Cemetery and the busy blocks which lie just below its heights. If you will look on the map, you will see that an incurving line drawn between these will take in the heights of Fort Greene Park, Prospect Park, and the Cemetery; here, then, you have a sketchy map of the great battle which was the first avowed battle fought in our nation's war for independence.

In an afternoon's stroll over these vicinities you can to-day re-fight that battle in your memory. You will, at times, follow old roads, walk in old footsteps, overlook old prospects. On a slope which invites loafing, which tempts babies to roll, you may hear the clank of military metal. On the heights associated with the contest, one is reminded of the remark of a certain real-estate dealer— that "armies always did have a leaning toward fine building sites."

Fort Greene Park, the height which the city long ago took over to be a green spot and pleasure ground for the people, lies between Myrtle and De Kalb avenues, and offers a refreshing glimpse of grass and trees in down-town Brooklyn. Call to mind the position of the American and British forces 139 years ago.

Washington had driven the British from Boston and had brought his army down to New York in the spring of that year—1776. Perhaps the American forces had not had as much to do with the British evacuation, however, as had strategic motives on the enemy's part. The British intended to make New York the center of their operations; they had regarded the campaign around Boston as a preliminary, and the real opening of the war was to take place around New York. In June of 1776 the signs of British occupation were shown.

General Howe proceeded to set forth his array in New York Harbor. Seven weeks after the beginning of this move he had more than four hundred vessels and thirty thousand troops there, the troops being encamped on Staten

Island. To meet this array, Washington could not call together twenty thousand effective men. Some of these, opposing all the completeness of British training and equipment, marched as they would walk behind the plow, and wielded, by way of weapon, a straightened scythe fastened to a pole.

Howe, having studied the situation and fortifications of the Americans, decided that his best move would be not to attack the center and right of the Americans, which included Governor's Island, the Battery, and the Hudson River defenses; although he believed his troops capable of making this attack victoriously, it offered the Americans too good an opportunity to retreat farther north along the island of Manhattan, and escape by way of Kingsbridge. The results would be better if he could outflank our army. The American left wing was stationed on Long Island, and Howe saw his opportunity to overcome the defenses on Brooklyn Heights and along the shore, to proceed up the East River, and to cut off the chance of retreat to the north.

When Washington had come to New York from Boston, he had spent the ensuing months in preparing for this British attack. Several points were strongly fortified, among them Brooklyn Heights. It offered a most favorable position, overlooking the entrance to the city of

New York, and there Washington had defenses built, there he placed General Greene with a large body of troops. But much sickness prevailed that summer, and in the middle of August Greene succumbed to an attack of bilious fever, and Sullivan was put in his place. Meanwhile General Putnam was arranging, by *chevaux-de-frise*, to stop the British vessels which might aim to enter and pass up the East River.

The design of the British was clearly worked out. It was on the twenty-second of August that definite activities began, when Howe landed twenty thousand men at Gravesend Bay, and from this spot set out to reach Brooklyn Heights. Four roads led thither: on the left, the Gowanus road which skirted the shore; on the right, the Jamaica road, curving inland; between these, two roads which crossed the wooded hills intervening and passed through the villages of Bedford and Flatbush.

Fort Greene Park, as it is known to-day, was a most vital point in the American defense. It was exposed to the enemy, and at the same time it gave the Americans their hold upon New York. It meant to New York what Bunker Hill and Dorchester Heights meant to Boston—namely, the command of the situation. About half the American army was therefore concentrated there—some nine thousand men. Because of the tremendous responsibility of the position,

The Monument to Civil War Heroes in Greenwood Cemetery.

The Civil War Soldiers' and Sailors' Arch at the Entrance to Prospect Park.

The View from Lookout Hill, where Maryland's Four Hundred Made their Great Defense in 1776.
(Prospect Park.)

Putnam was placed in supreme command, Sullivan still remaining.

The place, known as Fort Putnam before it was Fort Greene Park, is described by Lossing as a wooded hill near the Wallabout; a redoubt with five guns; when the trees were felled it commanded the East River as well as the roads approaching Brooklyn from the interior. Standing on its highest point to-day you can realize its value for a fortification.

The entrenchments which ran from Fort Putnam are difficult to trace in this century, owing to the over-riding growth of the city which has sprung up about them. It is known that one ran in a northwesterly direction down the hill toward a spring on the verge of the Wallabout. Another ran toward Freek's mill-pond, at the head of Gowanus Creek. There were various redoubts here and there; at the corner of Clinton and Atlantic streets, the site of the Athenæum of a later day, stood "Cobble Hill," an old fort. Three cannon were here; as the entrenchment made a spiral from top to bottom of the hill, it was called "Corkscrew Fort." The finding of arrowheads and buttons marked "42" (belonging to the 42d Highlanders), some half-century ago, recalled the position of Box Fort, near the termination of Hoyt Street at Carroll. Thus a fair sketch of the American position has been worked out; but many links in the chain have been debated.

For four days of that eventful August, Howe reconnoitered. The upshot was that he determined to approach Brooklyn Heights by all of the four roads, he himself choosing to take the Jamaica road which offered a roundabout eastern approach. On this journey he made his quarters in a building then known as Howard's Half-Way House, an old inn on the Jamaica road.

Washington's hour for swift and drastic measures had come. Having first sent reinforcements to Sullivan at Brooklyn, he had followed up this act by sending General Putnam to take charge of the entire affair. Putnam was a veteran at the time; he was in his fifty-ninth year and was mature in both life and war, equipped for the most important position which the situation of the Americans offered.

On the morning of August 24th, immediately upon receiving his appointment, Putnam crossed to Brooklyn. He had heard the sounds of the first skirmishing on Long Island, and he was chafing to be in the thick of it all. Although nearly sixty, his eagerness for action was as keen as that of a boy. His own enthusiasm had always fired the men under him, from the days of his Indian fighting; and now, as he arrived at Brooklyn Heights, loud and long cheering greeted the appearance of "Old Put."

Immediately a sense of confidence spread throughout the American forces and their sympathizers.

Putnam, with Burr, his aide-de-camp, set out at once to inspect the chain of defenses which had been put up during the summer. He had the situation clearly in mind now, and he was impatient for the battle to begin. Washington sent more troops across on the night of the 26th; those behind the Brooklyn works were under Putnam's personal command.

Howe now advanced, while Putnam prepared to meet the attack. By way of Bedford and Flatbush, through dense woods, General von Heister led the Hessians; these roads were defended by Sullivan. The Highland Regiments under General Grant followed the road along the shore; Stirling was ready for them. Howe himself, in his night march by way of the Jamaica road, was accompanied by Cornwallis, Clinton, and Percy, and aided by many British sympathizers along the route.

It was impossible to send enough men to meet Howe; so great was the British majority, that any force which the Americans might have sent would have been powerless. A patrol watched the Jamaica road, but it was captured at daybreak, and Bedford was gained by the British.

Sullivan was now bravely fighting against the advance of von Heister and his Hessians. But

Sullivan's position was between two fires. In spite of his efforts, Cornwallis found opportunity to attack him in the rear. The Americans were taken prisoners or driven to flee.

Stirling was being confronted by Grant with his five thousand men, three thousand more than Stirling had; nevertheless the brave American general formed a battle line all the way from Gowanus Bay over Battle Hill in Greenwood Cemetery.

Before going on to the other scenes of the conflict, you can take a look aside at the shaft rising before you, on the summit of Fort Greene Hill. It is the prison soldiers' monument, or Martyrs' Tomb, relating the last and saddest chapter of this battle story. Here were brought the bodies of those victims of the prison ship *Jersey*, who suffered such tortures after their capture by the British. The monument is flanked by cannon, and its height of 125 feet is surmounted by a bronze urn twenty feet high. The contributions which erected it came from city, state, United States Government, and the Prison Ship Martyrs' Association.

Your next step in tracing the battle story lies toward Prospect Park. You enter under the Soldiers' and Sailors' arch—a memorial dedicated to the defenders of our Union who fought from 1861 to 1865, and standing only a short distance from the spot where our soldiers of almost a century earlier defended our nation.

If you will turn into the Eastern Drive after entering the Park, follow it past the children's playground, and look sharply to your left after passing the playground, you will suddenly discover a gray bowlder retired among the trees near the Drive. Its tablet bears this inscription: "Line of Defense. August 27, 1776. Battle of Long Island. 175 feet south. Site of Valley Grove House, 150 feet north."

This tells its own story. You are approaching the thick of the fray.

Now follow on along the Eastern Drive until it bends into the Central Drive, pass the lake, and find your way to Lookout Hill. This land which is now one of the finest parks in the United States, a triumph of landscape gardening, and thronged with merry-making crowds, was once trampled by throngs of soldiers, drenched with blood, and given over to the horrors of battle.

Climb the slope of Lookout Hill and picture the prospect as it was on that August day when the gallant Marylanders fought here. A simple shaft rises, in their memory; on the one side you may read: "In honor of Maryland's Four Hundred, who on this Battle Field, August 27, 1776, saved the American army." And on the other side, George Washington's words quoted: "Good God! What brave fellows I must this day lose!"

Von Heister with his Hessians had overcome Sullivan in short order, with the assistance of the forces which had closed in from behind. Stirling and Grant, meeting on the shore road, had fought the first fight in which Americans had ever met British troops in the open field and in regular line of battle. Stirling had fought magnificently but he too was assaulted in the rear; his one effort now was to save his command from capture.

With the remnant of the Maryland men he formed a line and made one of the most terrific fights in the annals of the Revolution. The Maryland men were famous throughout the war for their personal gallantry, the battle at Eutaw Springs being one of their great feats, in which they drove Britain's finest infantry at the point of the bayonet. In this Long Island battle Stirling himself was captured, but to the Maryland regiment was due the fact that the retreat of hundreds of Americans was made possible. It was a frightful retreat—a mere fleeing mob, officers mingled with privates, no formation left, but still the vestige of an American division to be received at Putnam's headquarters on the Heights.

Going on to Greenwood Cemetery, you come to another historic spot. Entering at the gate where the cemetery offices stand, passing these buildings and following the path's curve to the right, you come into sight of the bay. Turn with the gravel road; pass the Civil War monument which was dedicated by the city of New York to the 148,000 soldiers enlisted by this city for that war; just beyond it you come to Fern Avenue, and at the intersection of this path with Greenbank Path lies Battle Hill. Near this did Stirling take his position.

During the time that the fierce fighting was going on, Putnam and his men were watching some of it from the Brooklyn works. They could see the Americans approaching the works, driven by the British, who, it appeared, were undertaking to make an assault upon the fortifications. Putnam was ready for this event. He passed to and fro among the men who waited behind the defenses, issuing quick orders, drawing their resistance taut along with his own. A story has been told of him at this time, reported to one Carson Brevoort by a man named Remsen who was present at the defenses. It is recorded in the *Memoirs* of the Long Island Historical Society:

"A few paces in the rear of the firing parties General Putnam was constantly stalking back and forth, at every return enforcing anew his favorite command, which Bunker Hill had made so famous: 'Don't fire, boys, until you can see the whites of their eyes.' The eminent success of this injunction in that battle had given it an importance in the mind of the old Indian fighter which quite justified its frequent repetition. . . .

"A soldier of one of the Connecticut regiments was crouching behind the breastwork and was busily employed in loading his own and his comrade's gun, which were fired, however, only by the latter, a Maryland soldier, who was kneeling to rest his piece upon the parapet and with deliberate aim picking off the enemy's troops. This partnership of courage and poltroonery . . . at length arrested the attention of the promenading General. The angry blood, which fired so readily at the call of his hot temper, flamed in an instant on his countenance, and with a few quick strides he reached the side of the couchant hero who remained unconscious of the proximity of his angry General. The flat side of his sword fell with stinging force on the back of the culprit as he exclaimed, 'Get up, you damned coward, and fire your own gun.'"

In spite of Putnam's indomitable spirit in the face of overwhelming odds, the American forces were powerless against an enemy so great in numbers, so complete in training and equipment. As many historians have commented, the wonder is, not that the Americans were forced to give up, but that they gave Howe a whole day of the hardest fighting, and caused him heavy losses, in defeating them. Moreover, the delay gave

Miss Matilda Hall's House, where the Secessionist Hung his Flag out until he was Raided. (Chapel Hill.)

Martyrs' Monument, Fort Greene Park.

The Place of Worship from which Chapel Hill Took its Name.

Washington time to plan his remarkable withdrawal.

Howe did not undertake to carry the Brooklyn works by storm. But, having driven the Americans back to where Putnam gallantly held his shattered forces together, he watched. Apparently no move lay open to the Americans. But Washington, hastening across the river from Manhattan, assembled at the Brooklyn ferry all the boats obtainable, and, under cover of the foggy night, removed his vanquished army to the other side of the river, while the British, officers and men, slept undisturbed.

How the thing was accomplished without rousing the victors has always remained inexplicable. Washington himself superintended the embarkation; Fiske says, he "collected every sloop, yacht, fishing-smack, yawl, scow, or row-boat that could be found in either water from the Battery to Kingsbridge or Hell Gate; and after nightfall of the 29th, these craft were all assembled at the Brooklyn ferry, and wisely manned by the fishermen of Marblehead and Gloucester from Glover's Essex Regiment, experts, every one of them, whether at oar or sail."

Washington did not leave the ground until every one of his men was off. Seven in the morning saw not only every American landed on the New York side, but cannon and small arms as well, tools, horses, ammunition, and larder. Fiske concludes, "When the bewildered British climbed into the empty works they did not find so much as a biscuit or a glass of rum wherewith to console themselves."

If you will cross Brooklyn to the Navy Yard, you can follow in imagination the sorry fate of our men confined in British prison ships. Here, looking out over Wallabout Bay, you recall the horrors of the old hulks which the British moored here, and kept as floating prisons, the *Jersey* being the most famous of these. She was called by her prisoners "the hell afloat." This vessel served as prison ship till the end of the war; it was a hotbed of filth and disease, men were left in rags, crowded beyond all conception of crowding, poisoned by spoiled food, and tortured with countless cruelties.

Until the year 1873 the bones of these martyred prisoners lay in a vault just outside the Navy Yard. Then they were removed to Fort Greene Park. The Martyrs' Tomb in that park contains the remains of eleven thousand American heroes.

Until the end of the Revolution, Brooklyn remained in the hands of the British. Washington, having removed his army to New York, now stationed the most of it along the Harlem River, Putnam being placed in command of a strong detachment in the city.

TOWARD THE SOUTH

CHAPTER VI

THE HIGHLANDS AND SANDY HOOK

LONG before summer-resorters disported themselves in parti-colored bathing suits, before processions of gay parasols paraded along board-walks, before husbands pined in Manhattan's August solitude, the same stately highlands rose above the gleaming sand of the New Jersey shore. The same lean peninsula of Sandy Hook crooked its finger out into the same Atlantic Ocean, and the Navesink River opened its wide mouth as now, near the Horseshoe of Sandy Hook Bay. Although we of to-day associate this country with the bathing suits and the parasols of lively beaches, its earlier chapters are a different sort of tale. Here lay country that Washington knew well, and Clinton too—country that figured in the stirring tales of the Revolution. And here the Pine Robbers, the terror of Monmouth County, burrowed their caves in the sand-hills.

You will recall the suggestions quoted in Chapter I from a guide-book of more than a century ago—for a "convenient number" of gentlemen to charter a boat of their own to visit "Sandy Hook and the Sea-Bass Banks." To-day it is not necessary to charter a boat, nor to leave the ladies behind on account of hardships. The regular line of steamboats sailing from Manhattan to the Atlantic Highlands will carry all travelers, and afford them a sketchy view of the Upper Bay, the Narrows, the Lower Bay, and finally Sandy Hook Bay.

Setting sail from North River you pass out into New York Bay, with its three historic islands in sight: Ellis, Governor's, and Bedloe's.

The first of these was the Gibbet Island, on which, we have already heard, the pirate Gibbs was hung.[1] It took its name from that distinguished person, and for a long time was known thus. Previous to this it had been called Oyster Island, by the Dutch who enjoyed feasts of the bivalve on its shores. In 1808 the National Government bought it from the State, placed a magazine there, and in 1891 turned it into an immigrant station. It is now used for this purpose, and can be visited by any one who obtains a pass from the Commissioner of Immigration.

Governor's Island is one of our most interesting national defenses. The Indians used to call this spot of land "Pagganck," and the Dutch who followed them named it Nut Island. Wouter

[1] Chapter IV.

Van Twiller bought it from the Indians in 1637 and made himself a home thereon, establishing a saw-mill. About the end of the same century, the Assembly set it aside for the benefit of the royal governors, and its present name was given the island.

There were fortifications there in the time of the Revolution, held by the Americans until their defeat on Long Island, after which the British took Governor's Island. The old well belonging to the early works is still to be seen on the east side, but other relics have disappeared. In 1794 the beginning of the present works was made. Military prisoners were confined here during the Civil War.

Bedloe's Island, like Ellis, also bore the name of Oyster Island in early days. Isaac Bedloe obtained this land by patent from Governor Nicoll, and held it until his death, when it passed into the hands of Captain Kennedy. It came into the possession of the United States Government at the beginning of the last century. Fort Wood was built upon it, and in 1883 the Statue of Liberty was erected. France presented the giant bronze, Bartholdi being chosen as sculptor.

Through the Narrows you pass out between Forts Hamilton and Wadsworth into the Lower Bay. Together they frown formidably upon any unwelcome entrance to our harbor. Fort

Hamilton was named for Colonel Archibald Hamilton who was a well-known commander of British forces. At this point Stonewall Jackson and General Robert E. Lee were stationed before the Civil War drew them into active service. The site of the old Simon Cortelyou house is within the limits of the fort, a building which once served as Howe's headquarters.

Cortelyou was disliked by Americans, being a hot Tory, and a most cruel one in his treatment of American prisoners.

Beyond, on the left, lies Gravesend Bay, that curve of water which Coney Island forms with the line of the mainland of Long Island. Here you catch glimmers of Revolutionary history; it was on this shore that Howe landed his troops, to lead them to the Battle of Long Island. In this bay were kept the British prison ships, cattle transports used for the confinement of prisoners taken in battle, and many Americans were carried to them after the Brooklyn defeat. Later, when the British took possession of New York, they were removed to various prisons in the city.

Coney Island gets its present name from the Dutch, Conynge Hook. Guyspert Op Dyck obtained this curiously shaped strip of land by grant from Governor Kieft. In later years it was divided into lots; Thomas Stilwell bought the entire strip in 1734. Almost a century later the first hotel was built there, showing that its value as a resort had been discovered; by the middle of the Nineteenth Century it had entered upon its famous career as an amusement center.

Entering Sandy Hook Bay, you pass the long Hook itself, with its famous lighthouse near the tip.

And now your journey bears toward the land —into New Jersey. You are to find an old road, clearly defined on maps a century old, running from the Navesink Highlands back inland.

One such map shows the road running in a westerly direction toward Middletown and dotted by a few farms, marked "S. Taylor," "E. Taylor," and "D. Conover." These names, and some of the homes of that period, are to be found to-day along the old road. In fact, there lies on this highway a hamlet of thirteen houses which is almost intact, the whole hamlet practically as it was in Revolutionary days. Such a discovery is rare in our hurrying America. Two or three of the dwellings are called by the townspeople "new"; we were told modestly by one resident that her home "wasn't old at all. Why, it was only built for grandmother to come to when she was a bride," the young matron said deprecatingly, her own offspring playing in the yard while she discussed the matter. But for a house which has known four generations to be counted "new" in any community of the United States speaks well for that community's love of tradition.

This part of New Jersey throbbed in Revolutionary days; not many miles away was fought the Battle of Monmouth, and hereabouts soldiers marched and tarried. The journeyer of to-day who seeks the old road must allow a long day for the water-and-land trip, and avail himself of a lunch wherever it offers, for old Cornelius Mount's inn has passed into a memory these many years, and no longer are his genial smile and his brimming mug awaiting the wayfarer.

From the boat-landing at Atlantic Highlands, the next step in the jaunt is to Leonardo. Where the trolley line is intersected by the road to Chapel Hill stands a fine old white house of colonial period surrounded by broad grounds. This house has been in the Leonard family for many generations. James and Henry were the pioneers of the family in this region, coming from Massachusetts where they had settled in 1642. They had built ironworks in New England, and they came to Monmouth County in New Jersey to build ironworks for James Grover. Evidently they were a progressive family, for we hear of "Ye Leonard's Mill in Middletown," being a successful saw-mill there. So prominent did they become that the town Leonardo was named for them. The house,

Cornelius Mount's Inn, where the Duel Challenge was Spoken in Verse.

The Village Smithy Containing the Ancient Anvil, at Chapel Hill.

The Old Leonard House at Leonardo.

nucleus of all the village around, is preserved almost in its original form, and the fine old rafters and fireplaces are to be seen to-day by the visitor who enters the colonial doorway.

The Chapel Hill road which runs from this house back to the old road, leading for perhaps a mile up the hill, is a most picturesque way for the pedestrian. For a stretch it passes through unbroken woodland, again fertile farms spread beyond it; here, in a wild blackberry patch, a group of freckled, pigtailed little girls are staining fingers and lips. Birds chant a chorus, and the gorgeous butterfly-weed blazes among many equally lovely wild flowers.

Climbing steadily through all this varied midsummer beauty, you see no goal beyond the road's windings. You are beginning to draw the conclusion that Chapel Hill, the hamlet which you were told would mark the old Middletown road, is a myth. Just ahead you see a low gray roof, but it apparently is merely another isolated farmhouse along the winding road—which winds once again; suddenly the roof is surrounded by others, and you find yourself confronted by a hamlet on this lonely height—the vision of it is as sudden, as unexpected as if it had been waved into being by a wand. Here, between the little white houses which face each other in gossipy intimacy, runs the ancient road you are seeking.

Chapel Hill, although it played no leading rôle in our nation's history, is perhaps the quaintest spot within thirty miles of New York. "From Bill's to Hosford's" it extends, this curious, changeless village of thirteen houses. Around it lie towns of far greater importance both in the present and past: Keyport, Port Monmouth, Middletown, Red Bank, Shrewsbury; but the visitor to Chapel Hill will call the trip worth while as presenting a picture remarkably unique; calling up not historic events, but historic times. It is as if one came suddenly upon a typical American village of Revolutionary times which had been in some magic way embalmed, preserved with all its remoteness and withdrawal from the progressing world. The inn, the "store" the village blacksmith shop, still gather with the villagers' homes along the street. Nobody ever goes to it (the motorist speeds by, but doesn't know its name), it is on hardly any map, it draws itself within itself here on the Jersey heights. The houses are associated with such names as Mount, Conover, Taylor, Hopping, and others, all familiar in the Revolutionary period of Monmouth County.

Cornelius Mount's inn stands to-day used as the home of one of his lineal descendants, Mrs. Patterson. The old fireplace around which the genial Mount's patrons once gathered is in the living-room, and a portrait of the well-known

Hopping, another member of the family, hangs opposite. This was the only public inn of all the region except at Middletown, and great was the gayety it witnessed. Edwin Salter, in his *History of Monmouth and Ocean Counties*, gives a characteristic entry from an inn book of that period in New Jersey, and Mr. Mount's entries were doubtless very similar.

1767.	DOLLEY HAGEMAN.	*Dr.*
Jan. 2.	To 1 mug of Cider & ½ Dram	6
	To 1 mug of Beer	6
	To ½ Dram	2
	To 2 Mugs of Beer	1
Apr. 8.	To 1 Dram	4
	To ½ Dram	2
		0.2.8

Thus did the frequenters of all such inns regale themselves in those days. But not even in those days could every inn boast a duel challenge—and such a challenge! It stands to-day in the annals of the old Mount house that one temperamental gentleman, probably somewhat the worse and the wittier for his drams, thus declared himself to his adversary:

> I will meet you at Chapel Hill,
> At Sam Cooper's Still,
> Or Loofburrow's Mill,
> In case you will.

John Loofburrow had a mill on Maclise Creek

in 1684, and for many years this creek was navigable for sloops and schooners within a half-mile of it.

Three of the Taylors lived near by and were famous Tories. One of the largest houses in Chapel Hill belongs to the family.

Near the western end of the village street the village smithy stands. The smith is not exactly a mighty man in appearance, but he is a very quaint figure, white-haired, lean, and alert. For thirty-eight years D. H. Irwin has toiled at that old forge in the little shop which was old when he fell heir to it. The anvil used by one of the original Mounts is standing beside the one in present use, and dates so far back that "the Mr. Mount who lately died at more than threescore-and-ten told me that it was old when he was a boy and his father was using it!" Miss Matilda Hall informed us.

Miss Hall will lead you down the street into her own house, and down cellar to a mysterious corner where lurk tomato pickles and spiced currants and all the delightful things that people don't put up nowadays; and there she will point out the deep fireplace with its old Holland bricks, brought over when there were no other bricks convenient to Monmouth County; and will tell you that in this warm corner the original dwellers in the house hid from Indian assaults, shooting up through the cellar window.

Still another tradition clings to this house. It is said that here, during the Civil War, dwelt one Glentworth, a stout Secessionist who used to buy up ammunition for Jeff Davis. In the midst of the loyal Unionists who filled this region, he hung out his Southern flag, much to the indignation of all who saw it. Soon there came news of a raid plotted at Navesink—a mob to come up the old road and make short work of dealing with the Secessionist. Their plans were carefully laid, and the raiders set out for Chapel Hill, their appetite lusty for the encounter. But upon arriving at the summit, all they saw was an innocent Union flag peacefully fluttering from the window. Mr. Glentworth had been apprised of the mob's intentions, and his loyalty appeared less valuable to him than his neck.

The chapel from which this village acquired its name shows the only sign of modern changes in the group of buildings. It has been turned into a stable and garage, which event marks the final chapter of the little church's history. For many years the place had been known as "High Point," until about 1800, when this Baptist meeting-house was erected, and the name "Chapel Hill" was given. The church was organized as the "Independent Baptist Society and Congregation at High Point, Middletown." In 1829 a Methodist society bought it, later it was sold to Deacon Andrew Brown of Middletown, and, as the flicker of life gradually faded from the little village on the hill, it resigned itself to the past.

From Middletown to Water Witch the old road stretches, a motor road of much popularity to-day. Starting along it in the direction of the coast, you can visit, by means of a short detour, the Chapel Hill Lighthouse, one of the range lights established by an Act of Congress in 1852. It is 224 feet above the sea and has a second order lens. This light and Conover Beacon on the beach below are the range lights for the old ship channel, for outward-bound vessels. The two are almost two miles apart. The view from the tower of this light commands the long strip of Sandy Hook, the bay, the ocean beyond, even Manhattan and Brooklyn, as well as miles of the New Jersey shore.

The present keeper, Mr. Wright, sets the light shining forth every evening; as it falls, its first ray strikes a certain grave in the old cemetery below. This is the grave of Captain George Porter, former keeper of the light, who for years tended it in the same tower. Porter had been in the Battle of Mobile Bay under Farragut, and was the only signal boy in the Navy.

As you return and follow the road which leads toward the Navesink Highlands, you find the stories of the Battle of Monmouth recurring to your mind. From some of the Chapel Hill houses, so runs the tradition, mugs of ale and bread and meat were passed out to the red-coats by the Tories who dwelt in this village side by side with Whigs, when marches led the soldiers to this road. When the battle was over, Sir Henry Clinton, after remaining a few days on the high grounds of Middletown, led his army in this direction and passed them over from Sandy Hook to New York.

In his official dispatch to Lord Germain he wrote: "Having reposed the troops until ten at night to avoid the excessive heat of the day, I took advantage of the moonlight to rejoin General Knyphausen"; which report caused much unholy glee among patriots, as the moon was new at the time.

It is said that Monmouth suffered more than any other Jersey county during the Revolution, not only from outrages committed by the British army, but from the depredations of the organized outcasts known as Pine Robbers. They pretended to be Tories, but they robbed Tories and Whigs with equal facility. Their burrowed caves in the sand hereabouts concealed them, also the pine woods, and thence they sallied forth to plunder and murder.

One Fenton was the arch-fiend among them—a former blacksmith of Freehold. When the vigilance committee warned him that, if he did not return his plunder, he would be shot, he sent back the clothing he had taken from a tailor's shop, but added in a note, "I have returned your damned rags. In a short time I am coming to burn your barns and houses, and roast you all like a pack of kittens!" At the head of a gang he attempted to do this, but was shot by a soldier.

The Refugees had a strongly fortified settlement at Sandy Hook known as "Refugees' Town." British war vessels were always in the vicinity, cannon defended its lighthouse, and raids were made. Captain Joseph Covenhoven was one of their prisoners.

It was near the Highlands that Captain Joshua Huddy was cruelly hung in 1782. "The Hero of Tom's River," of the artillery regiment, was taken while commanding a blockhouse situated near the bridge at the village of Tom's River. Lossing gives the following account of the ardent Whig's tragedy:

"It [the blockhouse] was attacked by some refugees from New York, and his ammunition giving out, Huddy was obliged to surrender. Himself and companions were taken to New York, and afterward back to Sandy Hook and placed, heavily ironed, on board a guard-ship. On the 12th of April, sixteen refugees, under Captain Lippincott, took Huddy to Gravelly Point, on the shore at the foot of the Navesink Hills, near the lighthouses, and hung him upon a gallows made of three rails. He met his fate with composure. Upon the barrel on which he stood for execution, he wrote his will with an unfaltering hand. His murderers falsely charged him with being concerned in the death of a desperate Tory, named Philip White, which occurred while Huddy was a prisoner in New York. To the breast of Huddy, the infamous Lippincott affixed the following label: 'We, the refugees, having long with grief beheld the cruel murders of our brethren, and finding nothing but such measures daily carrying into execution; we therefore determine not to suffer, without taking vengeance for the numerous cruelties; and thus begin, having made use of Captain Huddy as the first object to present to your view; and further determine to hang man for man, while there is a refugee existing.

'UP GOES HUDDY FOR PHILIP WHITE!'

"Huddy's body was carried to Freehold, and buried with the honors of war."

The country was aroused with indignation over this murder, as it was declared to be. Washington wrote to Sir Henry Clinton, stating that the murderers of Huddy must be given up, or he should take retaliation measures. Upon Clinton's refusal to comply, it was determined, by lot, that young Captain Asgill, a British officer, should be executed. But the color of affairs changed; it was found, in a court-martial of Lippincott, that he had received from the president of the Board of Associated Loyalists, orders to hang Huddy and he was acquitted. Sir Guy Carleton, having succeeded Clinton, wrote to Washington reprobating the death of Huddy and stating that he had brought this Board to an end. Young Asgill's mother, and the French minister, had meantime written to Washington interceding for the young officer, and he was finally set free. Lossing adds, "In a humorous poem, entitled *Rivington's Reflections*, Philip Freneau thus alludes to the case of Asgill. He makes Rivington (the Tory printer in New York) say,

'I'll petition the rebels (if York is forsaken)
For a place in their Zion which ne'er shall be shaken.
I am sure they'll be clever; it seems their whole study;
They hung not young Asgill for old Captain Huddy;
And it must be a truth that admits no denying—
If they spare us for *murder*, they'll spare us for *lying*.'"

The point known as Water Witch was named from Cooper's novel, traditions of which fill this locality. It is said that he lived in a cottage here while writing the book.

A tradition of Atlantic Highlands is connected with a spring, from which it is supposed that Hendrick Hudson supplied the *Half-Moon* with fresh water before she entered the Hudson River in 1609.

Chapel Hill Lighthouse, Government Range Light, 224 Feet above the Sea, Commanding One of the most Remarkable Views of New York Harbor.

From a photograph by George Wright.

The Old Vanderbilt House, where the Commodore Spent his Boyhood.

The Village Blacksmith at Chapel Hill.

Photograph by A. R. Coleman.

The nature-lover will find much of interest in the vicinity of the Highlands. Both plant- and bird-life are here to be studied in great variety. Many fish-hawks' nests are built in the dead tree-tops a little way back from the shore, and we surprised one pair with the camera; the mother bird's head being thrust up from the nest toward her arrogant mate, perched above.

CHAPTER VII

ON STATEN ISLAND TO OUDE DORP

STAATEN EYLAND, as Hendrick Hudson named it, had early communication with Manhattan Island, as well as with New Jersey. Ferries developed at many points, and, as time went on, roads led from their landings back into Staten Island, thus affording many opportunities to the journeyer from old New York.

The large island was called by the Indians "High Sandy Banks" and "The Place of Bad Woods," among many names. The Walloons had first settled in 1624; there had followed many hardships and difficulties, the Indians causing much trouble; the Walloons had removed to Long Island, and after this the dwelling houses which new settlers erected were near the Narrows, from this vicinity back to Old Town. In 1661 the Waldenses came to the island, later the Huguenots, and the settlements of Old Town and Fresh Kills grew. Before they arrived, the only roads were narrow paths leading through the forest, between these two places; as the people had intercourse with no one but the inhabitants of New Amsterdam, there was no demand for island roads. But now, with new settlers arriving, there came to be intercourse on the island itself, and roads developed. Islanders made ways to reach the two churches, that of the Waldenses at Stony Brook, and that of the Huguenots at Fresh Kills.

As more and more settlers arrived, locating for the most part along the shores, roads followed their courses of communication. These outlined the shores, then others intersected them, leading back into the island. As long ago as when Clute wrote his history, he stated that "the Clove Road is the only original one now left."

Staten Island began to be interesting historically as far back as the Seventeenth Century. When there were two hundred white families living within its limits, there were two thousand Indians. Difficulties naturally arose, and from that time on the island was the stage of many dramatic events. British and American conflicts took place on its soil, Indian raids, settlements from various lands with their attendant dramas; in fact, at no period in early America was the story of the island colorless.

Within a few miles stretching across the northeast corner of the borough of Richmond one may find enough reminders of colonial life, of Dutch settlements, of Revolutionary events to last for hours of prowling. In the early part of the Nineteenth Century a "common road" ran from what is now St. George around toward the southeast, keeping close to the shore, and leading on to the vicinity of Arrochar. In following Bay Street of to-day you are approximating this road.

In crossing from the Battery to St. George, review the story of New York's early quarantines as you pass their locations. Out to the right where the Statue of Liberty rises, on Bedloe's Island, was placed the first important quarantine station. There it was established in 1758, long before the Revolution, when our rapidly increasing commerce and the incoming of more and more vessels were bringing us many infectious diseases. The Government recognized the need of quarantine measures, and Bedloe's Island was chosen, and used for this purpose for thirty-eight years.

The station was then moved to Governor's Island, which lies at your left. So, until 1799, matters ran smoothly, when the yellow fever was suddenly imported to New York, and the cry of alarm arose, Governor's Island being thought too near the city. Commissioners were appointed, and they settled upon a parcel of land, thirty acres on the Staten Island shore, the property of St. Andrew's Church. Much disturbance was caused by this measure; the church objected, the islanders objected, but "the right of eminent domain" carried the day.

Therefore the quarantine was established. After you leave the ferry station at St. George you will cross a short bridge over railroad tracks and a short distance beyond, at the left, stands the Lighthouse Reservation; this enclosure is a part of the old quarantine. Good buildings were erected and the work of equipping them for wards went on, under protest from the first. During the first year there were twenty-five cases of imported disease on the island, outside the boundaries of the station, and twenty-four of the twenty-five were fatal. The indignation of the citizens waxed. The years that followed spread other diseases. Petitions brought promises but no fulfillment; it was said that the station was to be removed to Sandy Hook, but this was as far as the matter went. Finally the Board of Health of Castleton called upon the citizens, gathered them in a body, and the result was sensational and drastic action.

Fully prepared, absolutely cool in method, a body of citizens entered the quarantine, removed every patient with the utmost care (not one was in the least injured), then calmly set about burning down the buildings. Only one building survived. That one you can see to-day, a storage house now for the lighthouse supplies.

This reservation is full of interest for its present as well as for its past. It is headquarters for United States lighthouse supplies from the Atlantic to the Pacific; thence are sent forth lights, lenses, clocks, all the apparatus which keeps the lights shining from Casco Bay to the Golden Gate. Government buoys, too, are shipped from this point.

Near here, at 154 Stuyvesant Place, is a large, old-fashioned house marked "Public Museum." The collection includes many old documents, books, relics, coins, and so on relating to the colonial period on the island, and one of the treasures displayed is the original bell of the ancient Richmond courthouse. A complete model of the historic Billopp house is of particular interest to those who have not the courage to take the rather trying walk to ferret out this old residence in Tottenville.

The museum is under the auspices of the Staten Island Association of Arts and Sciences, and occupies two floors of the building. It is maintained by an annual budget appropriation from the city of New York. It possesses one of the most complete collections in existence of Staten Island Indian relics, claiming, under the head of archæology, about fifteen thousand native specimens.

Returning to the shore, and following along Bay Street, you will come to a dilapidated building standing at the corner of Grant Street, a sign of "Furnished Rooms" hanging before its door. Behind its decay, the building reveals a suggestion of ancient prosperity. It is well built of brick, with an old veranda running across the front and low windows above opening upon this; it has an old Dutch slant to its roof, with a chimney at each end; and the numerous windows which indicate a hostelry. This dingy, mournful, down-at-heel edifice was the famous old Planters' Hotel, where wealthy and aristocratic Southerners used to assemble and exchange genial southern stories in the early eighteen-hundreds. Here in Tompkinsville the building was erected by a Southerner in 1820 and conducted especially for southern visitors in New York, the early planters. In later years, when its clientage had melted away, it became a boys' academy, and since that period it has gradually degenerated. But its importance is indicated by the fact that upon Eddy's map of 1828 it is marked "Planters' Hotel" as if it represented a large local center.

Just to the south of it was the old Van Duzer's Ferry—this name of Dutch days being still perpetuated on the island. Vanderbilt's Periauger Ferry, from Stapleton, ran in opposition to it about 1800–17.

Continuing on Bay Street, you will come to the intersection of Clinton. By making a short detour here, turning up Clinton Street to the right, you will reach old Pavilion Hill, or Mt. Tompkins, or Mt. Pavilion, or Cow Hill, as the height has been disrespectfully called. All names have been applied to the one elevation which offers a stiff climb and a fine water view at the top. Not so very long ago there were still to be seen traces of the old fortifications; no sign remains now except a sort of excavation where some of the stonework stood. The view of shore and bay is one of the finest which Staten Island presents.

In 1776 Sir William Howe and his brother Lord Howe had arrived on the island. Half of their men were encamped there and they themselves were entertained at the Rose and Crown, a famous inn. The British now set about throwing up breastworks here and there near the shore, and two forts were built on Pavilion Hill, as it offered a most tempting position. During the stressful times of 1812 the Americans rebuilt these fortifications, and so for many years the hill was strongly fortified.

Long after it ceased to be used as a point of defense it became a popular Sunday resort and was known as Mt. Pavilion.

Returning to Bay Street and following it to the corner of Congress, you will find one of the Vanderbilt houses at the right. This one is huge and imposing, with massive colonial pillars framing its doorway. Although its yard is unkempt, and the encroachment of business has robbed it of its beauty, its magnificence is still sufficient to give it dramatic contrast with the other home of the same Cornelius Vanderbilt, only a few doors further on. The earlier home stands at the corner of Union Street; it is a humble little old white farmhouse, built by his mother, Mrs. Phœbe Vanderbilt; it was his boyhood's home before he erected his own mansion near by.

Morris tells an entertaining and illumining story of young Vanderbilt when fifteen years old. It seems that he had entertained fantastic and boyish visions of going to sea and adventuring; to make these dreams practical, his mother offered him a reward of one hundred dollars with which he might buy a boat, provided he accomplished an almost impossible farm task. Young Cornelius immediately laid the project before some of his boy friends, promised them sails in the boat if they would help him win it, and the task was forthwith accomplished. Instead of seeking treasure islands or playing hookey to loaf in his boat, he conceived the idea of ferrying passengers back and forth to the island, which he did for eighteen cents a trip. By the end of the first year he not only paid his mother for the boat, but had cleared one thousand dollars. By the end of the next year he had cleared another thousand and had secured a fractional interest in some more boats. He often went without his meals to carry excursion parties across. During the War of 1812 his business became tremendous. And so begins a story of transportation.

The small farmhouse is much dilapidated, but its outline is preserved, and it forms a good example of the old Dutch type of building. Here the Commodore's wife died.

Still further along on Bay Street you come to the Marine Hospital on high ground at your right, overlooking the bay. Just behind the modern building the old Seaman's Retreat was built more than a century ago; this was the original hospital building of the Marine Society of New York. Later the property was taken by the United States, and it was made over into a government hospital with fine modern equipment, accommodating many patients. At the western end of the land the Retreat laid out its cemetery; Clute says, "Here poor Jack finds a quiet resting place by the side of his comrades when his life of hardship, privations and peril is ended."

St. George, Tompkinsville, Stapleton, Clifton, and Rosebank are the villages passed along this northeastern shore. Rosebank offers a worth-while detour, to the house once occupied by Giuseppe Garibaldi. It is reached by turning

The Public Museum of St. George, where many Valuable Historic Relics are Shown.

The Old Planters' Hotel, the Resort of Wealthy Southerners almost a Century Ago, on Bay Street, Staten Island.

The Only Building Left of the Ancient Quarantine. Others Burned by Citizens in 1858. Near St. George Ferry.

The Garibaldi House, Staten Island.

into Chestnut Avenue, and is found on a knoll at the corner of Tompkins Avenue.

The memorial is curious in conception. So dilapidated was the house when public sentiment awakened to the thought of preserving it, that it was obvious it could not stand many years of weather-beating; therefore a substantial cement structure was built to enclose the old wooden building, leaving the latter open to the view of the public, although sheltered. A bronze bust of the Italian stands at the entrance, and a tablet.

During the years which Garibaldi spent in this country, he became a most popular citizen of Staten Island. He entered into business enterprises as if he were one of us; he made warm friends of his neighbors; he took the first three degrees in Freemasonry in Tompkins Lodge, No. 401, then at Tompkinsville.

It is natural that the ardent and democratic spirit of the Italian patriot should have appealed to the sympathies of Americans, and that these warm friendships should have arisen. His love of adventure, his roving life and shifting fortunes—he had been drover, shipbroker, and teacher of mathematics in South America, in addition to his better known lines of endeavor in Europe—were full of charm to a country still in the making, whose people had faced adventure and met shifting fortunes themselves. It has been said of him, "He will always remain the central figure in the story of Italian independence."

While in Staten Island he worked as a candle-maker for eighteen months, after which he became captain of various merchantmen. He returned to Italy in 1854.

Let us return to the shore. At the narrow point where the division between Upper and Lower New York Bay is formed by the close proximity of Staten and Long Islands, Fort Wadsworth stands. Opposite, on the Long Island shore, stands Fort Hamilton; together they command this entrance to our harbor. This situation was one of the points chosen by Sir William Howe in 1776, at the same time that he chose Pavilion Hill, for British fortifications.

He caused an especially strong defense to be erected here, and when it was abandoned at the end of the Revolution it remained as it was until the trouble of 1812 prompted the strengthening of its position. During that war time, Governor Daniel D. Tompkins of New York State had two stone forts, called Tompkins and Richmond, erected on these heights above the Narrows. Still another renaissance took place after this war was over, when, in 1847, the reservation was bought by the United States Government. The old forts were demolished and new works built, and the present Fort Wadsworth encloses the old Fort Tompkins and is kept up to date in its improvements.

The last shot of the Revolution was fired at this fort by a British gunboat on Evacuation Day in 1783, because the Staten Island onlookers were so openly derisive. This parting shot was apparently a sort of final expression of opinion—and the war was over.

A short walk along the line of the trolley brings you to the district known as Arrochar Park—"right where them two saloons stand on the top o' the hill," according to a local direction. Although nothing of particular interest catches the eye to-day, this part is of great historical importance, for it is the site of Oude Dorp, or Old Town, the first settlement by Europeans on Staten Island. Authorities have debated over the exact location of this ancient settlement, but it seems generally accepted that it lay to the west of Fort Wadsworth, near the blockhouse which was built on the heights, and that the present Arrochar practically corresponds with its location.

Here, in 1641, the little hamlet was commenced. Seven Dutch cottages were erected by diligent settlers. The building was with stones found on the shore, with lumber hewn from the virgin forest, with shells picked up on the shore and ground for mortar. The settlers engaged in fur trading and farming, and entered upon a peaceful, busy life.

It was not long, however, before trouble with the Indians began. Governor Kieft had a distillery which may have stood at Oude Dorp, at any rate on the island, and from it the Indians obtained rum which made them exceedingly intoxicated. Excited by drink, imposed upon by certain white persons, they took to disturbing the innocent settlers of Oude Dorp, and before the year was out five tribes had banded together, had descended upon the struggling little town, and burned it, slaying almost all the inhabitants. Those who escaped joined the soldiers at the blockhouse and made off across the Narrows.

A second time the town was built, and now eleven tribes banded together and repeated their destruction. Finally de Vries, the patroon of Staten Island, succeeded in making peace with the tribes and still again the farmhouses were built, in 1644. Such persistence and fortitude were characteristic of the Hollanders. But the following year trouble arose again. A squaw was seen by Hendrick Van Dyck, stealing peaches in his garden; he shot in sudden anger and killed the woman, and the famous "Peach War" opened. To avenge the squaw's death the tribes descended, sixty-four canoes arriving and nineteen hundred savage fighters, and in a short time Oude Dorp met its end. This was its end indeed; the Old Town never had the courage to rebuild, and the settlement vanished into a memory.

A little further on is South Beach, a people's playground, where peanut, ice-cream and chewing gum consumption is going on under the nose of history. The landmark of interest which formerly stood at this point has been demolished; it was the old Vreeland homestead, still another representative of the early Dutch farmhouses on the island.

The "common road" which followed the line of the shore a century ago swung westward at a point north of Fort Richmond and joined itself to another road leading from that fort inland. Converging, they made a southwesterly way, much as the Rapid Transit runs to-day; united, they brought up eventually at Tottenville, where the road continued in the form of a ferry to Perth Amboy.

CHAPTER VIII

TO OLD RICHMOND

IN the heart of Staten Island is the village of Richmond, once a most important center and county seat. A main road ran to it, penetrating one of the island's finest districts, both as farming land and from the standpoint of beauty; for the hills in and about Richmond offer the best of views. To-day the road running past Emerson Hill, Dongan Hills, and New Dorp, arrives at the same village and suggests the old route while not following it exactly.

The land rises from St. George on the beach, and reaches a fine height in Emerson Hill, named for the owner of the house which once stood there and its successor—Judge William Emerson. He was a brother of Ralph Waldo Emerson, and there are many Staten Island associations connected with both men. Judge Emerson was a New Englander, a Harvard graduate, and a close friend of his more famous brother. He built a house familiarly known as "The Snuggery" which stood on this steep tract of land; this was burned, and replaced by the building which now stands, a substantial old home of dignified proportions. Judge Emerson made his home on the hill from 1837 to 1856, and here his literary brother often visited him. It is supposed that the author wrote many of his poems here, and also his *Representative Men* lectures, which he delivered afterwards in England. The name "Snuggery" was especially fitting to the comfortable, genial, hospitable atmosphere which this family always created.

An interesting modern feature of Emerson Hill is the Japanese garden laid out by Mr. C. T. Brown. A curved Japanese bridge, sharp terraces, and curious ancient lamps are suggestive of the Orient in a spot adapted by nature to the picture.

From this point on toward Richmond, old houses marking early settlements are to be seen from time to time. One of these is the Perrine homestead at Dongan Hills, close beside the Richmond Road. It was built in 1668 and for two hundred years remained in the possession of one family. An addition has been built, but the old part still remains intact and can be recognized by its picturesque shabbiness of drooping roof and stained walls, and by the quaint bushes of wax berries which grow about its gate and worn path to the door.

Further along the road you will come to New

Dorp with its old Moravian church. The present building dates only from 1845, but the first worshipers of this faith on the island arrived much earlier. Captain Nicholas Garrison is said to have been the first Moravian to settle there. The story goes that he commanded a ship sailing from Georgia to New York, and on the voyage a violent storm was encountered. One of the passengers was Bishop Spangenburg; he remained calm during the peril, praying constantly for the survival of the ship. The storm subsided, all reached port in safety, and ever after the pious Bishop and the brave Captain were the firmest friends.

This vessel had been built for the use of the Moravians, or United Brethren, on Staten Island, between the years of 1745 and 1748, and Bishop Spangenburg had given almost its entire cost out of his liberal purse. For nine years the ship remained in the service of the church, crossing the Atlantic from New York to London or Amsterdam, and once traveling all the way to Greenland. She crossed the ocean twenty-four times in all, and bore an excellent reputation for seaworthiness.

During their earliest years on the island, the Moravians held services in a school. In 1756 it is said that there were only three communicant members on the island, these being Jacobus Vanderbilt and his wife Vettje, and Elizabeth

Inyard, a widow. It was not until 1762 that a number of persons applied for the establishment of a church. Cortelyou, Vanderbilt, and Perrine were among the names on this list. The original letter, expressing the desire that a church be established at New Dorp, near the home of the early colony of Waldenses, is now among the archives at Bethlehem, Pennsylvania.

In the following year (1763) the corner stone of the church and parsonage was laid. It was then the custom to erect these buildings all in one, and this building is still standing, although worship is held in the newer church.

The old building has seen stirring times. There was a night during the Revolution when British soldiers broke into the parsonage and wrought havoc, destroying all the furniture on which they could lay their hands. What was far more serious to the members of the old congregation, the enemy carried off the precious archives, and except for the law providing that duplicates of every official record shall be kept, there would now be a sadly broken line of history to record the Moravians' experiences.

Much wealth came into the church through the generosity of the Vanderbilt family. The mausoleum now to be seen on the hill behind the church is surrounded by a large tract of land, the entire cost of land and structure amounting to almost a million dollars. In both property and money the family gave largely to the church. William H. Vanderbilt, his son, and his grandson are all buried here.

The original building was given over to the uses of a school and a dwelling house when the new edifice was put up. It bears the tradition of being the first house of worship on the island in which an organ was used.

Across the street from the church and cemetery stands a dejected little residence, its lines practically unaltered from early days. This was the home of Aaron Cortelyou. Many years ago a burglary was committed in this house by a negro who paid the penalty on a gallows erected on the site of the present school at Richmond. This was the first legal execution in Richmond County.

You have passed beside Todt Hill while following the road; that hill whose name has led to many a debate among historians and many a facetious tale among fictionists. It rises from the Richmond Road at Garretsons, the district now known as Dongan Hills. Some of the early writers traced its name to a Dutch word, saying that during the days of battles with Indians on the island, a number of Dutch settlers were killed in a sharp conflict on this hill, and thus arose the name Todt, or Death Hill.

Others have claimed that the correct name was "Toad," and the tradition still lives of the

The Cortelyou Homestead at New Dorp.

The Moravian Church at New Dorp.

The Old Richmond Court-House.

The Old Perrine Homestead, Dongan Hills.

origin of this. It is said that a charming maiden resided on this hill, courted by more than one gallant. A certain one of the number was a most unwelcome guest at her home, and upon one occasion she secretly dropped a toad or two into his pockets, by way of practical joke. He took the hint that his society was not desired, and stayed away, but his friends learned of the joke and thereafter teased him to such an extent about his visits to "Toad Hill" that the name stuck.

Stony Brook is included in New Dorp. Here the Waldenses settled about the middle of the Seventeenth Century, thus forming the second settlement upon the island. The first courthouse, jail, and church were erected here. Witches who made themselves unpopular upon the island were punished at Stony Brook's ancient whipping post. Farmers gathered here with their produce on marketing days.

After the French and Indian War, General Monckton rested here with his army for a period of several weeks. Sir Jeffrey Amherst was invested with the Order of the Bath during this time, on October 25, 1761. During the Civil War there was a military post in New Dorp.

Beyond the Moravian Cemetery, still within the limits of New Dorp, the road curves, and at the curve, on a rambling building, hangs a sign which calls up some of the spiciest memories of Revolutionary days, when the rollicking British soldiers made their headquarters here, played their games and fought their duels. The sign, in modern lettering, is "Black Horse Tavern."

Fortunately the successive proprietors of the old road house have had enough sentiment, or eye for popularity, to preserve the name as it stood in the seventeen-hundreds when it was famous from end to end of the island. Originally there were two of these inns: (their stories are to be found in Morris's History) the Rose and Crown, where Sir William Howe stayed, and kept part of his staff, and summoned his generals in council; and the Black Horse, where other members of the staff stayed and where most of the revelry was carried on. The Rose and Crown has long since disappeared. The Black Horse has been altered and added to, but the main portion of the old building is to be seen.

Mine host of to-day is as ruddy and genial as we assume the host of old to have been. In his family dining-room he proudly displays the old beams, encased in pine, stretching sturdily across the ceiling. But his treasure of treasures is the ancient sign-board, the original, which used to sway before the door and beckon the passing soldier to the hospitality within.

It is said that one Lieutenant-Colonel Benton, a close friend of Howe's, was the possessor of a dashing black charger which had won a long list of races in old New Dorp Lane. At one time when Howe was reviewing some of his men, Benton mounted the animal and rode bravely forth to make a goodly display. The horse suddenly became alarmed and ran, Benton losing control completely, and in its fright the beast hurled itself against a wall of rock killing both itself and its rider. Curiously enough, it struck the fancy of the group of onlookers to call the tavern "The Black Horse" as a strange memorial to this incident. A British soldier who happened to have a knack with the brush painted the signboard. For long it swung outside the door, but the weathers of many winters were damaging it so much that it was taken down a few years ago and is now preserved indoors where any traveler may see it. The old painting is faint but still traceable, and the richly weathered wood is peppered with bullet holes.

The sign has had adventures of its own. After the Revolution it disappeared, and was not found until a neighboring barn, upon being torn down, revealed the shabby sign under its piles of rubbish. It was immediately restored to its old position.

Long years after the great war, the old proprietor of the inn used to receive visits from British officers who were living in Canada, and who, with their sons, liked to return to the old spot where they had seen some of their most adventurous days. The tavern was of great interest to them, also the knoll called Camp Hill, near the building. In the hollow west of the hill the dense woods used to screen many a duel during the time that the British were encamped at New Dorp. In fact the whole region teemed with their exploits, and came to be a sort of miniature Monte Carlo.

Half a block beyond the tavern is the old Fountain house. The lower part of it is the same stone building which was put up in 1668, and at the farther end an outcurving of bricks marks the old Dutch oven where many a substantial loaf used to be baked. The building to-day presents the appearance of a modern suburban cottage, but it is of genuine historical importance.

It is the remaining dwelling of that Waldensian–Huguenot settlement which dated back to the very early days of the island's white settlement, when the Waldensian church at Stony Brook was the first organized church there, as well as the first Waldensian church in North America. The denomination which grew from the belief of Peter Waldo in Lyons in the second half of the Twelfth Century had been persecuted in Europe and had been driven to wander much as the Huguenots were, and one group drifted to Staten Island. Here at Stony

Brook, near this old house, they built a quaint and humble little church which the Indians often attempted to destroy. Around the church grew up a loyal and thrifty congregation who made contented homes. The Fountain house is the best remaining relic of that period and group.

The road now soon arrives at Richmond. It was after the appointment of Governor Thomas Dongan, in 1683, that four counties were established: New York, Kings, Queens, and Richmond, the latter to include all of Staten Island, "and Shutter's Island, and the islands of meadow on the west side thereof." Stony Brook was the county seat, but this was later transferred to Richmond. The argument for this change was that "there is a bell by ye church which could be rung by ye high sheriff, and thus add dignity and respect to ye court of his Majesty ye King of Great Britain." The courthouse was built there, and in it, when court was not occupying its rooms, a village singing school was held.

The original courthouse has vanished, but the one which took its place is still standing, and this in itself is old. It is a large building at the head of a hilly block, and behind it the county jail stands. It has the look of age, and dates back to the eighteen-thirties. Opposite it is the old Surrogate's office, about a decade later in date and quaint in structure.

Down the hill, and only a short distance

beyond, is historic old St. Andrew's church which, in 1908, celebrated its two-hundredth anniversary and placed a tablet upon its wall in commemoration of the fact that it has held its own since the days when Queen Anne gave it the royal charter under which it was established. She gave likewise the silver communion service which is treasured in the Metropolitan Museum of Manhattan to-day, a duplicate of it being kept at the church. The bell, the prayer-books, and the pulpit cover which she gave have vanished in the course of time. The land which she gave still belongs to the church, and some of the land given in bequest by Ellis Duxbury, in Tompkinsville, for the maintenance of its minister, still assists in defraying the expenses of the parish.

A tablet on the wall of the church commemorates its famous Revolutionary event. It was in October, 1776, that General Hugh Mercer, who was in command of certain American forces in near-by New Jersey, crossed over to Staten Island to undertake an attack. He received the information that three companies of the enemy were stationed at Richmond; he therefore aimed his attack in that direction; a group of riflemen under Major Clarke were to advance to the east end of the village, along with Colonel Griffin who was detached with Colonel Patterson's battalion. On the other sides, so the plan was laid, the rest of the troops would attack Richmond.

It was on the night of October 15th that these troops from Perth Amboy crossed, and by daybreak Richmond was reached. Hearing of the Americans' approach, the British fled and the patriots halted, supposing the day to be theirs. But while they were halting, the sound of a volley of musketry astonished them, coming from the direction of St. Andrew's church; investigation proved that some of the enemy were remaining, using this spot as a defense. Then ensued a sharp battle. Major Clarke and his riflemen went forward to the attack, and found themselves confronted by a detachment of Skinner's men who were in front of the building. Firing a second volley, they retired within its walls. When a shot from a church window laid low one of Clarke's men directly beside him, he withheld no longer, and began the attack upon the church. By that time the American forces were gathered, and Colonel Griffin, who was in command, demanded that the British troops within the building surrender. They refused, and the Americans now stormed the building, shooting until every windowpane was shattered. Next the Americans began to throw rocks in at the windows, to save ammunition.

Upon this a soldier came to the door and stated that the troops within were ready to surrender, offering the explanation that the church was being used as a British hospital, and the sick and suffering lay within. The attacking party had not been aware of this fact, and Griffin mercifully permitted the surgeon to remain at his post with the sick while all others were marched out as prisoners.

The Americans started for Old Blazing Star Landing with their prisoners—their victory looked secure. But there were British troops ready to follow, and the upshot of the affair was that the prisoners were re-taken, along with those articles which the Americans had taken from the church—namely, forty-five muskets and other implements of war, and a standard of the British Light Horse. There were about twenty prisoners, all of whom had to be surrendered. It was with difficulty that the Americans themselves made their escape, and got across the ferry.

During the Revolution, while the British were in possession of the island, services were suspended in all its churches except this. It has been twice burned and restored, but it is easy to trace in the wall of to-day the original stones.

Among the headstones in the old churchyard are many of great age, their legends dim with the wear of years. One reads:

"Here lies the body of Sarah. She was a good neighbor, a tender mother to ten children, and

St. Andrew's Church.

Photograph by F. M. Simonson.

Cockloft Hall of "Salmagundi Papers."

A Bridge in the Japanese Garden of C. T. Brown, Emerson Hill, Staten Island.

The Old Fountain House at New Dorp, a Relic of the Waldensian Settlement. The Stone Lower Part Is the Original Building. House Dates back to 1668.

an obedient wife," thus summing up all the feminine virtues. And another:

Free from the busy cares of life,
  Here lies a prudent virtuous wife,
Who never caused a husband's sigh,
  But once, alas, that she must die.

CHAPTER IX

FROM TOTTENVILLE TO PERTH AMBOY

MORE than two hundred years ago Captain Christopher Billopp piled up the deck of his vessel with empty barrels and set sail to encircle Staten Island. Thereby hangs a much longer tale than the worthy Captain Billopp ever dreamed he was writing in the annals of New York State history.

Because it took him only a little over twenty-three hours to accomplish his trip, Staten Island was made a part of New York State, instead of New Jersey, and all because those empty barrels on Captain Billopp's deck gave him such excellent gain in sailing power.

The associations with the Billopp story lie in Tottenville, at the remote end of the island. This village perpetuates the honored name of Totten, long familiar in the island's history. Although in another State than Perth Amboy, the two have been inseparably linked by their position, so that old inhabitants of either refer to "the other side" as if they were one town. From a paper of 1737 this announcement was reprinted in Valentine's Manual:

"These are to inform all persons that there is a ferry settled from Amboy over to Staten Island, which is duly attended for the conveniency of those that have occasion to pass and repass that way. The ferriage is fourteen pence, Jersey currency, for man and horse, and five pence for a single passenger."

The railroad which whirls the traveler across the island to Tottenville carries him over a most surprising district when he considers the fact that he is within the limits of Greater New York. It is only a short time since the census estimate showed fewer than three inhabitants to the acre on this island, and the ride across many open miles in this direction makes the figures believable, in spite of the crowded Staten Island near the ferry, with which we are more familiar. At times the up-hill and down-dale country appears almost a wilderness, stretching away toward the water; a wilderness fertile and ready, waiting to be reclaimed.

The Billopp house, which is the pilgrim's goal, stands at some distance from the Tottenville station, and a walk of about a mile awaits one who does not travel in carriage or automobile. In general, the directions are: to turn to the left from the railroad track; follow the street up from the ferry to Elliott Avenue; now turn toward the right, and let Elliott Avenue lead you into a sandy road which cuts across a decidedly waste place. Kelley gives directions, "Follow Broadway, Main Street and Amboy Road to the Lane and Bentley Avenue," but the traveler will find the Billopp house more readily if he asks the way than by means of any printed rules.

It stands a little way beyond a group of farmhouses, and is surrounded by very large trees, generations old, with the sort of gigantic trunks that one seldom sees in this part of the world, where forest fires and reckless axes have wrought havoc. Here, under the shade of these trees, stands the famous old "Manor of Bentley," as the house was called in the days of its golden prime; now a battered, uncared-for relic, inhabited but neglected, forgotten except by the history lover.

With one exception, its features wear exactly the same appearance as in the past. The one change consists in the removal of the porch which used to run across the front of the building, with colonial pillars and a slant roof. This porch rotted until it had to be torn down; but the splendid stone-work of early days, when building was done for the future, is in excellent condition even now.

The Billopp house is of such interest in New York's history, that its decay is a melancholy sight. Built in 1668, it was from the first connected with some of the most interesting passages in the island's records.

After Staten Island had been discovered by Hendrick Hudson, there followed years of Dutch colonial government in it, during which this fine tidbit of land, in what came to be Tottenville, belonged to Nova Cæsarea, the name of that period for New Jersey.

Now James, the Duke of York and brother to Charles the Second, was given a sort of rulership over all the king's possessions in America. Provinces which had been under Dutch control passed into English hands. Staten Island became a scene of discord; to the English and Dutch dissensions the French added their quarrels, and matters began to look somewhat like a Kilkenny-cat controversy.

To settle matters, the Duke finally came to a decidedly original decision. He ordained that if the islands in the harbor of New York could be circumnavigated in twenty-four hours they should belong to the colony of New York; otherwise, Nova Cæsarea, or New Jersey, was to possess them. The next thing was to find the right man to attend to the circumnavigation.

It happened at the fortunate time that Captain Christopher Billopp was stopping at Perth Amboy. His vessel, called *The Bentley*, was a small one, probably belonging to the British navy, although there seems to be a question as to whether it was of the merchant service or not.

Billopp was chosen to perform the Duke's task. He was accounted an excellent seaman; but the feat did not promise to be easy, even so. He did not start out until he had thought over the matter carefully, to determine how he would be best able to accomplish it.

And thus he hit upon the idea of the empty barrels. If he were to cover his deck with them, he argued, he would gain much sailing power. Thus laden he set out, and we can picture the excitement which held New Yorkers and New Jerseyites in throbbing suspense.

Captain Billopp performed his feat. Nay, he more than performed it; a trifle over twenty-three hours sufficed for his sail, and Staten Island was New York's.

The Duke had a reward ready. So much pleased was he with Billopp's success, that, instead of letting him return to England to make his home, he presented the Captain with 1163 acres of land on Staten Island and invited him to remain there.

This land was at that corner of the island where you are now. So fine a plum had fallen into the worthy seaman's hands that he determined to make the most of it, and he set himself at once to building a suitable residence. He named it, for the vessel which had won him his laurels, the Manor of Bentley. The stones of which it was built were found in the vicinity, and were suitable for the best of walls; but Billopp sent to Belgium for the bricks needed, and to England for the cement.

The next thing for a wise sea-captain to do, having settled down in a home on dry land, was to take unto himself a wife—which he did. The daughter of Thomas Farmar, a judge who lived in Richmond County, looked comely to him, and her he chose.

Thus was established the Billopp household, destined to play an important part in local history. The Captain himself disappeared in the early seventeen-hundreds, before the Revolution came on; it is believed that his vessel, *The Bentley*, went down with him while he was making a voyage to England to visit his old home. He left a widow and one charming daughter, Miss Eugenia Billopp, who had received a fashionable education at the Perth Amboy Academy across the Kill. Miss Eugenia conceived an affection for her cousin, another Thomas Farmar, and the mother gave permission for the marriage to take place on the proviso that the happy groom should adopt the name of Billopp and make his home in the Manor of Bentley.

So the family name was perpetuated. The old Captain's grandson, likewise named Christopher, lived to be a loyalist and to be carried off by a group of American rangers who held him for ransom and kept him captive until an American prisoner was given in exchange. Once more he was taken captive, but at Howe's request General Washington set him free. He left this part of the country after the war, and took up his residence in the more sympathetic atmosphere of Nova Scotia.

A family burial ground was early established near the old house in Tottenville, and until recently some of the headstones were to be seen in their places. Members of the Billopp family, and their Indian friends, were laid near the house. At last only two headstones remained, and these were being so much damaged by the ubiquitous souvenir fiend, who chipped off bits to carry away, that they were removed to the cellar of the house.

The inscription on one of them reads (some letters being obliterated):

". . . Lyes ye Body of Thomas Billopp Esq, son of Thomas Farmar Esq. Dec^{d} August ye 2^{d} 1750 In ye 39th year of his age."

And the other:

"Here lyes ye Body of Evjenea y^{e} Wife of Thomas Billopp. Aged 23 years . . . March. . . ."

The old cellar has its own tradition. That black, cavernous doorway, which looks like a gulping mouth awaiting the unwary, points the way to the dungeon beyond. A veritable

"The Old Stone House in Willock's Lane," Used by the British during the Revolution. Built 1734. (Perth Amboy.)

Billopp House, Tottenville. Built 1668. Where Howe, Clinton, Cornwallis, and Burgoyne were Entertained.

"Dungeon" Approach, Billopp House, Tottenville. Through this Cellar Door Lies the Entrance to the Famous Dungeon where Patriots are Supposed to have been Imprisoned, and from which a Subway may have Led to the River.

The "Parker Castle" in Perth Amboy.

dungeon it is, probably as mysteriously legend-like as any cellar of an American citizen ever contained. You will grope your way from the dim light which surrounds the entrance, on into the growing dusk, until you reach a far corner where total blackness reigns. Stooping, striving to follow your guide, feeling your way, you enter at last a room like a cave, solidly walled and ominous.

Here, during that period of the Revolution when the house was held as a British outpost, it is said that this dungeon was put to stern uses. Our own American patriots are supposed to have been held captive there. Many a hardship did they suffer in this black cell. It is believed that an underground passage was made at that time, leading down to the river, a distance of two hundred yards; but to-day this cannot be traced. There is said to be a fairly good foundation for the theory.

But these gloomy tales of the dungeon, the suffering prisoners, and the underground passage, are only one side of the old house's history. Perhaps they are the more romantic side; when Cooper wrote *The Water Witch* he laid one of its scenes in this mysterious cellar. But gay and sparkling scenes took place above-stairs. Many a banquet did the old manor see; many a daintily brocaded lady, many a gallant ruffled and powdered gentleman tripped to light measure at the

Billopp balls. Colonel Billopp became famous for his magnificent entertainments. Such officers as Howe, Cornwallis, Clinton, Burgoyne, Knyphausen, and André were among his guests.

It was after the Battle of Long Island in 1776 that Howe went to the Billopp house to meet Benjamin Franklin, John Adams, and Edward Rutledge, who were chosen to confer upon the issues of the war. They hoped for peace, but when they found that Howe's offer was merely to resume old conditions, as before the war, the conference came to an end without results.

The village of Tottenville was once known as the Manor of Bentley, and the peninsula at its farthest point, later called Ward's Point, was originally Billopp's Point. Later on the village became simply "Bentley." Then along came the Totten family, and the town became divided against itself, for the lower section, hailing a new hero, desired that it be called after Totten. With the upper section battling for "Bentley," the lower for "Tottenville," the friction was bitter, until the victory of the lower half settled the question. The name of Totten stands in the records of old St. Andrew's Church, known for its "respectability and influence."

Looking over to the Jersey shore, your eye is crossing the Arthur Kill, which name is a corruption of the old Dutch "Achter Cull," and was the same as Staten Island Sound. Davis calls attention to a similar corruption in the name Kill van Kull, as we now abbreviate and spell it; this was once upon a time "Het Kill van het Cull," or "the stream of the bay."

Across the kills early ferries used to ply; crossings were adopted by the Indians, and later the white settlers followed in their paths. Several ferries were operated early at Port Richmond which lies across the Kill van Kull from Bayonne; Decker's Ferry is named as far back as 1777, and others followed it. From Staten Island to Elizabethtown Point a ferry was operated by Adoniah Schuyler in 1762. Crossing to-day from Tottenville to Perth Amboy you are traveling in practically the same line as the early ferry between these points.

With the modern industrial skyline of the Jersey shore ahead of you, and the crowding craft hovering all about you on the water, it is hard to realize that at one time these ferries were closed because there was no travel between the two shores, on account of animosity. So strong a tie now binds them that we can hardly think of Staten Island as a lone continent, unvisited by her neighbors. The Dutch did not release their hold willingly, and there were many struggles over the proprietorship, which brought about hard feeling that it took considerable time to heal.

Long ago Perth Amboy was reckoned a rival of New York, being a thriving and fashionable young city. It fell behind in the race, but remained to this day a town of much charm.

A number of old buildings stand, records of the days when it was a better-known center. Until recently it has been possible to see the old barracks used in the Revolution, but these have finally been torn down. The "Governor's Mansion" stands, in excellent condition, and lends dignity to the entire street upon which it is conspicuous. It is now used as a hotel, having changed hands several times since it was built in 1784, and being at present owned by John S. Hanson. It is at No. 149 Kearney Street.

The Board of Lords Proprietors of East Jersey erected it as a home for the colonial governor. The solid material of which it is built was brought over from England. Governor William Franklin occupied the house, and it was used as a headquarters for army officers during the Revolution. Previous to this it had been occupied by Governor Hamilton and other royal governors.

After the Revolution the place became a gay inn, and was known for its fashion and merry-makings. This famous hotel was called "The Brighton." Later on it changed its ways once more, and became a home for Presbyterian ministers, which it remained for a score of years.

Since it entered upon the career of a modern

hostelry many improvements have been made, but not in a way to alter the general aspect of the old building. There is now a sun parlor on the roof, with a view stretching away to Sandy Hook, and a modern garden in the rear, but these additions do not destroy the ancestral appearance of the mansion.

Going back in the direction of the ferry and turning up Water Street, you will come upon a somewhat dilapidated structure known as "Parker Castle." Several generations of the family have dwelt there since the days when James Parker built it. In the time of the Revolution it was known as one of the finest dwellings in this part of the country.

Parker himself took no part in the war, so his property was not confiscated; but he had connections on the royal side, therefore it was considered necessary to place him under restraint, and in 1777 he was kept in confinement in Morristown. The family long dwelt there, and its members have represented the law, the army, and the state. Other persons live there now, but many relics of the old days are preserved, among them, the kitchen's corner cupboard.

"The Old Stone House in Willock's Lane" is the familiar appellation applied to a quaint little structure standing to the south of Fayette Street. It is said that the house was built in 1734, and had the eventful experience of being occupied by British soldiers during the Revolutionary War. For many years it was the home of the Marsh family, well-known in Perth Amboy annals, and was afterwards sold to William B. Watson. It is now the property of William W. Pierce.

WESTWARD INTO NEW JERSEY

CHAPTER X

NEWARK, A TURNPIKE CENTER

NEWARK of a century ago was to its section of New Jersey much the same as any railway center is to-day. This was the era of the turnpike, and it was the main organ from which many arteries ran out in various directions into the State.

In its earliest days it had lived its own life, paying little attention to other communities. The first definite move toward outreaching was made in 1765, when, by act of the Assembly, the Plank Road was provided for. This road had always been Newark's outlet toward the lower part of the river, but now it became part of a system of communication with Powles Hook. The plank construction was an innovation and excited much comment. The Frenchman, Brissot de Warville, is quoted as saying: "Built wholly of wood, with much labor and perseverance, in the midst of water, on a soil that trembles under your feet, it proves to what point may be carried the patience of man, who is determined to conquer nature."

Urquhart traces the progress of travel, which now received a new impetus. Later in the same year a law was passed providing for the appointment of road commissioners to run out straight public roads, between New York and Philadelphia. In 1756, the first New York-Philadelphia stage had been put through, by way of Perth Amboy and Trenton, and now that the straightening of the road was undertaken, a second stage was established, to follow the new route. But popular travel still inclined to Elizabeth and its ferry instead of Newark, until after the Revolution. The first road travel was primitive and subject to some hardships, thus described by a graphic pen of that day:

"All the way to Newark (9 miles) is a very flat, marshy country, intersected with rivers; many cedar swamps, abounding with mosquitoes, which bit our legs, and hands, exceedingly; where they fix they will continue sucking our blood if not disturbed, till they swell four times their ordinary size, when they absolutely fall off and burst from their fulness. At two miles we cross a large cedar swamp; at three miles we intersect the road leading to Bergen, a Dutch town, half a mile on our right; at five miles we cross Hackensack (a little below the site of the present bridge at what was known as Dow's Ferry); at six we cross Passaic River (coachee and all) in a scoul, by means of pulling a rope fastened on the opposite side."

But the difficulties of this primitive travel were forgotten when the turnpike era brought prosperity and lively communication. The position of Newark made it a natural gateway to inner New Jersey, and one enterprise led to another, until it became a turnpike center. The Newark and Hackensack bridges were built, and a turnpike laid between them. Business was stimulated, and companies of individuals began to build similar roads, making a profit from the tolls. The Newark to Pompton Turnpike Company was incorporated in 1806, and it followed the line, with few changes, of the old Horseneck Road which had been laid down before the Revolution. Also in 1806, the Mt. Pleasant Turnpike Company sprang into being and stretched its work all the way to Morristown, following the old Crane Road, and earlier trails, by way of Whippany. And still another—the Springfield and Newark Company—organized to build a turnpike in this eventful year. The Newark and Morristown Turnpike opened in 1811, and others followed, until this section of New Jersey was a network of tollgate roads, veining out in every direction from the thriving center.

Newark is an old city of colorful history. When a place comes to be associated with the smokestacks and dinner pails of commerce, it takes an agile imagination to leap back to the times of tomahawks and redcoats, to visualize a horde of swashbuckling figures descending upon a farmhouse where factories now stand—"What ho, my good woman, a draught from yonder dairy, and right quickly!"—or to hear the beating of drums in streets where trolley bells now clang, summoning the townsmen to discuss the latest Indian peril. To call up these times in modern Newark, one must become deaf to a roar of railroads, trolleys, and automobiles, blind to crowded blocks of department-store show windows. Armies of human beings, factory workers, toilers in a great industrial system, have thronged in to take the place of a handful of Connecticut settlers who found the Passaic shore a likely land some two and a half centuries ago. Our trip thither to-day, shot through a sub-river tube, discharged lightly a few minutes later, fairly reproaches us with its ease and cheapness, when we consider the fact that these people struggled from Connecticut to New Jersey through such difficulties as might pertain to a long ocean voyage, and finally landed as worn and weary as escaped Huguenots or Pilgrim fathers upon long-looked-for shores.

Broad and Market streets meet at the center of Newark to-day as yesterday. Standing there, you can recall the fact that the intersection of these streets was the "Four Corners" of the original town, and was called so from the beginning. Here the settlers gathered whenever any matter of importance called them forth. Here the drum beating to summon them took place. And near here stands still the old Presbyterian Church which was the very pulse of the original settlement.

It was in 1666 that the group from Connecticut arrived. The settlement was made much as colonies in our Western States are created nowadays; that is to say, inducements were offered to come in and take up land. Nowadays railroads make special rates. At that time the colonists had to provide their own boat. But the fundamental principle was quite the same, and it interested Connecticut people, who always showed a tendency to pioneering. New Jersey was as much a pioneer country then as the Kansas plains were in the days of Frémont.

It was Governor Carteret who offered the inducements, and the dwellers of Milford, Connecticut, listened with attention. Robert Treat was sent to look the offer over, for a shrewd Yankee spirit was abroad in New England even then. Treat reported on the land with enthusiasm, and to his urging is credited the founding of Newark.

At this time, about 1665, all the region was a wilderness. The only roads through it were the trails of Indians and of wild animals. But the situation appeared to Treat to be excellent, here on the banks of the Passaic, and thirty families prepared to transport themselves in a ship commanded by Captain Samuel Swaine. It is reported that when the landing was about to be made, great rivalry arose among the passengers as to who should first set foot upon the new land, and at last it was voted that the Captain's fair daughter, Elizabeth, be given the privilege. Her lover, Josiah Ward, waded out knee-deep into the water to assist her to reach the land.

According to the custom of loyal Connecticut Presbyterians, the first thing done in the building of the new colony was to establish a church. The Rev. Abraham Pierson was the first pastor; fourteen others in succession have followed him. The church now standing is the third built upon this site, the first having been a little wooden temple, the next a simple stone structure erected in 1715, and the one now standing dating from 1791. The Rev. Aaron Burr, father of the statesman, was one of the famous men who held the pulpit in early days, and his portrait now hangs within the parish house.

The Old First Presbyterian Church in Newark.

Boxwood Hall, Elizabeth. Once the Home of Elias Boudinot.

The Schoolhouse at the Old Lyons Farms, where Washington Spoke to the Children.

The Lyons Farmhouse, Said to be the Oldest House in New Jersey.

This Aaron Burr later became a founder of Princeton College. Dr. James Richards, another of the distinguished line of pastors, gave up his church duties to become president of Auburn Theological Seminary. Dr. Edward Dorr Griffin became president of Williams. Abraham Pierson was identified with Yale. Portraits, and a tablet, are among the memorials to early days, and behind the church lies the old burying-ground with many a familiar and honored name engraved upon the stones.

They were stirring times when the residents of Newark—New Work was the first form of the name—gathered under the roof of this church, summoned by the roll of the town drums, to learn that there were signs of a new Indian outbreak in the air, and to discuss means of protection. It had been supposed that the Indians were settled into peace when the town was established, but this idea was soon disproved. The price paid them for the town was liberal for that day, and might have been sufficient to satisfy them, as prices went then; it was:

"Fifty double hands of powder, 100 bars of lead, twenty axes, twenty coats, ten guns, twenty pistols, ten kettles, ten swords, four blankets, four barrels of beer, ten pairs of breeches, fifty knives, twenty hoes, eight hundred and fifty fathoms of wampum, two ankers of liquors, and three troopers' coats." It has been pointed out by Mr. Urquhart, however, that in 1904 one lot near the church, a lot of just 100×38 feet, was sold for four hundred thousand dollars.

Under the roof of this ancient and historical church, some of the most modern forms of institutional work are going forward to-day. In the rear of the building is a girls' lunch room, where for a few cents the working girl of Newark is provided with a wholesome lunch, and she may rest in a comfortable lounging room. Boys' clubs and a gymnasium play their part in the Twentieth Century scheme of things.

On Broad Street stands picturesque old Trinity, younger in the city's annals than the "Old First," but historic for all that. Its spire is the original structure, although it caps a building much more recent than itself.

By turning into West Park Street, a few doors west of Broad you will come upon the building in which the New Jersey Historical Society has its headquarters. A large and valuable collection is displayed here. One of the documents on which the Society prides itself is the nine-foot parchment roll, signed when the Duke of York cut his possessions in half and gave to Lord John Berkeley and Sir George Carteret all the land which is now the State of New Jersey, this parchment roll being the agreement in formal shape. The Duke had received from his brother, King Charles, the royal charter for lands now including New York and New Jersey, and he handed over the latter to these gentlemen. The agreement was entitled, "The Concessions and Agreements of the Lords Proprietors of Nova Cæsarea or New Jersey, to and with all and every of the adventurers and all such as shall settle and plant there."

The Society has a remarkably full collection of photographs of historic houses in New Jersey—an example which every State would do well to follow, as each year sees one or more slipping from the muster roll, either through final decay, or to make way for the erection of new buildings.

Returning to Broad Street and following it north, you come to the House of Prayer, an Episcopal church beside which its rectory stands. The latter, at the corner of State Street, was known in other days as the old Plume homestead. It was built before the Revolution, and at that time it was beyond the town limits, although the railroad now booms in its ears and business pushes close upon it.

It is said that Aunt Nancy Visher Plume, as she was known to her friends, built the house, probably in 1710. Col. John I. Plume, known to the War of 1812, was born here. Being on the edge of town, it was a great stopping-place for soldiers when the Revolution came on, and the story is told that in 1777 some Hessians, trailing over this part of the country to see what disturbance they could cause, came across the hospitable farmhouse, entered, and took possession of its comforts. There was provender in the barn and milk in the dairy. The troopers flung their possessions about and made themselves entirely at home, demanding cream, wood, everything they fancied.

At last Mistress Plume became so indignant that her fear fled. Drawing herself up to all the feminine height she could muster, she faced the offenders. Oaths were foreign to her fair lips; but the stress of the moment overcame her, and she uttered such profanity as she would not have believed herself capable of.

"Ram's horn, if I die for it!" she cried with rage and determination.

Her violence amused the Hessian officer to such an extent that he roared with laughter, and ordered his men to conduct themselves with decency.

The house still preserves early treasures—big fireplaces, one having the old corner cupboard built above it; the finely hand-carved woodwork; the hand-made hinges with heavy rivets; even hand-made nails of huge dimensions have been found in making repairs, and kept as mementoes of Mistress Plume's day.

At the corner of Gouverneur Street and Mt.

Pleasant Avenue stands Cockloft Hall, conveniently reached from the Clinton Avenue car line. Clinton Avenue, by the way, is one of the oldest roads in Newark, being merely a broadening and straightening of an important Indian trail. The house stands two short blocks from it. It is withdrawn from the street, surrounded by a large lawn, and is well kept. Many years ago Washington Irving visited it, and wrote *Salmagundi* beneath its hospitable roof.

The house was built by the Gouverneur family and occupied by Gouverneur Kemble, and it was a famous resort for Irving, Paulding, and other men of letters. Irving and his friends were called the "Lads of Kilkenny" and known to everyone around as the merriest of companies. The host whom Irving describes was Isaac Gouverneur.

Even now the place has charm enough to explain those passages in which the author, walking on the Battery, reflects upon the crowded staleness of the city and the delights of the open.

"I all at once discovered that it was but to pack up my portmanteau, bid adieu for awhile to my elbow chair, and in a little time I should be transported from the region of smoke, and noise, and dust, to the enjoyment of a far sweeter prospect and a brighter sky. The next morning I was off full tilt to Cockloft Hall, leaving my man Pompey to follow at his leisure with my baggage. . . . The Hall is pleasantly situated on the banks of a sweet pastoral stream; not so near town as to invite an inundation of idle acquaintance, who come to lounge away an afternoon, nor so distant as to render it an absolute deed of charity or friendship to perform the journey. It is one of the oldest habitations in the country, and was built by my cousin Christopher's grandfather, to form a 'snug retreat, where he meant to sit himself down in his old days, and be comfortable for the rest of his life.'"

We hardly speak of the "sweet pastoral stream" which flows past commercial Newark in such poetical phrasing in these days, but when we picture the Newark of then, we can realize what a refuge this spot was to Irving when the city pressed close upon his heels.

"To such as have not yet lost the rural feeling, I address this picture," concludes the author, "and in the honest sincerity of a warm heart I invite them to turn aside from bustle, care and toil, to tarry with me for a season, in the hospitable mansion of the Cocklofts."

A little way behind Newark, on the road to Elizabeth, lies old Lyons Farms. This is not the district known to the real-estate agent and the bungalow dweller as Lyons Farms today. The latter is some distance further, much nearer to Elizabeth. The old district, first claimant to the name, is reached by following Elizabeth Avenue to where houses begin to thin out and fields appear. At the corner of Chancellor Street stands one of the old Lyons Farms buildings.

It is known now as an open-air school. Here is another striking instance, similar to that of the Presbyterian Church, of an ancient building, charged with our oldest United States tradition, dedicated to the most advanced of present-day uses. There is a certain charm in finding an old building of respected lineage keeping abreast of the times. For the wooden predecessor of this little old stone schoolhouse was built in the year 1728, when the ground on which it stands was purchased from the Hackensack Indians for the price of a quarter-pound of powder.

It grew to have an extremely high standing as an institution—in fact, it was known as the finest school in the State of New Jersey. So strong was its reputation for thoroughness and advancement, that the boys who attended it traveled hither from remote regions, to be prepared for college beneath its small roof.

This school played its part in the Revolution. During the brief time that Washington paused in Newark on his way to winter quarters in Morristown, he stopped here and spoke to the children. We can picture how those who lived to grow up used to remember his words and tell the story to their own grandchildren.

The building came to be a headquarters for public gatherings, and its yard, along with the surrounding fields, was used for the marshaling of five thousand soldiers, one of the largest bodies of those whom the State of New Jersey sent to the War for Independence. The little wooden building which originally stood on this spot was burned by Tory marauders, and in its place was erected the stone schoolhouse which now stands—Jersey brownstone is the material used for the stout walls.

Modern science and sympathy have worked together to construct a school which shall afford opportunities for good instruction, and at the same time reconstruct the health of children who are held back because of physical handicaps. An open-air addition has been built at one end, and here the youngsters of the Twentieth Century work and get into mischief much as those of George Washington's period did.

Standing on the height which surrounds the school you are within sight of the old Lyons farmhouse. It lies in a hollow near by. This building is said to be the oldest house in the State, dating back more than one hundred years before the Revolution.

William Meeker built it about 1670, and it housed seven generations of the same family.

It touched Revolutionary history many a time, harboring those who took part in the war and receiving disturbing calls from redcoats. The great-great-grandson of the builder, Josiah by name, served, in a way, in the war, although the care of his aged and feeble mother prevented him from leaving home to enter active service at the front. But his assistance rendered in frequently carrying messages did much to help the American cause.

The last of the long line of descent of this family was William Grummon, who dwelt in the house during a long lifetime. His death, in 1913, brought the line to an end. The present dwellers have no connection with the traditions of the place, and the building has slipped far into decay.

Powles Hook, which was the natural key to communication with Newark and the roads beyond, occupied the same spot as the Jersey City which was incorporated in 1820. There are almost a dozen spellings of the Dutch-born name. Its chief rôle in history was played when "Light-Horse Harry Lee" successfully attacked the British garrison stationed there in August, 1779.

Powles Hook was a farming district until the year 1764, when the establishment of a ferry took place, and thus did the early New Yorker set out for the lower Jersey shore. From that time on, business sprang up around the ferry. A tavern and ferry-house in one were erected by Michael Cornelisson, and here the travelers across North River paused to gossip and regale themselves.

CHAPTER XI

ELIZABETH, AND THE KING'S HIGHWAY

IN the days when powdered hair towered high upon fair heads, when waists were wasp-like and stiff silks rustled; when knee-breeches flourished and gentlemanly hats were cocked; when the strains of stately minuet music floated from ballroom windows; when the "scarlet fever," as Susannah Livingston dubbed it, was raging among American belles, because of all the fascinating redcoats turned loose in our land to wreck property, and hearts into the bargain—in those days Elizabethtown was at its height.

Few towns in our country's history record as glittering a tale of the past as does Elizabeth. Our national tradition is so largely composed of gallantly-borne hardships, of battle, persecution, and grimly-won victories, that the Elizabethan tales contrast with these as if they were glimpses of an early French court.

In Revolutionary times this town was one of the leading social centers of America. To a great extent this was due to its being accessible from many directions. The highway from Newark opened one easy way to it from New York; the same road continued on to Philadelphia, and made it thus open to both large cities. Besides this, the ferry, its early means of communication with the outer world, was much in use, and minor roads led inland to minor points.

In earliest days there was a road leading on past New Brunswick, and known as "the upper road." At times of high water this was not passable, as, in its course, the Raritan and the Delaware rivers both had to be forded. But in time these primitive fordings were done away with, the road was widened, straightened, and made smoother, and it was at last distinguished by the title of "The King's Highway." Along this Highway social life flowed for many years.

Elizabeth is fortunate in preserving a number of the old houses which are strongly associated with its early and sparkling history. In and about East Jersey Street you will find yourself in the midst of one of the most aristocratic residence sections of any of the New Jersey towns.

At No. 1105 East Jersey Street you will see a doctor's sign of the Twentieth Century hanging before an old and dignified door. This house, of good old colonial pattern, is the residence which Dr. William Barnet, that famously testy old physician, built in 1763, and which later became famous as the home of General Winfield Scott.

Dr. Barnet, its first occupant, was a surgeon in the American army during the War of Independence, and is said to have been the man who introduced vaccination into the town of Elizabeth, a matter of great importance in those days, because of the prevalence of smallpox. Dr. Barnet was so quick-tempered, tradition has it, that no patient could be sure in visiting him whether he would receive a pill, a scolding, or even a box on the ear—the latter, if Barnet believed the patient's ailment to be imaginary.

During 1781, when the British ran riot hereabouts, the doctor's house was plundered. It is recorded that he said indignantly: "They emptied my feather beds in the street, broke in windows, smashed my mirrors, and left our pantry and storeroom department bare. I could forgive them all, but that the rascals stole from my kitchen wall the finest string of red peppers in all Elizabethtown."

Later, Colonel Mayo bought the place, and his daughter became the bride of Lieut.-Gen. Winfield Scott. This was about the time that the eighteen-hundreds were ushered in. The first years of the young woman's married life were spent there happily with her husband; then followed the dark years when he was away at war. At last this cloudy period was over, and the

General came home for good, to spend his quiet years in a well-earned rest. The house, called Hampton Place, was conducted like a genuine old-time southern home (Elizabeth was a great summer resort for Southerners at that time), and it is said that General Scott was uncomfortable if he ever sat down to his dinner table without a guest. He was a Virginian of the old school, and Hampton Place was, in spirit, a Virginia home.

A little beyond, at No. 1073 in this street, is a house which appears plain enough at first glance, neither modern nor old in pattern; a second glance reveals the fact that old walls end at the top of the second story, and two newer stories have been added on. This is now the Home for Aged Women, but the brilliant old days knew it as Boxwood Hall, or the Boudinot mansion, one of the most aristocratic dwellings in the street.

If you will ring the bell and let a charmingly quaint little old lady show you in, you can see the fine broad hall, the spacious rooms, the old fireplaces which were there probably as early as the year 1750. The family brought carved mantels from France to adorn their home; they furnished in a manner which was accounted lavish in that period, and it is said that Washington himself once expressed great admiration for the house decorations when visiting there.

Samuel Woodruff came first, then the residence

The Old Fort, Elizabeth, Built in 1734.

The Old Château in Elizabeth, the Home of Cavalier Jouet.

The First Presbyterian Church, Elizabeth, Built in 1784. The Original Building was Burnt by the British.

House in Elizabeth, where General Winfield Scott Lived.

passed into the hands of Elias Boudinot, who dwelt in it during the Revolution. He was President of the Continental Congress, and, in that capacity, signed the treaty of peace with Great Britain. He gave the house its never-to-be-forgotten name of Boxwood Hall by planting a great number of boxwoods around it; these are now dead, but their tradition remains.

Many famous visitors were entertained at this home. In 1789 Washington stopped here on his way to the ceremonies of his inauguration. He met a committee of Congress and lunched in the great dining-room. It was at the Livingston home, by the way, that Mrs. Washington stopped on her way to join her husband during these same festivities; this was Liberty Hall, on the other side of town. Years later, when Jonathan Dayton lived at Boxwood he entertained Lafayette—in 1834.

During the war, Boxwood Hall was levied on by a party of redcoats, and the daughter Susan held her own in quick retort to the commanding officer. One of the members of the household had asked for British protection, she indignantly reminded him.

"It was not by your advice, I presume," he replied, and her fearless answer faced him:

"That it never was, I can tell you."

She was known to her father as his "little lamb," a name given in a mood of affectionate paternal satire.

This daughter of the Boudinots, with her swift-blooded French descent,—one of the old Huguenot families they were, fleeing to our land after the revocation of the Edict of Nantes —married and lived to become one of the famously brilliant women who surrounded the President's wife in Philadelphia, when it was the seat of our government. During the war, the Hon. Elias Boudinot spent much time in Philadelphia, but he settled down for a period of rest afterwards, among his boxwoods. He finally moved to Philadelphia, and the house fell into other hands; it has had various private occupants, has been a young ladies' boarding school, and is now a home for the aged. Its best-known occupants were the first, Samuel Woodruff, member of the board of aldermen, the mayor, and a trustee of the College of New Jersey; Boudinot himself; and General Dayton, prominent in Congress, and an early United States Senator from New Jersey.

A famous incident connected with the history of the building is that the slain body of Parson Caldwell, the "Fighting Parson" of the Presbyterian Church, was placed on view on the steps in front of the house. The funeral was held here and an address was made by Boudinot.

Across the street and a few doors beyond, at the southwest corner of Catherine Street, is a house now known as "the Dix home." This was the home of Governor Jonathan Belcher, so renowned for his saintliness that Whitefield said of him, "He is ripening for Heaven apace." This is a most interesting statement to reflect upon, as applied to a distinguished occupant of a high political position. But the fact that this saintly and esteemed gentleman dwelt here seems to hold a minor place in popular history, compared with the fact that perhaps the most brilliant wedding of the Revolution took place within these walls.

It meant bravery to give a conspicuous social function in those times, for the redcoats took it upon themselves to raid and make all sorts of trouble wherever they heard of such affairs going on. But when Miss "Caty" Smith, the daughter of William Peartree Smith, was to be married—although it was the troublous year 1778—it was determined that the Belcher house, where the ceremony was to be held, should be as gay as possible, and let the redcoats do their best to spoil the fun! "Caty" was to be married to young Boudinot, so the wedding was a great event in every way, and the most distinguished of Americans were to be present.

The great day came and the guests assembled. No less a person than Alexander Hamilton was master of ceremonies. Washington and Lafayette were guests. The lights poured forth into the quiet street, music and voices rang, the gayety reached an unprecedented height. Any nervousness which may have been felt at first, passed as the hours went by without molestation.

But a fortnight later the price of festivity was paid. A party of British soldiers, having heard of the affair, came to the house; finding the young husband absent, they raided, destroying the furniture and many valuable family portraits in a wanton manner. The poor young bride was so terrified that she could not remain in the house, and her husband was obliged to build a new home for her in Newark.

The house where all these events took place is unusually well preserved. Its carved mantel is one of the old features; the original narrow staircase with its newel post fixed by a wooden peg is in evidence; the corner cupboard of Governor Belcher, now brought down to the dining-room from his upstairs study; the ancient lock, with its huge key of early pattern; and great hinges spreading entirely across the front doors. Old Dutch tiles showing views of Holland scenery in blue on white rival the Biblical Dutch tiles of Boxwood Hall across the street.

Not far from this haughty old residence district is a humble little byway known as "Thompson's Lane." Just near Bridge Street, in this Lane, is the old fort, built in 1734 by Captain John Hunloke. It is modest in appearance, but examination reveals stout walls, ready to face the enemy.

Follow a little way along Bridge Street, trace Pearl Street to its foot, near the Elizabeth River, and you will come to the oldest house in the city. It is known as the Hetfield house, a dreary little structure to-day, in a lonely spot and a dismal district. But its supposed date of 1682 is enough to give it interest. There is a tradition that early councils between the whites and the Indians were held within these walls, which have evidently been considerably rebuilt since those days. The property was conveyed by Lubberson to Matthias Heathfield, who passed it on to his descendants.

Returning to Broad Street, you will find the old First Presbyterian Church, where the famous "Fighting Parson" Caldwell preached soon after he was ordained. The parish was one of the earliest in New Jersey, having been organized in 1664. In 1780, when times were stirring in Elizabethtown, and the homes of Americans were being raided, the church was burned down. But the site was retained, and in 1784 the Presbyterians rebuilt here. The spire and clock are visible for a long distance.

A side trip to 408 Rahway Avenue brings you to the old château, the Jouet house of history. It stands well back from the street and high above the sidewalk, a long, broad walk stretching up through the sweep of lawn to its door. Large trees shade it. Old-fashioned shutters protect the windows.

This estate belonged to Cavalier Jouet, a descendant of Daniel Jouet, the mayor of Angers in France; and of Marie Cavalier, who was a sister of Jean Cavalier, the famous "Camisard." During the time of Louis XIV he was the hero of the wars of the Cevennes.

Cavalier Jouet sided with the British during the Revolution, and was ardent in his Toryism with the ardor of his French blood. His property was confiscated. But for all its adventures and misadventures, the old house still remains in good preservation.

Liberty Hall is to be found by making still another side trip, in the direction of the Morris Turnpike. This was the mansion of William Livingston, the distinguished Revolutionary governor of New Jersey. The spirit of the house gave it the name of Liberty Hall during that period, and it is still known as that.

The brilliant trio of daughters, Sarah, Susan, and Kitty, did as much as the governor himself to make the Livingston home famous. The father, despite his distinction as lawyer, statesman, and patriot, prided himself on being a simple Jersey farmer, but the three young ladies caused the house to be a headquarters for continuous gayety.

Sarah, the eldest, was a renowned beauty, and so wonderful was her complexion that a wager as to its honesty was laid between the French minister and Don Juan de Miralles. The latter, vowing that only art could produce such coloring, insisted upon a test—and lost. This was when Sarah was in France, where she excited the admiration of Marie Antoinette.

The next daughter, Susan, or Susannah, was a mischief and a wit. She it was who, being forbidden by her father to drink tea after the tax was imposed, took to a beverage which she slyly brewed her self, and told him was merely "strawberry tea." It appeared to be a fruity drink, but in fact it was the prohibited herb, which she colored with strawberry juice to deceive her stern parent.

It was in the latter part of 1779 that this same Susannah performed her great feat of fooling a group of British soldiers. Two regiments, one thousand strong, had come to town with the intent to capture her father, and they approached the house late at night, thinking to take him in bed. He had left the house before their arrival, but the first division forced an entrance and demanded the Governor's dispatches. Only Susannah was ready to meet the emergency. She led them through the rooms while they searched every corner for the papers; at last they paused before a small secretary where, in fact, the papers were.

At this she broke into a nervous tremor. With downcast looks she begged the officer not to open this particular desk. Her love letters were within, she gave him to understand, and never did an embarrassed maiden play the rôle more blushingly. If they would leave her little secrets unseen and untouched, she would lead them to her father's dispatches, she promised at last; and the British fully believed her fib. She then conducted them to another spot, took down some wrapped and tied papers, and turned them over. The raiders gleefully stuffed them into the forage bags and made off, not learning until some time afterward that all they had for booty was a bundle of old law briefs, as worthless to them as blank paper.

In 1774 Sarah was married in the parlor of this house to John Jay. Years later Susannah's daughter eloped from a window with William Henry Harrison, who became the ninth President of the United States. Often the dwelling sheltered troops. When the British were foraging in the vicinity, the Livingstons had to desert the house. After the war was over Mrs. Washington stopped here on her way to her husband's inauguration festivities. These are but a few of the many traditions connected with the house.

In 1914 the inhabitants of Elizabeth celebrated the town's two-hundred-and-fiftieth birthday. Not many years before this a record showed that there were over forty houses there, built prior to the Revolution, and the number had not greatly diminished at the time of the celebration.

In 1609 the first old-world eye discovered the spot on which the town was built later; this was three days before the *Half-Moon* cast anchor in Sandy Hook Bay. A party explored the region, saw Indians, and found that there was a fine opening for a trade in peltries. This trade was opened with Holland, Manhattan being the means of communication; from Manhattan the Dutch merchants came to traffic with the natives for the fine skins they had captured. Later the spot became a Dutch colony. But Elizabethtown was not created until 1664; people came thither from Long Island, others from Connecticut, and a permanent settlement was established, the first in New Jersey.

A deed was executed by Mattano and other Indian chiefs, conveying all the land from the Raritan River north to the Passaic, and twice as great a stretch from east to west. The Governor confirmed the deed by a separate grant; dwellings began to rise. The earliest portion of the town lay along the river.

Sir George Carteret, one of the proprietors, had a wife Elizabeth, and from her the town got its name. Philip Carteret was appointed Governor; and it is told of him after his appointment he walked up from the landing place through the street carrying a hoe across his shoulder, to prove his pledge, that he would become a planter along with the settlers.

The town grew to importance. In 1747 Princeton College was opened here, Jonathan Dickinson being at its head. It was later moved to Newark, when he died.

And so Elizabethtown passed on to the brilliancy of social life which was at its height during the war period, although there were Revolutionary troubles to cast a shadow over its gayety. The Battle of Elizabethtown took place on June 8, 1780, the English and Hessians being repulsed by the citizens; on the site stands a statue of the Minute-Man, at Union Square. Raids were frequent. But after the war, the town once more resumed its gayety without check. Much stir accompanied the first inauguration, and from here Washington crossed on his way to the ceremony, by the ferry near the foot of Elizabeth Avenue.

Continuing on along the old turnpike from Elizabethtown, we come to Rahway, known to early history as Spank Town. Here a battle was fought during the Revolution—a battle only two hours long, but worth remembering as the last engagement of the Americans with the enemy when the latter was driven out of New Jersey, with the exception of Amboy and New

Brunswick, after their defeat at Trenton and Princeton in 1777.

Rahway's first saw-mill was built on the south side of the river in 1683, just above the railroad bridge of modern years. The following document records its establishment:

"A meeting of ye Inhabitants of Elizabeth-town, June ye 25, 1683: Voted that John Marsh have Liberty and Consent from ye towne soe far as they are concerned to gett timber to saw at his Saw-mill upon Land not Surveyed, lying upon Rawhay River or ye branches or elsewheare, so far as he shall have occasion to fetch timber for ye above mill.

"And the said John Marsh doth pledge him-self to ye inhabitants of ye towne to saw for them Logs if they bring them to ye mill, one-half of ye boards or timber for sawing the other, that is so much as is for their particular use."

David Oliver was one of the early landowners at Rahway, and his son, David Oliver, 2d, became a notorious Tory and refugee, and his name is connected with the annals of the town. An account in the *New Jersey Journal* of 1782 tells of his adventure the week before, when, along with a band of refugees from Staten Island, he attempted to carry off cattle from Elizabethtown. The party took a gunboat for the raid, and proceeded to the mouth of Elizabethtown Creek. They were waylaid by a party under Captain Jonathan Dayton, who had been informed of their move and was lying in wait for them. In the skirmish some of the refugees were shot, some captured; Oliver escaped to Rahway, where he was taken later in the night. He flourished under the popular appellation of "the dread of the inhabitants on the lines."

Another turnpike, forking from Elizabethtown, used to lead to Woodbridge. This was one of the oldest townships in Middlesex County, its charter being dated June 1, 1669. It was a peaceful, law-abiding community, with whose growth were identified some Puritans from New England, and many Quakers—the town came to be a headquarters for the Friends' Church. A glimpse of the thrifty, prosperous life of early dwellers in Woodbridge is caught in this quotation from Denton's *Brief Description:*

"Nature had furnished the country with all sorts of wild beasts and fowl, which gave them their food and much of their clothing. Fat venison, turkeys, geese, heath-hens, cranes, swans, ducks, pigeons and the like. The streams abounded with fish, etc. Here you need not trouble the shambles for meat, nor bakers and brewers for beer and bread, nor run to a linen-draper for a supply, everyone making their own linen and a great part of their woolen cloth for their ordinary wearing. Here one may . . . travel

. . . and if one chance to meet with an Indian town they shall give him the best entertainment they have, and upon his desire direct him on his way."

Returning to the main road running south from Elizabethtown and Rahway, the old Middlesex and Essex Turnpike, you continue to New Brunswick. This town was at one time Inians' Ferry, named for one John Inians; previous to this, during the Seventeenth Century, it had been Prigmore's Swamp. The first inhabitant is said to have been Daniel Cooper who kept a ferry, his home being at the point where the post road of later years crossed the river. About the year 1730 a group of Dutch families from Albany, New York, arrived here, built themselves houses from the building materials they brought along with them, and named the road upon which these houses fronted, "Albany Street." The settlement now began to wear the appearance of a budding village.

It continued to grow, and at the time of the Revolution was a town of importance. Its history during that war was full of distress, for New Brunswick lay in the path of both armies as they repeatedly crossed back and forth through the State. It passed from the hands of the Americans into the hands of the enemy, and during the winter of 1776–77 it was occupied by the British, under Cornwallis.

Here the enemy made themselves at home for a long stay. Howe himself had headquarters in Burnet Street, in the home of Neilson. The Hessian commander was in the Van Nuise house in Queen Street. A post was erected at Raritan landing, another on Bennet's Island, two miles below the city; there were fortifications built on the hill beyond the theological seminary; British officers took and occupied the houses of citizens here and there; and the encampment was made on William Van Deursen's property, below New Street.

For six months the British owned the town, and the citizens were subjected to all the misery of such a situation. All their schools, churches, and business had to be closed, many had to surrender their homes, barns in the surrounding country were torn down to furnish timber for a temporary bridge across the river, and the farmers were compelled to hand over their stores to the greedy enemy. But although the period of occupancy caused great suffering among the American citizens, the British were not left in peace.

Several American officers with high-spirited patriots under them caused the British considerable disturbance. At one time, during the latter part of the winter, the enemy became cut off from supplies, the base being at Amboy. They looked for relief from a fleet loaded with provisions, which it was planned to send up the Raritan River. But the Americans planted a battery of six cannon on the shore, and just as the fleet was rounding the point in the morning the cannon opened fire—to the end that five boats were disabled and sunk, the remainder sent back, a sadder and a wiser fleet, to Amboy.

Captain Hyler, famous for his gallant, adventurous spirit, commanded several large whaleboats, and a gunboat, the *Defiance*. He made a business of troubling the enemy's trading-vessels and plundering parties, going forth to any spot where he knew them to be—off Sandy Hook, near Staten Island, down the Raritan, and so on. One of his excursions resulted in the capture of five vessels in a quarter-hour's work.

And so, by skirmishing with the British outposts about New Brunswick, by interfering with their supplies, by meeting and driving back their foraging parties emerging from the town, several American officers caused this half-year to be one of not undisturbed peace to Howe and Cornwallis.

CHAPTER XII

WITH THE STAGECOACH TO PLAINFIELD, AND ON TO BOUND BROOK

IF we had the eyes to look along a certain New Jersey road and see emerging from the cloud of dust, not a thirty-horse-power, wind-shielded scarlet machine of to-day, but a totally different type of vehicle, we might travel along that same road to Yesterday. The vehicle of the imagination is of quaint construction, both broad and high, mounted upon wide straps of leather and swinging freely with an easy, ship-like motion. Its vigorous driver is cracking his whip over hurrying horses' heads. Some century ago the ancient stagecoach plied the old New Jersey road to Westfield, and to Plainfield, and beyond.

Both were changing points for the stage horses in the early eighteen-hundreds—points at which halts were made before going into the deeper country and on to more remote towns. In fact it was not until 1838 that the mails in that direction were carried by railroad as far as

The Hetfield House, the Oldest House in Elizabeth, Built about 1682.

House at South Bound Brook, where Baron Steuben had Quarters and Entertained Washington.

Mounted Cannon on Washington's Camp Ground above Bound Brook.

The Battle Monument at Bound Brook, on the Site of the Battle of 1777.

Plainfield, and even then the stage had still to carry them to points beyond for a number of years. The most traveled local roads before 1800 were one from Quibbleton (now New Market) to Scotch Plains, and a road to Rahway, beginning at a point near where Peace Street now is. Common roads interwove among the towns in this direction, connecting them with Elizabeth and Newark more or less directly. To-day the trolley passes from Westfield through Scotch Plains, Plainfield, and Bound Brook, suggesting the route of the old coach which alternately rocked and lurched the traveler of a century ago.

Westfield is an old town, having been laid out as the *western field* of the borough of Elizabeth about the year 1720. The early settlers were much disturbed by Indians, and there were several more or less serious frays with them, until the French war drew the peace-disturbers to Canada. The early history of the town and surroundings abounds in woes; not only were Indians thick, but wolves as well, to such an extent that a bounty of thirty shillings was offered for the death of a wolf. And a report from Ash Swamp, Short Hills, in 1750, states: "About ten days ago a shower of hail as big as hens' eggs destroyed fields of wheat and corn, limbs of trees broke to pieces, and of birds and fowls scarce one was saved." The heaping-up of troubles recalls the history of bleeding Kansas later on.

But there is a brighter side to Westfield lore. It surrounds the merry inn kept by Charles Gilman, on the main street opposite the road to Rahway. It was known as "The Stage House" and was famed throughout the surrounding country as a headquarters for most genial company. It acquired a special reputation for its flip, a favorite beverage of that period, for which Clayton gives the following recipe:

"A quart jug nearly filled with malt-beer, sweetened, a red-hot poker being thrust into the liquid and kept there until a foam is produced, when a half-pint of rum is poured in and some nutmeg grated upon it."

Mr. Gilman, in his blue coat with brass buttons, welcomed all travelers at the door, invited them in to a mug of flip at the price of three pence, and a meal of beans, cabbage, corn-bread, and bacon at 3*s*. 6*d*. So familiar and well-loved was his figure that upon his passing away a bard sang, in paraphrase of the lines on "Old Grimes,"

> Old Gilman is dead, that good old man,
> We ne'er shall see him more;
> He used to wear a long blue coat
> All buttoned down before.

Upon his demise his widow assumed charge of the hostelry and became known as Aunt Polly

Gilman. The inn has long since been removed and only its tradition remains.

Assuming that you are a traveler aboard the rolling old vehicle of a century ago, and that you are continuing along a dusty road into Plainfield of yesterday; and that the coach has halted for a change of horses and refreshments at some old inn with its swinging sign-board; you may dismount and have a look at several historic points

Most familiar of all is the Quaker Church. The trolley of to-day enters the town near where this old gray building stands, at the corner of Watchung Street and North Avenue. Its sign reads: "1788. Religious Society of Friends. Public Worship First Day at 11 A.M., Fourth Day Evening 7:45. All are welcome."

At the summons of this simple and welcoming sign did the early-day Quakers come plodding for worship every First Day, some afoot from farms miles away, some riding on horseback, some, the older members of the families, enthroned upon the seat of chaise or gig. They had settled all through this region, clearing the virgin forest and building houses of the timber which they hewed. Their headquarters had been at Woodbridge, but so remote were some of the homes from that center that they established a meeting at Plainfield, and in 1787 it was agreed that a house of worship should be built.

All of this portion of New Jersey is strongly identified with the history of the Quaker Church in America, and the Friends are the foundation stones of much of the prosperity and soundness that has made the State. Their first step was always to clear the forests and build themselves homes; the instinct of substantial and conservative home-building was like that of the Dutch. Pioneering with both of these groups was pioneering for the sake of a base, and was rarely touched by the spirit of adventure, although adventure was often forced upon them.

From the original headquarters at Woodbridge, ramifications of Quakerdom stretched. Here, there, everywhere, Quaker farmhouses sprang up; firmly constructed, firmly adhered to. Men hewed wood and broke ground; women knitted, wove cloth of their own spinning, plied all the household arts of that day, such as the making of soap, candles, and cheese.

About the period of 1787, when it was decided that Plainfield must become a new center, this town was merely a slightly settled rural district. It consisted of a few scattered houses, a mill, and a school, grouped near a cross-road. After much debate it was decided to purchase three acres of land near the house of John Webster, 3d, and start a meeting here. A house of thirty-four by forty-eight feet was arranged for, and upwards of three hundred pounds was subscribed. The

Friends, who had begun to settle in Plainfield township almost seventy years before, and had struggled through the hardships of the war period, now had a comfortable and restful spot for their Sabbath pilgrimage's end, and from that day on they have maintained their services in the sturdy old building which those three hundred pounds started.

Adjoining the building is to be seen the simple little cemetery. There are no imposing headstones or ornate monuments—only the plainest stones, a mere record of the bare fact of death. Not a lot is to be had for money—according to tradition, a resting-spot for the dead is always freely given.

A short walk beyond this old Quaker headquarters is the center of the original town—the corner of Front and Somerset streets. Here, at the beginning of the last century, a population of 215 persons centered; here they hailed the news brought in by the stages; and here they discussed this news between the stages' visits, while eagerly awaiting more. Three times a week the "Swiftsure" line sent a vehicle between New York and Philadelphia, and we can picture the Plainfielders of that day gathering in the store of Thomas Nesbit, later of John Fitz Randolph, and exchanging gossip and comment with feet aloft, while the storekeeper bartered his "dry goods, groceries, boots and shoes" for "skines, furs, tallow, wax and honny."

On this corner stood the store; just around the corner stood the ancient mill which was the very nucleus of "Mill Town" as the original Plainfield was called. Here ran the brook just as it runs now, and here, in 1755, was built the original mill whither the farmers brought their grists from miles around of fertile farming land. The mill changed hands a number of times, and was rebuilt in 1853, but the lineal descendant of the first building, now in itself a very old mill, stands back from Somerset Street, just around the corner from Front Street, on the right-hand side. It is used as a barn, and stands behind the garage, on the property of Mr. French; it may be recognized by its bright green paint. The old landmark is preserved in excellent condition, and a few steps up the poplar lane will lead you where you can observe it, and get a glimpse of the brook which once ran its wheel.

Around here once clustered many an old log house. The mill property in old days included not only a grist-mill, but a saw-mill, a cider-mill, and a distillery as well. Moreover, several hundred hogs disported themselves in a hog yard, which fact, although adding nothing to the poetry or picturesqueness of history, adds interest to the commercial beginnings of this enterprising town.

That Plainfield was a stirring center for all the life of this section is witnessed by the account of a local historian, who recalls that it was the general show place for early circuses traveling through this part of New Jersey. He has preserved one of the dodgers of such an entertainment, dated October 22, 1835. It announced that a "Menagerie and Aviary will be exhibited in this village on Tuesday the 3rd of November next, the largest collection of animals ever exhibited in this place, embracing 2 Elephants, Camels, Lions, Tigers, Bears, Panthers, Wolves, 1 Rhinocerous, weighing upwards of 5000 pounds. The Menagerie and Aviary occupies 36 spacious Carriages, Waggons &c., and are drawn by 112 splendid gray horses—and 60 men (including 14 musicians) are required to complete its operations."

A modern building of interest in Plainfield is the Job Male Library. Its scrapbook records of local history are entertaining and of value. It possesses a fine collection of Japanese porcelains and cloisonné made by F. X. Schoonmaker.

Continuing in the direction of the old stage, you turn toward Bound Brook. On the way thither there is a fine side trip for the pedestrian or motorist to Washington Rock. The distance of the rock from the nearest trolley point is about two miles, across the valley and up the mountain side toward your right. Another side trip from the town of Plainfield is to North Plainfield, where a provincial hotel of old pattern stands, known as "Washington's Headquarters." It has the upper and lower verandas and sloping roof with two end chimneys of old design. Washington is said to have stayed here during some of the time that the army was encamped near Bound Brook.

To reach the rock, you must approach the mountains from Dunellen. It stands solitary on the brow of the hill, and has come to be a popular spot for picnickers, offering a magnificent view and many woodsy rambles near by.

Historically, it is one of the most important points hereabouts, and the trip lies over attractive country roads, gradually mounting to wooded slopes, achieving at last the wonderful summit, the superb outlook from which our great General watched so often the movements of the enemy during the hard period of early 1777. From the twenty-eighth of May in that year until the middle or end of June, Washington retired to this rock day after day, watching, sweeping with his powerful telescope all the region for a circuit of sixty miles. The elevation of this remarkable rock is about four hundred feet above sea level; in itself it is twenty-five feet high, and its curious projection makes it a most unique lookout point. To the left, on a clear day, the view reaches as far as the New York City skyscrapers and the bay; includes the towns of Rahway, Elizabeth, Newark, and New Brighton. To the right, New Brunswick is seen, and the heights of Trenton and Princeton. Fronting one are the bays of Amboy and Raritan. The heights of far-off Navesink and the plains of Monmouth intervening lie to the southeast. This is the panorama which lay, map-like and clear, before Washington.

Many a gloomy hour did the General pass upon this height as he scanned the war's prospect. He had broken the winter camp at Morristown after the frightful months of terrific hardships and cold, and had moved it to this vicinity. The victories at Trenton and at Princeton had not been sufficient to put new heart into the Americans, for the depression caused by Stirling's defeat on Long Island, by the conquests of Fort Washington and Fort Lee, by the retreat of Washington across New Jersey, could not yet be overcome in spirit. Washington knew now, as summer approached, that the possession of Philadelphia was Howe's fixed purpose, and there must have been many a day when he feared the outcome in spite of his resolute efforts. From the rock he looked over upon the British camp at New Brunswick and faced facts—not encouraging facts. On the night of June 13th Howe led his troops from this camp toward Somerville, meaning to cross the Delaware and proceed to Philadelphia. Perhaps his ultimate downfall was due to the vision, both physical and mental, which this solitary, withdrawn lookout spot afforded the American leader.

Almost a half century ago a monument was placed upon this rock, and in 1912 a new one was erected—from a central cairn of rough stone a flagstaff rises, a gilded eagle surmounting the staff.

Turning back to the Bound Brook road, you will enter Main Street of that town and come upon its battle monument in the middle of the street. "This stone marks the site of the Battle of Bound Brook fought April 13, 1777, between 500 American soldiers under General Benjamin Lincoln and 4000 British troops under Lord Cornwallis," is the inscription. That in brief tells the story of a sharp skirmish which gave this village a position of some importance in Revolutionary history.

Lincoln, whose quarters were at the other end of the village in the only two-story house it possessed, was stationed here on the Raritan River with an extent of five or six miles to guard and a force of even less than five hundred men fit for duty. On the thirteenth of April, owing to the negligence of his patrol, ran his statement, he was surprised by a large party of the enemy under Cornwallis and Grant, who came upon him so suddenly that the General and one of his aides had barely time to get on horseback; the other side was taken, as were also a few pieces of artillery. Lincoln was obliged to retreat after a struggle; terrified by the overwhelming British force, every inhabitant of Bound Brook took to his heels and fled to the mountains. One dead soldier remained, a poor chap who had been shot down in the blockhouse; he was the only American left in the village.

This town has for long years boasted of many fine old houses, dwellings of the Revolutionary period and earlier; but of late they have been melting away to make room for modern residence and business buildings. However, one of the most interesting of all still stands in excellent preservation—the "La Tourette House" it is familiarly called. Leaving the monument and turning toward the river, you can cross the bridge to South Bound Brook; where streets fork at this point, choose the left, follow it for almost a mile, and you will suddenly come within sight of a fine old farmhouse with spreading lawn, smothering vines, and sloping roof, its walls painted a deep cream color. It looks substantial enough for the wear-and-tear of many years to come, and it was erected by Abraham Staats in pre-Revolutionary days.

The old hand-made shingles still sturdily protect the firm walls, and within are preserved many pieces of old furniture and other relics of the seventeen-hundreds. This is the house in which Baron Steuben had his winter quarters in 1778 and 1779. Here he debated many a vital matter of generalship, conferred with other officers, gave orders, and accomplished vast and important work. Here could be seen his diamond-set medal of gold, a gift from his Prussian king, Frederick the Great, designating the order of "Fidelity."

The serious side of life and war was only one phase of this house's spirit during those months. Baron Steuben entertained frequently and delightfully, and the most distinguished Americans, including General and Mrs. Washington, were his guests. Just before the encampment of Middlebrook was broken up in June of 1779, the Baron wound up festivities by a magnificent entertainment to the American officers, for which tables were spread in the grove surrounding the house, and great was the revelry in what is now the retired and quiet La Tourette dwelling.

At the far end of Bound Brook lies the camp ground of Washington. It is this town's proudest historic feature; it has been marked by a flag and mounted cannon, and here the townspeople assemble on every safe-and-sane Fourth of July for their patriotic orations combined with lemonade and crackerjack. Even beneath

The Monument and Tablet on Washington's Rock, Plainfield.

Photograph by Collier.

The Quaker Church in Plainfield, Built in 1788.

The Washington Headquarters, Morristown.

The Wick House on the Old Jockey Hollow Road, Morristown.

By permission of Rev. Andrew M. Sherman.

the thoughts of lemonade there is doubtless plenty of good sound American patriotism throbbing.

By following Main Street to Mountain Avenue, then turning into this cross street, you will be led directly toward the mountains, arriving at the spot which Washington chose for his camp—one of the finest hill-brows in all this region, and a stiff climb from the foot.

On the way out Mountain Avenue one passes the public library; just beyond it is a cemetery old enough to be worth a glance from the landmark lover. Even on stones not more than a half-century old there are some quaint inscriptions, such as,

> Dear mother is gone, from sorrow free,
> Her face on earth no more we'll see.
> With angels above she dwells on high;
> We hope to meet her when called to die.

This part of New Jersey has older epitaphs than this. Not many miles away in a Dunellen cemetery is the stone of Luke Covert, who died in 1828 in the ninety-fourth year of his age. There is certainly a note of triumph in its inscription, and a triumph rather of this world than of another:

> Come look upon my grave,
>   All you that pass by;
> Where one doth live to such an age
>   Thousands do younger die.

To return to Mountain Avenue. It leads past the links and grounds of a country club, past half-rural homes, decidedly rural homes, and then, of a sudden, the road begins to ascend sharply and you seem to be led back into mountain fastnesses. There is at last a decisive turn in the road; a stony branch starts toward the left, directly along the brow of the hill, and by following this for perhaps a quarter-mile you emerge at last into the open, and find below you a marvelous panorama of plain, towns, buildings, woods—this is the old camp ground.

It is recognized by its mounted cannon and the flag flying above them. Here, as at Plainfield, Washington surveyed the scene below and summed up the situation. Chimney Rock is another point from which a remarkable outlook can be had to-day as in the days of the Revolution.

CHAPTER XIII

BY THE OLD TURNPIKE TO MORRISTOWN

A PILGRIMAGE out through the Springfield region, made famous by its "Fighting Parson" of long ago—on through the hilly and open country of New Jersey, where travelers of old climbed for refreshment to Bottle Hill—leads you at last to historic Morristown, which teems with Revolutionary tradition, even to possessing the coat and hat in which George Washington was inaugurated.

Such a pilgrimage carries you over two important old turnpikes, at least approximately. From Newark, the Springfield Turnpike led a little south of west; at Springfield started the Morris Turnpike, leading on northwest, and penetrating the hilly country until it reached Morristown. This latter road passed through the Short Hills, crossed the county line from Essex into Morris County, and provided travelers with way-stations at Chatham and Bottle Hill.

You will recognize Springfield by its church-tower clock, which rises slim and white in the midst of the town. Follow that tower to its base, and you come to a little old white church, and near it the weather-beaten stones of an old-time burying-ground. In that churchyard is a modern monument commemorating the great event in Springfield's history.

"The first British advance," states the inscription, "was stayed at the bridge east of the village June 7, 1780. The Battle of Springfield was fought June 23rd. The Americans under General Greene on that day, near the stream west of the Church, checked the enemy, who in their retreat burned the Church and village. From this Church Parson Caldwell took psalm-books during the fight and flung them to the Americans for wadding, crying, 'Put Watts into 'em, boys!'"

This is the story in a nutshell. Previous to the battle, Washington had moved his camp to Rockaway Bridge, his suspicions having been aroused by the movement of some British troops up the Hudson River. Acting upon the idea that the enemy had certain subterfuge in mind, he made the move on June 22d, and gave the post at Short Hills into the charge of Major-General Greene. The following day, early in the morning, two divisions under Knyphausen arrived at Springfield from Elizabethtown. They amounted to about six thousand infantry, cavalry, and artillery.

The right column of the British aimed to drive Major Lee's dragoons from one of the bridges which crossed the Passaic, but it must first ford the stream. Dayton's regiment was so bravely resisting the left, that Knyphausen was almost unable to force his way forward; only his great superiority in numbers made this possible. His troops were drawn up, and had begun a heavy cannonade, but, although Greene was ready to fight, Knyphausen, for some reason, did not enter into an engagement. The British, at Springfield, made a stand of several hours, after which they fell upon the town, plundering the inhabitants, burning, until it was only a heap of ashes, and finally retreating to Elizabethtown Point.

The conflict would be counted of less importance in American annals had it not been for the heroism of Parson Caldwell. He was pastor of the Presbyterian Church, a man well-known throughout this part of the State, having studied for the ministry at Princeton College in Newark, when Burr was its president; and having held the pastorate of the First Church in Elizabethtown.

He was innately a patriot, with an inherited instinct of revolt against tyranny. His ancestors had been French Huguenots who had fled to Scotland after the revocation of the Edict of Nantes; again they had fled from persecution, this time of Claverhouse, seeking a home in Ireland. Caldwell's parents came to this country from Ireland, and he was born in Virginia, in 1734.

At the outbreak of the Revolution James Caldwell showed ardent patriotism, and came to be known as an active patriot. "There are times when it is righteous to fight as well as to pray," was part of his creed. His church followers sustained him in his Revolutionary spirit, and were in sympathy with him when he became, in June, 1776, Chaplain of the Jersey Brigade under Colonel Dayton. From this time on his efforts in behalf of patriotism increased. When the army camped at Morristown he used to work at getting provisions for the half-starved troops, and his great popularity made it possible for him to collect large supplies of stores from all over the region—which stores he distributed himself.

He became deputy quartermaster-general, with an office at Chatham. Over his office door appeared the letters "D.Q.M.G." and the story is told by Shaw that Caldwell's friend Abraham Clark, puzzling over the initials, finally said: "I don't know what the letters mean, but I think they must indicate that you're a Devilish Queer Minister of the Gospel."

His "queerness" was the sort that made him beloved, even though it took such forms as preaching with a pair of pistols on the desk beside the Bible—for there was often danger of a raid, and the "Fighting Parson" did not mean to be surprised. The soldiers were devoted to him—one day he would be distributing stores among them, the next, preaching the sort of sermon that put new courage into their very weary souls.

It was the week before the Battle of Springfield that all his fire had been roused to the utmost by the brutal killing of his wife Hannah, who was shot down in her home by a redcoat while the Parson was away. Armed with all the sense of outrage which such an act inspired, he entered the battle a few days later, and Bret Harte has told his story in the poem *Caldwell of Springfield.*

. . . Stay one moment; you've heard
Of Caldwell, the parson, who once preached the word
Down at Springfield? What, no? Come—that's bad; why he had
All the Jerseys aflame! And they gave him the name
Of the "rebel high priest." He stuck in their gorge,
For he loved the Lord God—and he hated King George!

He had cause, you might say! When the Hessians that day
Marched up with Knyphausen, they stopped on their way
At the "farms," where his wife, with a child in her arms,
Sat alone in the house. How it happened none knew

But God—and that one of the hireling crew
Who fired the shot! Enough!—there she lay,
And Caldwell, the chaplain, her husband, away!

Did he preach—did he pray? Think of him as you stand
By the old church to-day,—think of him and his band
Of militant ploughboys! See the smoke and the heat
Of that reckless advance, of that straggling retreat!
Keep the ghost of that wife, foully slain, in your view—
And what could you, what should you, what would *you* do?

Why, just what *he* did! They were left in the lurch
For the want of more wadding. He ran to the church,
Broke the door, stripped the pews, and dashed out in the road
With his arms full of hymn-books, and threw down his load
At their feet! Then above all the shouting and shots
Rang his voice: "Put Watts into 'em! Boys, give 'em Watts!"

And they did. That is all. Grasses spring, flowers blow,
Pretty much as they did ninety-three years ago.
You may dig anywhere and you'll turn up a ball—
But not always a hero like this—and that's all.

Following in the direction of the old Morris Turnpike, you soon pass beyond Essex County and approach Chatham, one of the places noted on the maps of a century ago. This village was settled by early New Englanders, and offered good opportunities by virtue of the iron ore found hereabouts. In fact the region came to be known as "The Old Forges."

It was customary to carry leather bags of the ore on the backs of horses, bring them here from the mines, and, after the ore was manufactured into iron, the bars were put once more, in their new form, into leather bags, and carried in the same manner to Elizabethtown and Newark, where they were loaded on to boats and shipped to New York. This business became so thriving that it led to the opening of new roads.

Farther on, where the pretty town of Madison stands on an elevation, one would never suspect that beneath its name such an appellation as "Bottle Hill" is hidden away. Yet Bottle Hill the town was for many a year.

This came of the fact that the keeper of an early inn, instead of having an elaborate signboard painted to indicate his line of business, merely swung a bottle to a post in front of his establishment, trusting to the public to supply the statement. Some say that this inn-keeper was an Indian, accustomed to sign language—at any rate, his history seems to be blurred by time. But there is no doubt that such a sign did hang from such a post, and its unique simplicity naturally clung to the memory of travelers, who gave the village its name.

As the place developed, a French element grew there, tracing its ancestry back to Vincent

Boisaubin, who had been an officer in the bodyguard of Louis XVI. He preferred America to France for a home, and so cultured a gentleman, so public-spirited a citizen was he, that he was welcomed in Bottle Hill. It is claimed that his act was the origin of the familiar story, told often with countless variations—the story of the poor citizen who had lost his cow. "What can we do to help him?" someone asked, and Boisaubin reached into his generous pocket with the observation, "I am sorry for that man five dollars."

This is the town in which General Wayne made his headquarters during the American army's first encampment at Morristown. Deacon Ephraim Sayre's house was the one used by Wayne as headquarters, and one of the recollections passed down from that day is of the little mulatto whom Wayne kept as servant, and who always carried about a wooden sword with its edges sharpened, so much was he imbued with the martial spirit.

As you enter Morristown by the road from Springfield, you are almost immediately confronted by the most famous of all its historic buildings. This is the Washington headquarters, a treasure-house containing relics of such value that it ranks with the small group of such buildings which are of national, rather than local, importance. It is somewhat amusing to observe the rivalry that exists among the guardians of these treasure-houses. "No, we have no old fireplace oven," apologetically admitted the little lady who showed us about, "I'm sorry. They have one at Mt. Vernon. But," brightening, "we've got Washington's inauguration suit upstairs!"

This building was the home of Col. Jacob Ford in 1779, when it was turned over to Washington for his headquarters. The *New Jersey Gazette* of that year printed this news item:

"We understand that the headquarters of the American Army is established at Morris-Town in the Vicinity of which the troops are now hutting."

The main body of the army went into quarters here for the winter of 1779–80, at first in tents, later in log huts, as the weather grew almost unbearable. They were about two miles from headquarters; the life-guard were in log huts only a few rods southeast of the Ford house. This residence has been carefully preserved and left unchanged; the house and the surrounding large grounds are the same that they were when Martha Washington looked forth from the windows upon the bleak winter landscape.

To the left of the front door is the dining-room used by Washington. Two log additions made for him served as kitchen and offices. To-day you are shown the desk and table where he wrote, the table used by Hamilton, the old kitchen oven and spinning-wheel, and a host of old pieces of furniture brought from interesting sources. There are sidelights on early American housekeeping thrown by some of these relics, one being the flour barrel scooped out of a tree-trunk.

Mrs. Thompson was that keen Irish housekeeper who, during a dearth of provisions here, coaxed the General to let her be given an order for six bushels of salt. As it was worth eight dollars a bushel, the farmers around were delighted to exchange their fresh beef for it, and Mrs. Thompson surprised her chief with a banquet.

Washington's dishes, brought over from Philadelphia, are on display. In the case where the inauguration suit is preserved, modestly abiding in the shadow of her great husband's garments, cuddle the blue satin and the white satin slippers worn by Mrs. Washington. The most valuable paper contained in the cabinet of documents is the great General's commission as Commander of the Army. From nine to five o'clock the house is open to the public except on Sunday.

Continuing on along the road toward the center of town, you should turn in first at Oliphant Lane which lies at your right just before you cross the railroad. Here, the first house on your right, stands a modest little residence

The Springfield Church, Made Famous by the "Fighting Parson."

The Old Arnold Tavern where "Arnold's Light-Horse Troop" Gathered, Morristown.

The Old Dutch Church of Passaic.

The Van Wagoner Homestead, Passaic.

which once sheltered one of the romances of American history. It used to be known as Dr. John Cochran's quarters; Dr. Cochran was surgeon-general of the American army, and his wife, the sister of General Philip Schuyler, entertained Schuyler's daughter Elizabeth in this dwelling during the army's winter at Morristown.

It so happened that Alexander Hamilton, being one of Washington's aides, was stopping at the Ford mansion; and he found it extremely convenient to drop in frequently around the corner of this lane to the house where Miss Betty was visiting.

On one occasion Colonel Hamilton left the house so much preoccupied with thoughts of Betty, that when the sentinel propounded to him the question, "Who comes there?" he was at a loss for the password. The sentinel recognized his superior, but he held to his duty and refused to let the Colonel pass.

Hamilton was in despair, when at last he caught sight of young Ford through the darkness; calling the boy, to whom he himself had given the countersign, he asked for it and received it. But even then it was with reluctance that the sentinel stretched a rule and let the officer pass.

The subsequent romance and marriage of Alexander Hamilton and Betty Schuyler are familiarly known.

Still continuing along the same road, you will come to the Memorial Hospital, which will be your guide in locating an old and dilapidated dwelling directly opposite, and back from the street. It used to stand on the site of the present hospital. In Revolutionary days it was the home of Parson Timothy Johnes, that old Presbyterian minister who came on horseback to Morristown in 1743, brought his wife and two children, and was given a home by his parishioners, who cut the wood themselves for this residence, planted and gathered the pastor's crops for him, and furnished the house by their sewing bees. Parson Johnes welcomed Washington to his communion table, although the General was an Episcopalian.

"Ours is not the Presbyterians' table, General, it is the Lord's," he said.

The part of Morristown first settled is in the vicinity of Spring and Water streets. At this corner you will to-day find Dickerson's Tavern, known to the neighborhood as "the old yellow house." Its original form is more or less altered, but the main part of the house remains, on the original site, and stories of the past hover about it.

Here the meeting of May 1, 1775, was held by the men of Morris County, for the defense of that county against possible invasion. Here it was ordered that three hundred volunteers be recruited, that five hundred pounds of powder be bought, and one ton of lead. Peaceful Morristown was to be peaceful no longer.

Captain Peter Dickerson, one of the early Long Island captains, was largely instrumental in all these moves. He made his tavern headquarters for discussions of this kind. He bore personally the entire expense of the company commanded by him, and the sum thus expended was never repaid; it now stands to his credit in the nation's capital.

Reaching the Green, you are in the heart of historic Morristown. Quartermaster-General Greene's headquarters used to stand on the corner of Morris and South streets, on the site of a present drugstore. The burying-place of many soldiers was near by. The early Presbyterian Church stood where the present one stands, and was used as a hospital for soldiers in 1777. The bell of this church was presented to Morristown by the King of Great Britain and was stamped with the impress of the British Crown.

A short walk out Mt. Kemble Avenue brings you to some old buildings. On the right, the white house with immense grounds sloping up behind it, is the one-time General Doughty house. Handsome as it is, judged by present standards, one can realize that in a less ambitious period this was a veritable palace.

Gen. John Doughty was a graduate of King's

College, now Columbia University, in the class of 1770. He entered the army at the opening of the Revolution and was fast promoted. When peace was declared at last, he was sent west to establish forts on the Ohio River and at even more wildly western points; this experience led to spicier adventures than he had seen in the Revolution.

At one time, when going down the Tennessee River in a barge with sixteen soldiers, he was attacked by a large number of Indians in canoes; it was not until his aim felled the savage old chief that the battle was brought to a happy ending. After a long period of such hairbreadth escapes, he was content to settle down on his four hundred acres in Morristown and devote the remaining portion of his life to "agricultural pursuits, the cultivation of literature, and the exercise of a generous and elegant hospitality."

A few blocks beyond stands All Souls' Hospital. This building has been remodeled to suit its present needs; old times knew it as "the Arnold Tavern." It used to stand on the site of the present Hoffman building.

In January, 1777, Washington arrived in town, and went directly to this tavern, where he made his headquarters. During the winter it is said that he was attacked by quinsy, and that his wife came here to care for him.

When the building was removed to this site,

a strange old spear was found in its cellar—a five-foot pike, such as the English heavy-armed troops once bore. This was no doubt a relic left by Col. Jacob Arnold's Light-Horse Troop, who were armed each with this kind of spear. The tavern was built by Arnold's father, and afterwards passed into the hands of his son.

Fort Nonsense lies not far from the center of town. By following Court Street you will reach the hill at the top of which that fantastic fort was built—a fort never to be used, intended merely to keep idle troops out of mischief during the long winter of 1779–80. The view of the hills and valleys around is worth the climb, and a monument marking the site of the nonsensical old fort is at the summit besides. Here embankments, ditches, and blockhouses were made by busy soldiers; this was a characteristically shrewd move on Washington's part to avoid the perils of idleness among his men.

By starting out on Western Avenue and going about four miles, you enter the historic associations which lie along the old Jockey Hollow Road. One of the old soldiers' bake-ovens used to be visible on this road, and there were other similar ovens near it. Even to-day there are spots where a few stones mark the locality of camps.

It was down the Jockey Hollow Road that trouble during the mutiny of the Pennsylvania troops occurred, which Lossing calls "the only serious and decided mutiny in the American army during the Revolution." New Year's Day of 1781 saw the beginning of it. The mutineers had suffered every hardship and privation, and the war was dragging slowly and hopelessly. The men were paid little or no money, promises of Congress were not always fulfilled, and riot began at last.

One incident of the period leading to mutiny is associated with an old house which you will find now standing, beside the road. It is the Wick house. From this building were brought several of the old pieces of furniture now displayed in the Washington headquarters.

Here lived that gallant young patriot, Miss Tempe Wick, the daughter of the house. During the disorder some of the troops down this road became disgracefully drunk, and set out to make trouble. They rioted in the neighborhood of the house, causing especial disturbance to Mrs. Wick who was very ill at the time. It was necessary to call the doctor, who lived a mile away; no one could go on the errand save Tempe, so she carried her sick mother to the cellar for safety and set out on her favorite horse to ride for the doctor.

Returning, she was confronted by a group of noisy soldiers who ordered her to dismount. But instead of losing her nerve and giving up to them, she kept to her horse, held her head high, and galloped away down the road where they could not follow. Returning again, she rode her horse straight into the house, out of danger, through the kitchen, and shut the pet animal into the spare bedchamber, where he remained a captive for several days until all danger of his being stolen was past, and the rioters disappeared from the neighborhood.

CHAPTER XIV

A VOYAGE UP THE PASSAIC

"MRS. S., with her mother, aunt, two brothers and sister, took passage on a schooner at New York, at the dock near Cortlandt Street, for Acquackanonk Landing. The Captain had several other passengers. The Captain started at 10:45 A.M., expecting to run up in half a day; but the wind was treacherous, and he was that day and night and the next day and part of the night on the way, having been a half day aground in the mud. Meanwhile the whole party got out of provisions, and the last day there was nothing to eat. Mrs. S.'s sister, about twelve, and her two brothers, who were growing children, suffered until the passengers broke open a barrel of flour and made paste pudding and flour cakes. They landed finally at the dock at Acquackanonk Landing at 11 o'clock on a November night, when the tide was so high that they had to wade a distance through the water over their shoes, having left their goods on the schooner; and as there were no vacant accommodations at the landing place, and being told that it was only a 'short step' to Paterson, where they were destined, the entire party, hungry, wet and miserable, followed the road up through the fog and rain, the night being also very dark. They had been seven weeks on the ocean, but did not know what suffering was until they made their inland journey. The next day their goods were brought on a wagon from the Landing."

Thus *The News History* reprints an early description of a voyage to the town of Passaic, then known as Acquackanonk Landing. Being at the head of tidewater on the Passaic River, it soon grew to be an important headquarters for water travel, in the days when we made better use of our rivers than we do to-day. At that time, sloops and schooners of goodly size were able to carry commerce up the stream, and, as may be seen from the above harrowing tale, passengers traveled at times in company with the flour barrels. In fact there was a considerable amount of water travel by early dwellers in New Jersey; they came to Acquackanonk from all the surrounding country, and there took boats to New York.

By the beginning of the Eighteenth Century, there were roads from all directions converging at this town, and passengers for Newark and New York could choose between a boat running down the Passaic, or a stagecoach. Later on, a turnpike connected Acquackanonk with Paterson and the Great Falls, and from there another, the Hamburg and Paterson Turnpike, ran northwest to the remoter country, toward Pompton.

The motorist of the Twentieth Century can start from Newark, and follow avenues and drives along the shore of the Passaic River, tracing fairly well the direction of the old turnpike, and keeping in mind that time when Acquackanonk was so far away that it required paste pudding and flour cakes to sustain nature on the journey.

The County Bridge crosses the river and enters the town near where Main and Gregory avenues meet, the heart of the original town. Hereabouts it was settled by early Holland Dutch, on the site of an Indian village.

Jacob Stoffelson is supposed to have been the first white man to set foot in what is now Passaic. He was a highly esteemed though little educated man, whose friendship with the Indians led him to be more or less a power. Before 1678 he arrived here, looking for land which he was to purchase for his friend Christopher Hoaglandt, a New York merchant from Holland. Stoffelson had ridden overland from Jersey City, making his way through miles of wilderness.

From this time on the spot came to be known as having a most valuable situation, and before long it was a settlement of thriving Dutch. At the corner of Main and Gregory avenues is still standing a relic of the Dutch period, the old Van Wagoner homestead, its stone walls screened by weeping willows. This house is almost all that is left to call up pictures of Dutch life here.

This house was commenced before the Revolution, interrupted by the war, and its building was resumed in 1788. For years it remained in the hands of the Van Wagoners, one of the sturdiest and finest of the old Holland families. They were of the same stock as the Gerritsens; some members of the family changed the name to signify that they came from the town of Wagening, and thus the new name developed in the same line.

The original Gerritsen brought a certificate from the "burgomasters, schepens and counsellors of the city of Wagening," to the effect that these worthy gentlemen "have testified and certified that they have good knowledge of Gerrit Gerritsen and Annetje Hermansse, his wife, as to their life and conversation, and that they have always been considered and esteemed as pious and honest people, and that no complaint of evil or disorderly conduct has ever reached their ears; on the contrary, they have always led pious, quiet, and honest lives, as it becomes pious and honest persons. They especially testify that they govern their family well and bring up their children in the fear of God and in all modesty and respectability."

Many branches of the Gerritsens (spelled variously) and the Van Wagoners lived to become fruitful and multiply and replenish the earth for many miles around New York. One, called "Manus" Van Wagoner, was prominent in the Revolution, remaining neutral and entertaining distinguished members of both sides. One Mrs. Gerritsen was far from neutral; some lively stories of her partisanship are related, one to the effect that she chased from her house with the tongs some old neighbors who had become British informers; at another time she charged upon a peddler whom she suspected of being a spy, and pushed him out over the lower half of her Dutch door.

If you will turn to the old Dutch church just around the corner from the Van Wagoner homestead, you will find many familiar old names of that period inscribed on the headstones in the yard. The Polish now use the church building for their services.

The bridge which leads into town here is not far from the site of the original bridge of Acquackanonk. The original crossed about 250 feet to the north, and came out directly opposite the famous old Tap House on the Hill. A little farther down, where Paulison Avenue ends, there was a ferry. Some claim that Washington, in his retreat from Fort Lee and from Hackensack, crossed the river at the original bridge here, and camped in the village overnight, although authorities differ on this detail. Part of Cornwallis' army is said to have followed to this bridge and found it destroyed, with three thousand men waiting and ready to intercept; the British wheeled, and crossed further to the north.

The territory which was once included under the name Acquackanonk was very extensive, and the deeds to the property were direct from Sir George Carteret and the Lords Proprietors of the province which was known as East New Jersey. For many years the village was eclipsed by the Landing; navigation to New York was lively every fall and spring, and the roads leading to the Landing often displayed a veritable procession of wagons, coming from every direction, bringing in products to the large storehouses and docks. From the agricultural regions came grain, hay, and farm produce. From the woods came barrel staves, hoop poles, and timber. From the mines of Morris County came iron ore. From forest districts beyond came furs. All these goods were brought to Acquackanonk Landing for shipment. In the midst of all this lawful prosperity, there is a somewhat adventurous tale of the Ludlow brothers, Cornelius V. C. and John, who took advantage of the excellent shipping situation to furnish the British with cannon which they obtained at Ringwood above Pompton, during the War of 1812.

Continuing on to Paterson, we may trace one of the most remarkable stories in the records of industrial America. We associate the name of Alexander Hamilton so constantly with his soldierhood and statesmanship that we forget his rôle as a master of industry. The colossal scheme of organized industry which he visualized might have eclipsed his other works, had it matured under his hands. The country and its industrial methods were hardly ripe enough in the seventeen-hundreds to develop his plans; probably they were too advanced, as a matter of fact, for his own powers of execution. But much of the nation's industrial prosperity owes its beginning to Alexander Hamilton and his discovery, in a manufacturing sense, of the Great Falls of the Passaic River.

As you approach the Falls, you pass through dingy streets, beside crowded mills, in the midst of much that is sordid and dismal. Suddenly the road swings about a sweeping curve, and before you gapes a gorge, sheer and wicked as a bit of Rocky Mountain scenery, with men like ants toiling at the foot of its plunge.

A new building appears glued to the rock at the bottom of the chasm. Above its door you may read, "1791–1914," and between the dates the three significant letters, "S. U. M." This, in brief, is the story.

Soon after the Revolution, when the United States was settling down from the disturbance of war and beginning to take up constructive thought, Alexander Hamilton, the first Secretary of the Treasury under Washington, conceived the idea of a great association. It was to organize American manufactures—every kind of manufacture, from a spool of thread to a plow. It was to establish the real independence of the young country. As soon as this offspring of Britain should learn to make her own wares she would be genuinely quit of apron strings, and would cease to be an importer. Furthermore, in time she would compete with foreign countries, would become an exporter on a vast scale.

Having seen this vision of the future unrolling before him, Hamilton looked about for a place suitable to begin operations. He thoroughly scoured the country surrounding New York. At last he sifted the matter down; no situation, according to his idea, held such promise as the Great Falls of the Passaic at a point then included in the town of Acquackanonk. Paterson did not then exist; Ottawa, a tiny village across the river, was the nearest hamlet.

So enthusiastic was the great financier, and so logical did his plan appear, that he succeeded in interesting many capitalists in the venture. Five thousand shares of stock were subscribed, at one hundred dollars each, though only 2267 were ever fully paid for. The organization was launched in 1791, the Legislature of New Jersey passing an act incorporating it; and its name was announced as "The Society for Establishing Useful Manufactures." It created such enthusiasm, such faith, that both individuals and the State were ready to yield to its every request; it was authorized to put through canals, to claim whatever it needed for its purposes in numberless ways. The start was made with a mill for the making of cotton cloth.

The tale of the rise and fall of this society reads like the tale of a mere bursting bubble. But in essence this dream was more than a bubble, for all its outward bursting. It paved the way, despite its own failure, for a vast industrial life which might never have reached its present proportions but for Hamilton's vision.

When only this one small cotton factory was as yet under way, the crash came. It appears that an adventurer of a reckless and spendthrift disposition, Major L'Enfant by name, became influential in the organization and brought about its demise. His visions were as mad as Hamilton's had been sane, and he plunged the funds into a ship canal which he planned to build from Paterson to the head of

The Passaic River, near the Site of the Old Acquackanonck Bridge.

The Monument to Alexander Hamilton at Weehawken.

The Old House at Huyler's Landing, Built before the Revolution.

The Cornwallis Headquarters at Alpine.

tidewater in the Passaic. Thus ended the prosperity of the S. U. M.

But the organization was not dead. It possessed a perpetual charter, and held jurisdiction and rights over the watershed. The corporation survives to-day in the water company of this district, which perpetuates the name and history; and Hamilton's discovery of the manufacturing value of the Passaic led to the sudden forging ahead of American industry. Other factories sprang up around the great nucleus; within a little over a century, more than a hundred silk mills clustered there, with two hundred times as many operatives. The manufactures of the present have spread far beyond that of silk; machinery, locomotives, and so on are made here.

During the summer, the hundred feet of precipitous rock lie bare in the heat. Through the winter the Falls present a wonderful picture —a picture which the Indians knew long before any white person had ever seen it, in the latter part of the Seventeenth Century. The Indians named the Falls Totowa, which means to sink, or to be forced down beneath the water by weight. They told tales of the marvelous rainbows which formed above the cataract, of the glen called the Valley of the Rocks, where Washington and Lafayette both wandered in later days.

Even before the Revolution, tourists were making excursions to the Great Falls so frequently, as their fame grew, that it appeared worth while to Abraham Godwin to establish a public house in the neighborhood. An announcement issued November 28, 1774, reads:

"This is to acquaint the public that there is a stage-waggon erected to go from the house of Abraham Godwin, near the Great Falls, to Powles Hook."

Still later the Falls became known as the scene of dare-devil exploits, such as Niagara has boasted of. The story of Sam Patch is the most familiar. Some have walked tight ropes stretched across the ravine; one of these performances was by Mons. de Lave, as long ago as 1860. There have been terrific accidents and sensational rescues here; James W. McKee, the song writer, once snatched the reins from a team and made a life-line which he threw to a man and a boy who had been dashed over the edge, and they actually clung to the line and were safely landed.

Back in the main part of town we find a few historic buildings. One is the old hotel at the foot of Bank Street, where River Street intersects; this was the one built about 1774 by Abraham Godwin. A little west of it stands the stone house which Cornelius Van Winkle erected in 1770. On Water Street, between Hamburgh Avenue and Temple Street, stands the Doremus house, which is the oldest dwelling in the city.

On Main Street stands the First Presbyterian Church, more than a century old. Among its early documents is preserved a paper headed:

"SUBSCRIPTION FOR A HEARSE, 1825.

"We the subscribers, members of the First Presbyterian Congregation in Paterson, considering it to be desirable and important that a Hearse should be procured, which shall be the property of the Congregation, to be used for the accommodation of the members of this Congregation—and also for the accommodation of others, when convenient—Promise to pay to the Trustees of the First Presbyterian Society in Paterson the sums annexed to our respective names for the above mentioned object."

"Easy rolling grades, fine views," is the road note printed on a recent automobile map, where the road from Paterson to Pompton continues along the Passaic Valley. The way was less easy when Washington's army crossed Pompton Township, as it did several times, going between West Point and Morristown. In the valley of Ringwood, the place where Washington had his horses shod is still pointed out. Near this Robert Erskine was buried; he had been given the management of the iron mines in this district for the London company before the Revolution, but at the outbreak of that war he joined the American forces. Washington was a close friend of his, and Erskine was made Geographer and Surveyor-General to the Army of the United States.

If the motorist of the nineteen-hundreds returns to New York from Paterson and Passaic by way of the Paterson Plank Road, he will arrive at Weehawken, where the story of Alexander Hamilton was brought to its close. Going east to the heights which rise above the vista of New York and her thronged waters, below which trains, ready to start in dozens of different directions, lie like serpents stretched in lean lines below, and countless boats crawl hither and thither, he will find, at the edge of the Boulevard, the monument which marks Hamilton's end.

This was in 1804. Hamilton had been active in politics for a long time. In 1795 he had resigned his office as Secretary of the Treasury, having accomplished enough in that office to entitle him to a comparative rest. He had carried a measure for the funding of the domestic debt, in order to reëstablish public credit; had founded a national bank; and had rearranged the system of duties. Moreover, he had been of inestimable aid to the administration in matters outside the scope of his own department.

But although he resumed his private law practice in New York after six years of work for the new government, he was leader of the Federal party, and the fierce party strife of 1801 brought him forward into public life again. In the winter of 1804 he and Aaron Burr crossed political swords, and the upshot was a duel challenge by Burr. Hamilton had great abhorrence of the practice of dueling, but the challenge was so made that he felt it impossible in honor, to refuse; and on the morning of July 11th, Hamilton and Burr met just at the foot of this cliff, below where the monument now stands. It was the same spot where Hamilton's eldest son had been killed in a duel three years before.

He fell at the first shot from Burr's pistol. He made no attempt to answer the fire. He was mortally wounded; being carried across the river to the home of Mr. Bayard, near Greenwich Village, he died the following day, soon after the arrival of his wife and children. Such was the nation's sympathy with him and indignation toward his opponent that Burr was practically exiled. Hamilton's widow lived until 1854, and was much beloved and honored.

The bowlder against which Hamilton fell in the duel was preserved.

CHAPTER XV

ALONG THE PALISADES

NESTLING at the foot of the Palisades was old Closter Landing. Above it, now as then, the height is cloaked by a mass of dense green foliage. It is not far from the highest point of the entire wall; from here up to Indian Head, opposite Hastings, the Palisades rise to their greatest height. The Landing is known to-day as Alpine, and lies opposite the town of Yonkers.

When the Palisades Interstate Park Commission took the west bank of the Hudson River and made it a pleasure ground for the people, it included the stretch all the way from Newburgh in New York State, south to Fort Lee in New Jersey. There is no finer strip along the shore than that near Alpine—here you can penetrate woodsy trails that suggest the Catskills, and scramble over wave-lashed rocks that remind you of the coast of Maine.

Where the little rowboat of old days crossed the river, you can now take the ferry from

Yonkers and cross in a few minutes. Straight ahead of you, as you approach the further shore, lies a deep pass known as Alpine Gorge, and here an old road winds up to the summit and on to the town of Closter. Here is Harrington Township, named for Peter Haring who came from North Holland in the early part of the Seventeenth Century. The Great Chip Rock Reach was the name once applied to the stretch along the river where you are landing.

It is a calm enough picture to-day. The woods lie green and still, the river slaps quietly on the shore, picnickers land and hurry away with their bulging baskets, a park patrolman in full regalia marches solitary along the rocks. Only one lonely white house stands near, to link the comfortable present with the war-torn past.

A century and a half ago it was built, from the stones that strewed the shore, from the timber yielded by the virgin forest. Its heavy walls have withstood time and weather. It is preserved as the Cornwallis Headquarters.

On November 19, 1776, Cornwallis crossed the river and arrived where you are to-day, at Closter Landing. He brought six thousand men. He had with him the first and second battalions of light infantry. There were also two companies of chasseurs, the 33d and 42d regiments of the line, and two battalions of guards.

The American forces at Fort Lee were the object of his pursuit. Having landed upon the west bank and being near his destination, he looked about for a comfortable headquarters and found this dwelling immediately at hand. Here he ate, drank, and gave commands, and here the tradition of the British stay has ever since clung—and will cling permanently, for the house is preserved by the Park Commission as a landmark.

A partly obliterated road leads from just south of the house to the crest above. It is hardly more than a steep trail through a wilderness at present; so steep, that anyone who attempts it now must realize what it meant to the British army to scale the summit.

Here Cornwallis' men mounted to the top of the Palisades. On the edge of the bluff above, you stand where the British general stood before he proceeded south to Fort Lee. It was a two-hour march on a November morning, made while the retreat of Washington began, and one of the darkest days of Revolutionary history was dawning upon our army.

At old Closter Landing the *Half-Moon* has been making headquarters much of the time since her first voyage up the Hudson River in 1909, at the Hudson–Fulton celebration. In the year 1609 her ancestor, whose name she bears, sailed slowly up the river as far as Indian Head, just above this point. There the first anchor that ever was lowered into the Indians' Ma-hi-can-ittuc River cut the blue water, and the original *Half-Moon* lay at rest. In the morning, twenty-eight canoes filled with men, women, and children made out to the vessel, bearing oysters and beans which the Dutch purchased. No doubt curiosity was a stronger incentive than the sale of oysters and beans.

If the traveler of to-day follows the British march to Fort Lee, he must keep to the top of the bluff. But the walk along the shore reveals several interesting landmarks. The next landing below Alpine was known in early times as Lower Closter. It is now called Huyler's Landing, and the broad white house which guards it shines across the river, a familiar sight from the east shore, at Ludlow. It stands almost at the water's edge, and is of about the same period as the Cornwallis Headquarters. It must have been equally well built, and more pretentious. The substantial appearance of both buildings offers a silent comment on the get-built-quick domiciles of the hasty present.

Just south is another house of pre-Revolutionary period, but not cared for as the other two are.

Continuing still to the south, you come at last to a little old cemetery—you can easily miss it if you do not look sharply to the right.

A group of worn tombstones is to be discovered, half smothered in the tangle of green which covers the slope. If you will break your way through the tangle, and part concealing branches, you can make out dates a century old, and the names of various members of the Van Wagoner family who dwelt hereabouts as early as the Revolution. The Van Wagoners lived, died, and were buried here, in Undercliff Settlement, a succession of generations.

Above, on the brow of the cliff, you may see Hermit's Point jutting out. You are approaching the one-time Englewood Pier, now a landing place for the Dykman Street Ferry. Still further south, near where the Fort Lee Ferry runs from 130th Street in Manhattan to-day, was the old Burdett's Ferry of Revolutionary days.

This route was important, being the continuation of the Hackensack Turnpike. The road snaked its way from the valley beyond, and approached the water at a point near the old Burdett home—representatives of this family have ever since been living at Fort Lee. The proudest tradition of the family is said to be that one Mrs. Peter Burdett cooked the flapjacks on which General Washington and his officers breakfasted during their stay in the neighborhood.

Burdett's Ferry was the only means of communication between the sister forts, Washington and Lee, and while Mollie Sneden was operating the ferry at Sneden's Landing, five miles above Alpine, the loyal patriot Peter Burdett was assisting our army to transport ammunition and supplies as well as soldiers from shore to shore, while his better half displayed her patriotism in flapjacks.

The old Burdett homestead was for many years a landmark of Fort Lee, but it has at last been demolished. Etienne Burdett, son of one of the early Huguenots in this country, cleared a spot in the forest of the Palisades and there built him a dwelling. Acres surrounding belonged to him. His brother Peter fell heir to the home, and it long remained in the family.

On the Palisades at Fort Lee we are on the historic ground of the American fort—the point toward which Cornwallis was left marching from Closter Landing. Thomas Paine has left the best-known description of the evacuation of this post; as an aide-de-camp to Greene he saw all the retreat; he was with the troops here, and he marched with them back to the edge of Pennsylvania.

In the center of the town is Monument Square, with its Revolutionary monument which was erected in 1908 by the State of New Jersey under the auspices of the Fort Lee Revolutionary Monument Association. It is the work of the sculptor Carl E. Tefft. Two bronze figures of Continental soldiers seem to be scaling the great bowlders which form the base, one fairly at the top, the other struggling to reach it; these bowlders are the very stuff of the Palisades themselves, and the conception of the soldiers' purpose is to achieve that crest.

Arthur C. Mack's volume, *The Palisades of the Hudson*, traces these localities in detail. Turning toward the south, you come upon a small stone church which has no stirring history of its own, but is in the midst of historic sites. Directly in front of where this modern Episcopal church stands was Washington's well. Somewhat further down and toward the north, the ancient army oven is known to have been.

West from the church, across the trolley track and a little beyond, is Hook's Ice Pond, where workmen in 1898 dug up quantities of relics. There were found cannon balls, bayonets, shoe buckles, stirrups, bullets, and bullet molds. Long ago, on the west side of the pond, there were piles of stones which had once been fireplaces in the soldiers' huts.

North of the church again, north, too, of the monument and just east of Parker Avenue (the street on which the church faces) you will find the main site of fortification, lying between Cedar and English streets. In this immediate vicinity there have been dug up bullets, bullet molds, and cannon balls within recent years.

Continuing still further north, and eastward,

out toward the edge of the height, you will find the old Bluff Point, the site of the works enclosed by the abatis. This site is out toward the river from the end of Main Street. Some distance further up along the edge is the site of the redoubt which commanded the sunken obstructions between Fort Washington and Fort Lee.

This was the situation in '76. The Palisades' bluff jutting out here at Fort Lee had been fortified early in the year by two redoubts; the lower and lesser was called Fort Constitution, and the upper, the main one, was named after Charles Lee, who later attempted to buy his freedom from British captors by offering them a plan for conquering Washington's army. His name has not, therefore, been a popular one, and few of us, in using the name of the fort, ever think of its origin. Lee was taken back into the American army and reappointed second in command, but his treachery at Monmouth, and other misdeeds, led to his final dismissal, and he died a sad and disgraced death in later years.

At the beginning of the Fort Lee story, Fort Washington, across the river, had fallen. This fortification stood on the hill between 181st and 186th streets of the present. Congress had insisted that General Washington should hold this fort in spite of his wish to evacuate—but in the end Howe had contrived to get a supply of flatboats to King's Bridge, and thus reach Fort

Washington. It was then a fairly simple matter for the British to proceed. Magaw found himself wholly in the power of the enemy, and he and his garrison became prisoners of war. He had made a stubborn defense, having refused Howe's first summons to surrender; but the end found the garrison of more than two thousand men in the jails of New York.

Washington, meanwhile, was on the west shore of the Hudson. Both Greene and Magaw had believed that the fort on the east side could be defended, and Magaw's reply to Howe's first summons, November 15th, showed his spirit:

"Actuated by the most glorious cause that mankind ever fought in, I am determined to defend this post to the very last extremity."

As the danger had increased, Greene had sent a messenger across the river to Washington, informing him of the situation; but at the same time he sent reinforcements to Magaw, anticipating a happy outcome. The message disturbed Washington, but the sender was hopeful. At nightfall Washington had arrived at Fort Lee; Greene and Putnam were at Fort Washington. Irving says: "He threw himself into a boat and had partly crossed the river, when he met those generals returning. They informed him of the garrison's having been reinforced. . . . It was with difficulty however that they could prevail

The Monument at Fort Lee, to Soldiers of the Revolution.

The "Half-Moon" Anchored at Historic "Closter Landing."

The Old Dutch Church of Hackensack, whose Records Date back to 1686.

Mansion House at Hackensack, where Washington Stayed during his Retreat.

on him to return with them to the Jersey shore, for he was excessively excited."

And Bacon adds: "Less discreet historians than Irving have not hesitated to say that the Father of His Country on that occasion expressed his excitement in language of much greater vigor than is countenanced by polite custom. In other words, this is believed to have been one of the rare occasions upon which Washington swore."

Fort Washington was not to be saved, however. Lossing says: "Washington, standing upon Fort Lee with his general officers, and the author of *Common Sense*, saw some of the slaughter near the doomed fortress, and with streaming eyes he beheld the meteor flag of England flashing above its ramparts in the bright November sun."

The abandonment of Fort Lee was now a foregone conclusion, for it was obviously the next move for the British to take the sister fort. The flight was made in reckless haste. Camp kettles were left on the fires, more than four hundred tents were left standing, and more than three months' provision for three thousand men. A few blankets, a little baggage, were hauled away in wagons, while all the cannon remained except two twelve-pounders. Thomas Paine wrote:

"As I was with the troops at Fort Lee and marched with them to the edge of Pennsylvania, I am well acquainted with many circumstances which those who lived at a distance knew little of. Our situation there was exceedingly cramped, the place being on a narrow neck of land between the Hackensack and North Rivers. Our force was inconsiderable, being not one-fourth as great as Howe could bring against us. We had no army at hand to have relieved the garrison, had we shut ourselves up and stood on the defense. Our ammunition, light artillery, and the best part of our stores had been removed upon the apprehension that Howe would endeavor to penetrate the Jerseys, in which case Fort Lee could be of no use to us. . . . Such was our situation and condition at Fort Lee on the morning of the 20th of November, when an officer arrived with information that the enemy with two hundred boats had landed seven or eight miles above. Major-General Greene, who commanded the garrison, immediately ordered them under arms, and sent an express to his Excellency, General Washington, at Hackensack, distant six miles. Our first object was to secure the bridge across the Hackensack. General Washington arrived in about three-quarters of an hour and marched at the head of his troops. . . . We brought off as much baggage as the wagons could contain. The rest was lost. . . . The simple object was to bring off the garrison and march them on till they could be strengthened by the Pennsylvania or Jersey militia."

The melancholy retreat over the six miles back to Hackensack left only a deserted fort for Cornwallis when he arrived from Closter Landing. The conquest was easy for the English forces, and it is probable that they might have captured the American army had they continued with vigor.

If you follow the retreat back to where it arrived at Hackensack, you can picture a cold, rainy dusk. In such a dusk the Americans arrived. They came marching two abreast; they were barefooted, their feet torn by the rough roads; their garments were so worn and torn that they were exposed to the cold rain, except for wrapping their blankets around them as they marched. Toward the Mansion House they trod that path of defeat and hardship, and were drawn up in the square which you now find crisply trimmed and watered and green, adorned with a fountain, prosperous, and at peace.

There the pitiful group, huddling in their blankets against the rain, waited for the next duty. Their march was by no means over.

Facing the square stands the Mansion House, now a hotel, but in those days the private residence of Peter Zabriskie. Washington had been making it his headquarters, and he returned to it now for the period before continuing his march. A tablet has been placed upon the building by the Bergen County Historical Society "to mark the site of the Mansion House occupied as headquarters by General George Washington during the retreat from Fort Lee in 1776."

It is a spacious, old-fashioned structure, coming out to a line with Main Street and only slightly withdrawn from the sidewalk on its front, Washington Place. The house has been altered and added to since the days of Peter Zabriskie, but the main part of the building is the same as in 1776.

At the farther end of the small park is the old Dutch church, the First Reformed Church of Hackensack, full of early history. Records of the original building date back to 1686. It is known that the church was established soon after the beginning of the town, which was in 1640, when the Dutch settled it, naming it for the Indians who dwelt thereabouts. The name "Hackensack" meant to the Indians "a river in a marsh," and distinguished this stream from the "Passaic," "a river in a valley."

The churchyard surrounds the building, and its stones bear many familiar old names. Some of the materials of which the Dutch church of 1696 was constructed are now to be seen in the eastern wall.

Here and there are old names carved in the stones used in the walls; one stone reveals the words, "Jacob Brinker hoff 1792," and another, "Peter Zabrsky 1791," with the long "s."

Little is known of some of the owners of these names. Some stones display ornamentation accompanying the letters—crude carvings of grotesque figures, similar to those often found on headstones in old churchyards.

A monument standing in the open space before the church, and opposite the Bergen County Court House, is dedicated to the memory of Brigadier-General Enoch Poor, by the New Jersey Sons of the American Revolution. Poor was born in Andover, Massachusetts, but much of his life was associated with Hackensack, and he died near this town in 1780. In command of a New Hampshire brigade he rendered signal service at many battles, especially Stillwater, Saratoga, Newtown, and Monmouth.

At Valley Forge he displayed his courage and unselfishness in providing for the comfort of his soldiers. He won the high regard not only of the men under him, but of Washington and Lafayette. A military funeral closed his career; soldiers marched to his grave beside the old Dutch church which now looks upon his monument; a quaint record reports that the drums were muffled in black crêpe and that the officers wore crêpe around their left arms.

For the present-day pilgrim who does not care to leave the shores of the Hudson, and follow Washington's retreat inland to Hackensack, it is worth while to continue south from Fort Lee and search out the landing place of the old Bull's Ferry, which was one of the three important crossings (Fort Lee Ferry and Weehawken Ferry being the others) some hundred years ago. Shadyside of modern times is the name given this point. Near the old ferry a blockhouse was erected during the Revolution, and this was garrisoned by a detachment of British troops. It served as protection to the plundering loyalists who lived round about, safeguarding them in their seizing of cattle and horses. When the Continentals attacked the blockhouse in order to get back their property, they were repulsed by the garrison and forced to give up the attack, having lost sixty men.

NORTH—FROM THE SHORES OF THE HUDSON TO LONG ISLAND SOUND AND EAST RIVER

CHAPTER XVI

IN ANDRÉ'S FOOTSTEPS TO TAPPAN

SNEDEN'S LANDING, or Paramus Landing as it was previously called, is in Rockland County, New York. It may be reached in the Twentieth Century by a ferryboat which is the lineal descendant of the dugout in which Jeremiah Dobbs used to ferry his chance passengers across the Hudson.

This same Jeremiah Dobbs was a Swede, a tenant of the Philipses. He was a fisherman by rights; but the income derived from selling fish not being sufficient, apparently, to maintain even his modest ways of living, he put his dugout to use, and offered it as a means of crossing the river at the point now known by his name. So rapidly did his trade increase, and so well known did his ferry become, that the village springing up at its eastern terminus came to be called "Dobbs Ferry"; this is a deep regret to many residents of the present town. In fact, there have been public meetings held to agitate the question of this name, and several attempts made to induce the Legislature to change it. In 1830, Van Brugh Livingston filed deeds under the name of Livingston's Landing, and for a period of thirty years this name was in current use. In 1870 a meeting was held to arrange for the formal adoption of a name, and Jenkins gives the following account of the affair:

"That [name] of Paulding, one of the captors of André, was almost agreed upon when a gentleman arose and made a speech in a serious vein to the following effect. He said he was no worshipper of Dobbs; he disliked that his home should be identified with such a low place as a ferry; double names especially were uncouth and undesirable; and he had known Paulding personally and could not brook him. Van Wart, who had also aided in the capture of André, was a Christian gentleman; he, therefore, moved that instead of calling the place Paulding-on-Hudson, the Van of Van Wart be stricken off and the place be called 'Wart-on-Hudson.' The speech gave such a ridiculous turn to the whole affair that the meeting broke up and nothing further was attempted at that time."

Other efforts have been made to drive away the ghost of old Dobbs, but they have been unavailing. It appears that he is there to stay. From the days when he was one of the first settlers, dwelling in a shanty on Willow Point, he must have traveled far toward prosperity, for he and his ferry were of great importance.

The boat in which he carried his first passengers was a canoe, dug out of a tree-trunk. The one used now is a light motor-boat, propelled by a power which would no doubt seem as satanic to old Dobbs as did the Headless Horseman to his neighbor, Ichabod Crane. Nevertheless, the methods of this modern ferry are somewhat primitive. To summon the present boat, one approaches a signal—an upright white square of wood—which stands at the water's edge; pulls a rope which springs a trap door, and thus displays a black square on the white. The boatman, who may be reposing over at Sneden's Landing, puts off for the eastern shore, and it is well for the traveler if he be not in desperate haste.

In the motor-boat you are tossed across the Hudson just where the passengers of Dobbs were tossed in colonial times, and later, those of Molly Sneden, the ferry mistress of the Revolution. That one end of the route should commemorate his name, the other hers, seems a fair division of fame. The ferry of to-day is used by a few dwellers on the west shore and is little known to the general traveler, the larger and more systematic boats from Tarrytown to Nyack carrying most of the passengers for this region.

Here where you have crossed, the British fleet was stationed from 1776 to 1783; and here the British navy first saluted the American flag, obeying the instruction of Parliament.

Turning toward the land, you will see before you the house where Molly Sneden dwelt. It has been somewhat altered by the addition of a modern veranda, but if you will look at its rear side you will see the original house with the modern veranda blotted out, and the unbroken line of stone masonry, the old-time shutters, preserving the traditions of past days.

Molly Sneden controlled the ferry after old Dobbs had laid down his oars. The Sneden family (Sneeden and Snyden are other spellings of the name) were hot Tories, and many an adventure did the ferry participate in. Molly was a brave woman, and her grave, in the old cemetery above at Palisades, is preserved with honor.

Tradition has it that in 1775 Martha Washington crossed this ferry to reach General Washington who was then at Cambridge.

Near the Sneden house stands another dwelling of the same period, in which the roughly shaped stones of the Palisades themselves were laid for stout walls, as firm and weather-worthy to-day as in the seventeen-hundreds.

To follow all of history's story which lies written through this part of the Hudson River district, you must climb the steep road leading from the ferry landing up the wall of rock. The road zigzags from one fine view to another, a series of delightful river and land pictures accompanying you all the way to the top.

By the sign of a flag-pole you may know when, in following this road, you have reached that building known as "The Big House." Just beyond the flag, on a green knoll which slopes on one side toward a bit of woodland, on the other toward the river, stands this mansion whose date of building is given as 1685—that is, the foundation of its kitchen is said to have been laid in that year, almost a century before the Revolution. In its hall is a mahogany table at which Washington is said to have sat, and this inscription commemorates the fact:

"At this table Gen. Washington is said to have dined in The Big House, Palisades, Rockland County, New York, during the Revolutionary War. Property of the Palisades Library Association. Aug. 30, 1899."

Above it, along the broad hall, stretch the giant beams of old days. A portion of the house is now used as a library.

To the road again. It is smooth and wide and well-shaded much of the way. It leads to Tappan, the old town around which centers the strongest historic interest of this trip, it being the spot upon which was written the last chapter of André's story.

Tappan is about two miles from the ferry below, in the midst of a fertile valley. This

16

region was known during the Revolution as having abundant forage. It was well situated for an army encampment, and the Americans used the ridge to the southwest for this purpose; the shelter of the hills and the nearness of the river gave it value. When, in September, 1778, Lieutenant-Colonel Baylor was sent with a regiment of light horse to watch the British movements, and to intercept scouts and foragers, he made his headquarters at Tappan.

As a result, the place became the scene of a serious event. His troops were camping in barns more than two miles below the village and were unarmed. Cornwallis saw an opportunity to take the Americans by surprise, as they were in a position of great insecurity. He sent General Grey, with some light infantry and other troops, to approach from the western side, and ordered that an approach on the east be made by a corps from Knyphausen's division, Knyphausen being then at Dobbs Ferry. The plan was to surround Baylor's camp, also Wayne's body of militia who were not far off. Wayne's men were warned of the plan, but Baylor's remained in ignorance.

It was midnight when Grey silently approached the camp of sleeping men. They were entirely at the mercy of the enemy, and mercy was refused. Grey ordered that no quarter be given, soldiers were bayoneted outright, and

The Home of Molly Sneden, the Ferry Mistress, at Sneden's Landing.

"The Big House," at Palisades, N. Y., where Washington Sat at Table. The Table is now to be Seen there.

The "'76 Stone House," where André was Imprisoned at Tappan.

The Present Ferryboat, a Lineal Descendant of Jeremiah Dobbs's Dugout.

sixty-seven of the one hundred and four men were wounded or killed. Baylor was taken prisoner, having been first wounded.

Grey won for himself the reputation of hardness during the war in more ways than one. He was called "The No-Flint General," owing to his custom of forcing his men to take the flints out of their muskets, in order that they should be obliged to use the bayonet.

That portion of the André story which was written hereabouts calls for a refreshed memory of the earlier portion which involved his capture at Tarrytown[1]—when, with the perilous papers crammed inside the soles of his stockings, he was taken by the three Americans, scorned when he showed Benedict Arnold's pass, searched, and summed up in Paulding's declaration, "By God, he is a spy!"

He had written frankly to Washington, telling his story quite fully—how he had gone up the river on the sloop of war *Vulture*, had met Arnold for the secret conference near Stony Point in the clump of fir trees. He had stopped at the house of Joshua Smith along with Arnold, and during that stop the *Vulture*, lying waiting for him in the river, had been fired upon, and André had made his escape with difficulty. To Washington he explained this situation; but his honesty could not save him.

[1] Chapter XVII.

It was on September 28, 1780, that he was taken across the river. Major Tallmadge was put in charge of the prisoner, and together the two men set out for Tappan. During that sad journey Tallmadge acquired a warm interest in the brave and charming young officer. Riding horseback side by side, they fell into a conversation that partook of intimacy. André asked what feeling the American officers were likely to show regarding his case. Tallmadge held silence at first, thinking of the fate of Nathan Hale who had been his classmate at Yale College and whom General Howe had hanged four years before for an act of the same nature as André's. At length, the question being repeated, Tallmadge referred to the fate of his friend. "But surely you do not consider his case and mine alike!" André responded with surprise. Tallmadge was forced to answer: "They are precisely similar, and similar will be your fate."

Reaching the railroad station at Tappan, you must cross the track and continue along the same road beyond to find the building used as a prison during this incident. On the way you will pass an old residence now known as the William Rogers house, the sixth on your left; local tradition calls this the Washington Headquarters. The rear of the house is more indicative of its age than the front, which has been extended on the side toward the Sparkill River by which the lawn is flanked. The house is said to have been built in 1700.

A little further along you come to the red church, the original of which was the building in which André's trial was held. Fiske says:

"A military commission of fourteen generals was assembled, with Greene presiding, to sit in judgment on the unfortunate young officer. 'It is impossible to save him,' said the kindly Steuben, who was one of the judges. 'Would to God the wretch who has drawn him to his death might be made to suffer in his stead!' The opinion of the court was unanimous that André had acted as a spy, and incurred the penalty of death. Washington allowed a brief respite, that Sir Henry Clinton's views might be considered. The British commander, in his sore distress over the danger of his young friend, could find no better grounds to allege in his defense than that he had, presumably, gone ashore under a flag of truce, and that when taken he certainly was travelling under the protection of a pass which Arnold, in the ordinary exercise of his authority, had a right to grant. But clearly these safeguards were vitiated by the treasonable purpose of the commander who granted them, and in availing himself of them André, who was privy to this treasonable purpose, took his life in his hands as completely as any ordinary spy would do. André himself had already candidly admitted before the court 'that it was impossible for him to suppose that he came ashore under the sanction of a flag'; and Washington struck to the root of the matter, as he invariably did, in his letter to Clinton, where he said that André 'was employed in the execution of measures very foreign to the objects of flags of truce, and such as they were never meant to authorize or countenance in the most distant degree.' The argument was conclusive, but it was not strange that the British general should have been slow to admit its force. He begged that the question might be submitted to an impartial committee, consisting of Knyphausen from the one army and Rochambeau from the other; but as no question had arisen which the military commission was not thoroughly competent to decide, Washington very properly refused to permit such an unusual proceeding. Lastly, Clinton asked that André might be exchanged for Christopher Gadsden, who had been taken in the capture of Charleston, and was then imprisoned at St. Augustine. At the same time, a letter from Arnold to Washington, with characteristic want of tact, hinting at retaliation upon the persons of sundry South Carolinian prisoners, was received with silent contempt.

"There was a general feeling in the American

army that if Arnold himself could be surrendered to justice, it might perhaps be well to set free the less guilty victim by an act of executive clemency; and Greene gave expression to this feeling in an interview with Lieutenant-General Robertson, whom Clinton sent up on Sunday, the first of October, to plead for André's life. No such suggestion could be made in the form of an official proposal. Under no circumstances could Clinton be expected to betray the man from whose crime he had sought to profit, and who had now thrown himself upon him for protection. Nevertheless, in a roundabout way the suggestion was made. On Saturday, Captain Ogden, with an escort of twenty-five men and a flag of truce, was sent down to Paulus Hook with letters for Clinton, and he contrived to whisper to the commandant there that if in any way Arnold might be suffered to slip into the hands of the Americans André would be set free. It was Lafayette who had authorized Ogden to offer the suggestion, and so, apparently, Washington must have connived at it; but Clinton, naturally, refused to entertain the idea for a moment. The conference between Greene and Robertson led to nothing. A petition from André, in which he begged to be shot rather than hanged, was duly considered and rejected; and, accordingly, on Monday, the second of October, the ninth day after his capture by the yeomen at Tarrytown, the adjutant-general of the British army was led to the gallows."

The building in which the young British officer was imprisoned during these swift, bitter days is only a short distance beyond the church. "The '76 Stone House" it is called, and to-day its historic inscriptions are displayed amidst the announcements of a road house and the refreshments offered therein. Lossing, in describing his visit to this building more than half a century ago, states that "its whole appearance has been materially changed," and adds, "The room wherein the unfortunate prisoner was confined, and which was kept with care in its original condition more than half a century, has been enlarged and *improved* for the purposes *of a ball-room!* I was there a few years ago, when the then owner was committing the sacrilege, and he boasted, with great satisfaction, that he had received a 'whole dollar for the old lock that fastened up Major Andrew!' " Could Lossing visit the place to-day, with its billiard-room and liquor store within, its lager beer signs without, he would reflect even more sadly now than then that "sentiment does not obey the laws of trade—it seems to cheapen with a decrease of supply." A picture of André, and some ancient relics, including a fiddle and oxbow, are to be seen within the building.

From this building André was led forth and

up the slope beyond, where you follow the road. Turning to the left on a branch that leads toward a knoll, you will reach the spot where the execution took place. A circle of iron fence surrounds a simple stone. The inscription states that: "Here died, October 2, 1780, Major John André of the British Army, who, entering the American lines on a secret mission to Benedict Arnold for the surrender of West Point, was taken prisoner and condemned as a spy. His death, though according to the stern code of war, moved even his enemies to pity, and both armies mourned the fate of one so young and so brave. In 1821 his remains were removed to Westminster Abbey. A hundred years after his execution this stone was placed above the spot where he lay, not to perpetuate the record of strife, but in token of those better feelings which have since united two nations, one in race, in language and in religion, with the earnest hope that this friendly union will never be broken."

André met death gallantly, although the bitterness of dying as a spy, not a soldier, tortured him to the end. The execution took place at twelve o'clock. "The principal guard-officer," wrote Dr. Thatcher, an army surgeon, who was present, "who was constantly in the room with the prisoner, relates that when the hour of execution was announced to him in the morning, he received it without emotion, and, while all present were affected with silent gloom, he retained a firm countenance. . . . Observing his servant enter his room in tears, he exclaimed, 'Leave me, until you can show yourself more manly'. . . . Major André walked from the stone house in which he had been confined between two of our subaltern officers, arm-in-arm. . . . It was his earnest desire to be shot, as being the mode of death most comformable to the feelings of a military man, and he had indulged the hope that his request would be granted. At the moment, therefore, when suddenly he came in view of the gallows, he involuntarily started backward and made a pause. 'Why this emotion, sir?' said an officer by his side. Instantly recovering his composure, he said, 'I am reconciled to my death, but I detest the mode.' "

On the previous day he had made a last appeal in a letter to Washington, asking that he might die a soldier's death. N. P. Willis translated the brave and dignified request into verse in this wise:

It is not the fear of death
  That damps my brow;
It is not for another breath
  I ask thee now;
I can die with a lip unstirr'd,
  And a quiet heart—
Let but this prayer be heard
  Ere I depart.

I can give up my mother's look—
  My sister's kiss;
I can think of love—yet brook
  A death like this!
I can give up the young fame
  I burn'd to win;
All—but the spotless name
  I glory in.

Thine is the power to give,
  Thine to deny,
Joy for the hour I live,
  Calmness to die.
By all the brave should cherish,
  By my dying breath,
I ask that I may perish
  By a soldier's death.

CHAPTER XVII

BESIDE THE HUDSON TO SLEEPY HOLLOW

THERE is a drowsy little old churchyard overshadowed by thick branches, hummed to by lazy bees—a spot that means more than we have as yet estimated in our literature's history. Let us travel toward it along the Hudson's east shore.

Old Broadway, upon leaving Yonkers, began to climb a steep hill as it pushed on toward the north. The road being difficult, the Highland Turnpike Company took it in hand about 1806, straightened out its worst windings, smoothed it, and established a tollgate. Thus the name of "The Highland Turnpike" was applied to it, although the name that has remained through the years is that of the Albany Post Road.

Along the water's edge runs Warburton Avenue, lined with fine country estates. Above it, on the hill, runs the old turnpike, which has in its day also been flanked by many famous estates. One of these was the home of C. H. Lilienthal, with its battlemented tower of brownstone, visible from the river. A high gray tower marks the famous "Greystone," country house of Samuel J. Tilden, who was Governor, and candidate for the Presidency of the United States. He was called the "Sage of Greystone." Samuel Untermyer owns the property now, and has made a practice of throwing open the magnificent grounds, gardens, and hothouses of rare flowers to the enjoyment of the public.

Hastings lies next on old Broadway's route. Its site almost covers the old Post estate. One Peter Post formerly owned all this territory and occupied his small stone house here as far back as the time of the Revolution. But after that war the house, formerly a dwelling-place of good repute, fell into other hands, and came to be used as a tavern, and the good people round about were horrified by the genial company of cock-fighters and hard drinkers who gathered nightly under its roof. The resort grew to be notorious, but the worthy neighbors were eventually appeased when its career as a tavern closed and it passed once more back into the oblivion of respectability, coming to be described as "a neat cottage."

Peter Post's encounter with a group of Hessians is a Hastings tradition. He was a loyal patriot, and he assisted Colonel Sheldon to surprise a party of the troublesome Hessians, by leading them to believe that the Americans whom they were pursuing were further ahead, whereas these same Americans were hidden in the rear and merely awaiting their chance. The Hessians passed on, the Americans sallied forth, to the end that only one marauder was left to tell the tale. Dead bodies of the Hessians were strewn in all directions. But the survivor made off to Emmerick's camp, did in fact tell his tale, and Post was the victim of the enemy's rage. He was all but killed by the blows he received. The affair occurred in 1777.

From Hastings, Broadway pushes on to Dobbs Ferry. Here stands the so-called Livingston mansion. The house was built by a Dutch farmer, and it was probably not until many years after that the name of Livingston was connected with it. But it is best remembered as the home of Van Brugh Livingston; later it was owned by Stephen Archer, and the Hasbrouck family have been recent occupants.

The house has of late struggled bravely against decay. But although the yard and the roof and the veranda may be shabby, the treasures within-doors are carefully preserved. One room is shown in which the Evacuation papers were signed. This is in the middle of the building, the front portion having been built on since Revolutionary days. A rosewood table, with its accompanying rosewood and haircloth chairs, is called "the Lafayette table," tradition having it that in times of large entertainments this

The Monument near the Livingston Mansion, Recording the History of the Spot.

The Door of the Old Church at Sleepy Hollow.

The Glen at Dobbs Ferry, where the Indians are Supposed to have Camped.

The Old Bell Tower at Sunnyside.

long and groaning board would be stretched diagonally across the room.

In May of 1783, General Washington, with Clinton and their suites, went down the river to meet Sir Guy Carleton who was to come up the river in a frigate and meet them at Dobbs Ferry. Here at the Livingston Mansion the conference between the commanders took place. On May 8th the American party dined on board the sloop, where they were received with military honors and entertained with stately courtesy by General Carleton.

A monument standing near the house records the fact that "here, in 1781, the French allies under Rochambeau joined the American army. Here, in 1781, Washington planned the Yorktown campaign, which brought to a triumphant end the war for American independence. Here, in 1783, Washington and Carleton arranged for the evacuation of American soil by the British; and opposite this point a British sloop of war fired seventeen guns, the first salute by Great Britain to the United States of America."

Southwest of the house is the horseshoe-shaped embankment where the remains of the military fort were to be seen for many years. The ground has now been leveled over. Dobbs Ferry was within the "Neutral Ground" of the Revolution, and, like every other place within these limits, suffered from marauders and raiders of both sides. From the mouth of the Croton River east to the Sound ran the Americans' line of posts, that the enemy might be held off from the Highlands. The British line ran near the Harlem River, starting at Kingsbridge and reaching to Pelham and New Rochelle. The tract lying between, about a score of miles in width, belonging to neither side, was known as the Neutral Ground, and not only did the regular troops cause trouble to the dwellers within those twenty miles, but here the famous "Cowboys" of the British and "Skinners" of the Americans, mere lawless, marauding bands, robbed, burned, and murdered in their wild raids.

At the upper end of the town's main street you come upon a pretty glen crossed by a rustic bridge. There is a story to the effect that the glen at this point was an old camping place of Indians, and that the British later on used it as a camping ground. The Indians knew Dobbs Ferry as "The Place of the Bark Kettle," and their settlement was probably located at the mouth of Wicker's Creek.

At Irvington the post road enters what has come to be familiarly known as the land of Irving. A little blue sign reading simply "Sunnyside Lane" introduces the pilgrim to this land. You enter the shaded curves with a throb of beloved association: this is the lane that Irving tells you of, this is the brook—the wild brook, which "came babbling down the ravine and threw itself into the little cove where of yore the Water Guard harbored their whale-boats." The history of this home of Irving's is fully given in *Wolfert's Roost*, wherein he explains the origin of its curious name; how Wolfert "retired to this fastness in the wilderness, with the bitter determination to bury himself from the world, and live here for the rest of his days in peace and quiet. In token of that fixed purpose, he inscribed over his door his favorite Dutch motto, 'Lust in Rust' (pleasure in quiet). The mansion was thence called Wolfert's Rust, but by the uneducated, who did not understand Dutch, Wolfert's Roost."

At the end of the lane you enter the gates of the estate. Except upon the few days in the year when the present members of the Irving family reserve these grounds for their private enjoyment, these gates are open to visitors. Any weekday other than a holiday the public is admitted. The stranger within the gates may stroll down the paths and out into the opening where trees part and that wonderful picture of the Tappan Zee, one of Irving's keenest delights, suddenly meets the eye. Here stands the famous house; once the Roost, later named Sunnyside, that "little old-fashioned stone mansion, all made up of gable ends, and as full of angles and corners as an old cocked hat." It bears the same likeness to a cocked hat to-day that it did when Washington Irving chose it for his abiding place, in the land which he had loved from his boyhood, when he had played along this part of the Hudson's shore. The trunks of the old vines which drape the building are grown to tree-like dimensions. In the tower the old bell still hangs, the bell which in early days summoned farm hands to gather.

On the green circle in front of the house I found a very little chap in modern Buster Brown garments and a wide straw hat; on that green circle, face to face with the Tappan Zee where British ships of war were once anchored, where "stout galleys armed with eighteen-pounders and navigated with sails and oars, cruised about like hawks," the little chap was earnestly engaged in trying to fire a cannon of some four inches in length. "Why won't it go off?" he demanded, rolling it forward on its diminutive wheels until it commanded the Tappan Zee. "I want to shoot the enemy with it." From that "little Mediterranean" once "ploughed by hostile prows," there came not a sound; not even an excursion boat was to be seen; and at Wolfert's Roost, once a rallying place, a secret station from which the enemies of a nation could be watched, a point at which plots fermented and war hummed in the air, there was only a very little boy playing with a four-inch-long cannon.

The Tappan Zee is about two and a half miles wide and ten miles long. It has played its part both in actual history, and in lore. It was a source of inspiration to Irving for much that he wrote. We can imagine that the legend of "The Storm-Ship" took form upon paper when he was gazing forth upon this water which the ghostly ship was said to haunt.

"In the golden age of the province of the New Netherlands, the people of the Manhattoes were alarmed one sultry afternoon by a tremendous storm of thunder and lightning. Great was the terror of the good old women of the Manhattoes. They gathered their children together, and took refuge in the cellars; after having hung a shoe on the iron point of every bedpost, lest it should attract the lightning. At length the storm abated; the thunder sank into a growl, and the setting sun, breaking from under the fringed borders of the clouds, made the broad bosom of the bay to gleam like a sea of molten gold.

"The word was given from the fort that a ship was standing up the bay. It passed from mouth to mouth, and street to street, and soon put the little capital in a bustle. The arrival of a ship, in those early times of the settlement, was an event of vast importance to the inhabitants. The news from the fort, therefore, brought all the populace down to the Battery, to behold the wished-for sight. Many were the groups collected about the Battery. Here and there might be seen a burgomaster, of slow and pompous gravity, giving his opinion with great confidence to a crowd of old women and idle boys. At another place was a knot of old weather-beaten fellows, who had been seamen or fishermen in their times, and were great authorities on such occasions; these gave different opinions, and caused great disputes among their several adherents: but the man most looked up to, and followed and watched by the crowd, was Hans Van Pelt, an old Dutch sea-captain retired from service, the nautical oracle of the place. He reconnoitred the ship through an ancient telescope, hummed a Dutch tune to himself, and said nothing. A hum, however, from Hans Van Pelt, had always more weight with the public than a speech from another man.

"In the meantime the ship became more distinct to the naked eye: she was a stout, round, Dutch-built vessel, with high bow and poop, and bearing Dutch colors. The evening sun gilded her bellying canvas, and she came riding over the long waving billows. The sentinel who had given notice of her approach, declared, that he first got sight of her when she was in the center of the bay; and that she broke suddenly on his sight, just as if she had come out of the bosom of the black thunder-cloud. The by-standers looked at Hans Van Pelt, to see what he would say to this report; Hans Van Pelt screwed his mouth closer together, and said nothing; upon which some shook their heads, and others shrugged their shoulders.

"The ship was now repeatedly hailed, but made no reply, and passing by the fort, stood on up the Hudson. A gun was brought to bear on her, and, with some difficulty, loaded and fired by Hans Van Pelt. The shot seemed absolutely to pass through the ship, and to skip along the water on the other side, but no notice was taken of it! What was strange, she had all her sails set, and sailed right against wind and tide, which were both down the river. Upon this Hans Van Pelt set off to board her; but he turned without success. Sometimes he would get within one or two hundred yards of her, and then, in a twinkling, she would be half a mile off. He got near enough, however, to see the crew; who were all dressed in Dutch style, the officers in doublets and high hats and feathers; not a word was spoken by anyone on board; they stood as motionless as so many statues."

The tale goes on to relate how much the governor was disturbed by the appearance of this ship; how he called his council together repeatedly, sent messengers about, but could learn nothing of the ship and its mission. Captains of sloops seldom came in without bringing a report of having seen the strange ship at some point along the river; "sometimes it was by the flashes of the thunder-storm lighting up a pitchy night, and giving glimpses of her careering across Tappan Zee, or the wide waste of Haverstraw Bay. Her appearance was always just after, or just before, or just in the midst of unruly weather; and she was known among the skippers and voyagers of the Hudson by the name of 'the storm-ship.' "

Many theories were advanced concerning the origin of this vessel. Some "suggested, that, if it really was a supernatural apparition, as there was every natural reason to believe, it might be Hendrick Hudson, and his crew of the *Half-Moon*."

But "other events occurred to occupy the thoughts and doubts of the sage Wouter and his council, and the storm-ship ceased to be a subject of deliberation at the board. It continued, however, a matter of popular belief and marvellous anecdote through the whole time of the Dutch government, and particularly just before the capture of New Amsterdam, and the subjugation of the province by the English squadron. About that time the storm-ship was repeatedly seen in the Tappan Zee, and about Weehawk, and even down as far as Hoboken; and her appearance was supposed to be ominous of the approaching squall in public affairs, and the downfall of Dutch domination.

"Since that time we have no authentic accounts of her. People who live along the river insist that they sometimes see her in summer moonlight; and that in a deep still midnight they have heard the chant of her crew, as if heaving the lead; but sights and sounds are deceptive along the mountainous shores."

Jacob Van Tassel was owner of Wolfert's Roost at the outbreak of the Revolution, and his republican sympathies were well known He made the Roost a rendezvous for American land-scouts, and also water-guards who lurked in coves along the shore in their canoe-shaped boats called whaleboats, to obtain information concerning the enemy, sometimes cutting off boats which attempted to approach the shore from British vessels. Van Tassel often accompanied his friends in their expeditions, leaving as garrison at home his wife, his sister Nochie Van Wurmer, a blooming young daughter, and a negro woman.

On one occasion, when a boatful of armed men approched the shore from a vessel, landed, and attacked the house, the valiant garrison of four wielded broomsticks, shovels, and any other weapons of the kind available; but in spite of this noble defense the house was plundered and burned, and the beauty of the Roost was seized. Van Tassel's wife, sister, and the negro woman fought to get her back, battling down to the edge of the water; suddenly a voice from the frigate commanded that the prize be left behind, and, as Irving says, "the heroine of the Roost escaped with a mere rumpling of the feathers." Van Tassel's house was rebuilt upon the same site, and that second dwelling is the present house at Sunnyside.

Emerging from Sunnyside Lane, you continue on Broadway past the estates of many wealthy residents who, as Jenkins says, "thus far have succeeded in keeping the trolley cars from the historic highway, the last effort in that direction being in opposition to a bill before the Legislature of 1910. To mention these owners would be to give a list of the greatest and best in the business, political, literary, and professional life of New York for several generations." Lyndehurst, which became famous as the home of Miss Helen Miller Gould, now Mrs. Finley Shepard, is the most prominent of these residences. Its grounds, like those of the Irving home, stand open to the public except on Sundays and holidays. The castle-like house stands in the midst of vast gardens and trees. At the foot of the slope, near the river, is an attractive brown-shingled building which Miss Gould erected as a club for the girls of the village, with meetings on Saturdays for various classes. Adjoining it is a tennis court for the girls.

Years ago the estate was the home of Philip R. Paulding and was called "Paulding Manor";

Philip Hone called it "Paulding's Folly," on account of its extravagance. Later it was known as "Merritt's Folly," the then owner, Mr. Merritt, having spent more than one hundred thousand dollars in the conservatories and greenhouses which are still in use. Jay Gould was a later owner, and his daughter inherited Lyndehurst.

The post road leads you on to Tarrytown. The origin of this town's name is disputed. "Wheat Town" is said by some to have been the meaning of the original name, "Tarwe Dorp" in Dutch, which latter has been gradually corrupted into "Tarrytown." The name of two early settlers, the Terry brothers, is another origin ascribed. Irving offered the explanation that the farmers of the neighborhood used to bring their produce here to be shipped to New York, and on these occasions they tarried so long at the hospitable taverns around that the place came to be known as Tarrytown to these farmers' wives.

On Broadway, between Tarrytown and Sleepy Hollow beyond, stands a stately monument. It is of native marble, surmounted by the figure of a minute-man in bronze, resting upon his rifle. The scene of André's capture is depicted in bronze bas-relief on the monument's base. Here, in September, 1780, Major John André was captured by the three Americans, Isaac

Van Wart, John Paulding, and David Williams. André had just consummated his plot with Arnold and was attempting to reach New York.

According to Fiske, Sir Henry Clinton had warned the young officer not to carry any papers which might endanger him. But André did not heed the advice, and he took with him from Arnold six papers, five of them being in the traitor's handwriting. They contained descriptions of the fortresses and information concerning the disposition of the troops. André expected to tie up these papers with a stone in the bundle, so that he could drop them into the water in case of emergency; but in the meantime he placed them inside the soles of his stockings. With Joshua Smith he crossed the river from the west shore where he had met Arnold, and started on his ride toward White Plains. Smith showed such timidity on account of the Cowboys and Skinners who infested the region, that André was obliged to stop with him at a farmhouse overnight, though delay was dangerous; next morning Smith became so very nervous, when the journey was resumed, that André let him go back, and continued toward White Plains alone.

He now struck into the road which led through Tarrytown. He felt himself out of danger, and rode light-heartedly. But that morning a party

The Signal for the Ferryman at Dobbs Ferry.

The Livingston Mansion, Dobbs Ferry.

The Old Mill at Philipse Manor (now Demolished).

The Bridge at Sleepy Hollow.

of seven young men had come forth with the purpose of intercepting some Cowboys who were expected; and when André came riding toward them about nine o'clock, near the creek above Tarrytown, three of the young men sprang out at him from the bushes, calling "Halt!" They leveled their muskets at him because he was a stranger; had Smith, whom they knew, been along, there would probably have been nothing but a casual greeting.

Believing that these were Cowboys, one of them happening to have on a Hessian's coat, André frankly said that he was a British officer and that his business was important. Upon that John Paulding, he of the Hessian coat, stated that the party consisted of Americans, and ordered him to dismount.

The famous search followed, the papers were discovered in André's stockings, and Paulding uttered his well-known words, "By God, he is a spy!" The three young Americans showed their patriotism by refusing all bribes, and, taking their prisoner twelve miles up the river, they delivered him over to Colonel John Jameson who commanded a cavalry outpost at North Castle. Jameson sent the documents by an express-rider to Washington, but, being apparently of a credulous nature, he did not suspect the nature of the situation, and sent a letter to Arnold, which turned out to be the means of saving the traitor's life. Tallmadge happening to come in, Jameson talked over the matter with him, and the former immediately suspected that Arnold was not acting as he should; he wanted the letter, giving Arnold information, recalled, but it was too late.

Arnold and his wife happened to be entertaining Hamilton and a party at breakfast when the letter arrived; he opened it, and read Jameson's ingenuous message, that "one John Anderson had been taken with compromising documents in his possession."

Arnold kept his presence of mind. He merely put the letter in his pocket, explained that he was suddenly called across the river and would soon return, and made his escape immediately.

But André was prisoner. The rest of his story covered but a short period, until he was hanged as a spy on the knoll above Tappan, on the west side of the river. The names of his three captors have survived, as standing for true American alertness, force, and honesty.

Irving speaks of the tree which used to stand at the spot where André was taken, and of the mournful cries and wailings heard, and the funeral trains seen by the superstitious Dutch folk of Sleepy Hollow.

Pass the monument and continue along the old post road, and Sleepy Hollow itself comes in sight at last. It is a good many years since its scribe said that "a drowsy, dreamy influence seemed to hang over the land," yet the "listless repose of the place" is just the same to-day that it was in his time—save for the ubiquitous honk of the motor-car. Broadway cuts through the sleepy little hollow, and where Broadway leads the automobile is sure to go. Except for its whirr and honk, the spot still slumbers beside the Pocantico Creek.

It is highly probable that this famous vicinity is better known to the purposeful tourist from remote regions than it is to the average New Yorker—just because he has always lived so near it, and known so much about it in a general way, that he has never taken the pains to observe it very closely with his own eyes. The little churchyard is almost ignored by the motorist—he hies past it at the high-speed limit of his gasolene charger, or as near that limit as he dares, with maybe a careless observation on the Ichabod Crane legend. The pedestrian, to whom gasolene is merely a convenience for taking out spots, may pause and observe; but the pedestrian is usually of the immediate vicinity. A catechism on the Sleepy Hollow localities would reveal less ignorance in the man from Ohio or the traveling school-ma'am from Iowa than in the resident of New York, or I lose my wager.

Here is the creek beside which Ichabod Crane rode in his terrified efforts to escape the pursuit of the Headless Horseman. And here the bridge—" 'If I can but reach that bridge,' thought Ichabod, 'I am safe.' " "Just beyond swells the green knoll on which stands the white-washed church." Ichabod, you will remember, heard the black steed panting and blowing close behind him; he gave old Gunpowder a kick in the ribs, and the horse sprang upon the bridge; immediately thereafter the goblin rose in his stirrups and threw his head at the unfortunate schoolmaster.

The original bridge could not very well be standing to-day, as it was a crude affair, easily worn away by time and water. But in 1912 a handsome new bridge crossing the Pocantico at the same spot was dedicated, a memorial to the Sleepy Hollow tradition, and the gift of William Rockefeller. The visitor can stand upon it and gaze up the same slope toward the same church—the latter has suffered no change since that early day, and in it services are still held. The building was called "a monument of bygone days" even by Irving, for it had been built in the early days of the province, and the same tablet over the portal is as he described it—bearing the names of the church's founders, Frederick Filipson, the patroon of Yonkers, and his wife Katrina Van Courtland, of the Van Courtlands of Croton; a powerful family connection, as Irving observes, "with one foot resting on Spiting Devil Creek and the other on the Croton River."

All of the old graves cluster close around the church. Farther up the slope are newer ones, where members of the same old Dutch families have more recently been interred. Among these is the grave of Washington Irving.

Tracing the creek downward a short distance from the church bridge one comes upon the Philipse Manor house, which is dated earlier than the one at Yonkers, as the family lived first in the upper country and later moved nearer to New York City. The house is a spreading white building, stretched out under the shade of old trees. In its yard is one of the old wells of which Irving spoke as characteristic in all the Dutch yards; a "moss-covered bucket suspended to the long balancing-pole, according to antediluvian hydraulics." The creek makes a rather sharp curve near the kitchen door, and here are the few remaining timbers of the old mill. A section of one wall stands, showing a suggestion of door and windows. Beside it is a pile of lumber, gray from weather-beating, which has fallen from the other walls.

The creek, haunted along its path by Indians in early days, still loses itself here and there in a green, dark tangle, and it takes no more than an average imagination to invest the spot with all the mystery and romance of the old tales.

The whole place slumbers; the only sign of energy is at one point, just below the bridge, where a monument cutter diligently plies his trade.

CHAPTER XVIII

THE SAWMILL RIVER ROAD

THE old Sawmill River Road still pursues much the same course up into Westchester County, New York, that it did in the days when Washington included it in his study of available routes for military moves. Tracing the course of the stream for which it was named, keeping a bit to the east of that river, it zigzags along through meadows, beside country estates, and ferrets out some of the most picturesque localities in the whole county, not forgetting Elmsford, where the British guide hid in the currant bushes, and the Four Corners where Betty Flanagan mixed that historic beverage, her cocktail.

The road to-day is stamped on an automobile map with the heavy red line which testifies to its excellence for man, beast, and machine. Starting from Yonkers, it works its way between the Hudson River and the White Plains Road, skirting the Pocantico Hills.

A saw-mill which the old Dutchman, Van der

Donck, long ago erected on this Westchester County stream, gave it the name of de Zaag kill, meaning Sawmill River. "Nepperan" was the Indian name for the river, and it is sometimes called that to this day.

A Mohican village originally stood at the mouth of the Nepperan. Nappechemak is given as the first name of the village, a Mohican word later corrupted into Nepperan, and later giving way altogether to the present "Yonkers." The Indians had a strong settlement at this point when something significant occurred. Hendrick Hudson sailed up the Hudson River. The next event was the visiting of Dutch traders in his wake, and following this, the Dutch West India Company made settlements. The Indian days were already over.

Now, in 1639, came Adrien Van der Donck. He was a lawyer from Holland. He is described as having been a right royal spender—in fact, quite modern as to his way of holding his purse strings—and as "Lord Van der Donck" he was known to all the country round, for his distinction, his enterprise, and his lavishness. "The Jonkheer's land," meaning "Young Lord's land," came to be the name of the village which was practically his. "The Yonkers" (Dutch "j" being "y") was a natural corruption, and it was not until well into the Nineteenth Century that mere "Yonkers" was accepted.

Governor Stuyvesant and the young lord were far from friendly, and Van der Donck's desire to become a patroon, forming his purchases of 1646 into a patroonship, were thwarted for many years. In 1653, however, only two years before his death, his old wish was gratified, permitting him to be known to posterity as the patroon of Yonkers. His saw-mill was the pioneer of many mills, all utilizing the sturdy little Nepperan; many dams came, and the village eventually grew to be a milling city, manufacturing rugs and hats as well as the carpets for which it is best known. Until 1892 the stream was continuously used for these mills, but the dams at last came to be considered a menace to public health, and the authorities broke them. This closed a chapter in the working life of the Sawmill River.

The next figure of prominence in the story of Yonkers, following Van der Donck, was Frederick Philipse. "The Young Lord's" widow had fallen heir to the land, and in time she turned her property over to her brother, Elias Doughty, who broke it up and sold it in sections to several persons. Frederick Philipse was one of these, and he was so ambitious a landowner that he set about acquiring the rest of the land and more too, going as far as the Croton River with his purchases. The English called Philipse the "Dutch millionaire," and he was known to be the wealthiest man in the colony. He was greatly interested in contraband and piratical trade; according to Jenkins, "more than any other merchant, and his name was sent to England as one of those who should be investigated. He was one of the backers of Captain Kidd in Bellomont's time, and it is stated that Lord Bellomont remarked that 'if the coffers of Frederick Philipse were searched, Captain Kidd's missing treasures could easily be found.' As a result of Bellomont's attempts to suppress the 'free' trade, Philipse resigned from the council and retired to his manor about 1698 and spent the remaining years of his life in its development. He died in 1702 at the age of seventy-six."

Another Frederick Philipse, his grandson, succeeded as lord of the manor, and this lord's son, Colonel Frederick Philipse, followed in 1751. He was the last of the manor-lords. He was a British sympathizer during the Revolutionary War, and his estate was confiscated in 1779 according to the laws which the State Legislature had enacted against loyalists. He went to live in England and was there reimbursed for the loss of his possessions to the amount of three hundred thousand dollars.

The old manor-house is to-day preserved for its historic value. The date of its building was 1682, and the original house is a portion of the present one. The first Philipse erected a stone building which was used as a trading post and mills. The second Philipse added to it in 1745, and the structure of to-day was the result. Jenkins describes the house as magnificent in its day: "Workmen and materials were imported from England especially for the construction of the mansion; and the elaborate carvings and workmanship are visible to-day. Every kind of available tree and plant that would grow in this climate was imported and planted in the gardens, which reached down to the bank of the Hudson in a series of terraces. Some of the boxwood hedges were in 1830 ten feet high. Every person of distinction who visited the province was made welcome and entertained by the manor-lord. In the attic of the house, so it was said, there were quarters for fifty household servants alone; from which some idea may be gained of the lavish scale upon which these great landowners lived. Besides negro slaves, of which there were very few, the servants and employees consisted of bond-servants, or redemptioners. But these manor-lords were not landowners only; they were great merchants whose ships visited all parts of the world with which the navigation laws permitted them to trade and brought back the productions of every clime. Nor did they always obey these laws; for it is a notorious fact that about one third of the colonial trade was contraband, and that the great, noble, and wealthy merchants of all the colonies thought it no sin to cheat the king of his revenue whenever they could find or make the opportunity. In addition to their foreign trade, they carried on a fur trade with the Indians in the valley of the Mohawk and as far west as the French permitted them to go."

The famous romance of the old house, perhaps to be taken with a grain of salt, but altogether too charming to be lost from our illusions, is connected with Mary Philipse, daughter of the manor in pre-Revolutionary days. Here George Washington first met her, and here, tradition has it, his first love resulted. It is said that he grew exceedingly sentimental on the subject of the beautiful Mary, and that when he had to return south, to his plantation in Virginia, he engaged a friend in Westchester County to keep him informed of his fair lady's doings. "Colonel Roger Morris is pressing his suit!" suddenly wrote the friend. Just why Washington let Colonel Morris carry off the prize is vague in history. Some say that he did seek Mary Philipse's hand and was refused. Others claim that, overpressed by affairs, he let the vivid colors of his romance fade. At any rate he had immortalized Mary Philipse by falling in love with her.

The confiscated estates of Colonel Philipse were sold in 1785, and thus the old house

Old Headstones in Churchyard, and a Corner of the Sleepy Hollow Church.

The Old Dutch Church, Elmsford, Sister to the Sleepy Hollow Church.

The Old Door of St. John's Church, Yonkers.

The Featherstone House, Elmsford, where Washington and Rochambeau Conferred, and where the British Guide Hid in the Currant Bushes.

passed on to the possession of Cornelius P. Low. Lemuel Wells was the next owner, and when he died intestate his widow and heirs divided the land into lots which were sold under the orders of the Chancery Court.

It was Frederick Philipse, 2d, father of Miss Mary, who built the stone church of St. John about the middle of the Eighteenth Century as a sort of thank-offering for his well-prospered life. Its successor is a large Protestant Episcopal Church, facing on Getty Square. For many years the original church remained, a fine relic of colonial architecture; it was not until 1870 that the present building was erected in its place. The new building is spacious and handsome, with a fine brass pulpit, a carved font of Italian marble, and several good windows. The architecture is Gothic. A portion of the old wall is included in the south side of the modern building and can be readily picked out to-day, along with one of the ancient, low, arched doors.

The second manor-lord acquired his Church of England training from a devout English mother who brought him up in Barbados. His grandfather, the first Frederick Philipse, was a member of the Reformed Dutch Church; hence, only by this accident of the English mother's affiliations, did the church of St. John come into existence. For a while it did not sustain its own clergyman, but depended upon monthly visits from the rector of St. Peter's at Westchester. The first building was put up in 1752, and after the second manor-lord's death his son, Colonel Philipse, secured a glebe to the church, carrying on his father's work. But until 1787 it remained a mission. After 1764, it had certain ministers of its own, whom the Propagation Society in London furnished to it; the second of these, Luke Babcock, was involved in Revolutionary events to the extent of being captured by a party of raiders at the beginning of the war, for having been over-zealous in the king's cause. The affair was most cruel, and the clergyman died from the effects of the brutal treatment he received.

George Panton succeeded to Babcock's labors; but the Revolution caused his work to be most discouraging as well as involving him in considerable danger. The building was burned in 1791, but the next year saw it rebuilt, and this second edifice remained until 1870.

One of Yonkers' most interesting modern buildings is Hollywood Inn, also at Getty Square. William F. Cochran built it and presented it to the workingmen of the city, to be to them a club-house, unsectarian, a place where men could always find recreation and instruction in their idle hours without question of creed or money. It is said to be the pioneer workingmen's club in the United States, and it has been studied and copied by other similar institutions all over the country.

Jenkins suggests a theory that something in the atmosphere of Yonkers creates humor, calling attention to its noted humorists. "Flora McFlimsey of Madison Square," that famous lady of a generation ago who was afflicted by having nothing to wear, emanated from the pen of William Allen Butler of Yonkers. "Eli Perkins," whose name in real life was Melville D. Landon, lived and died there. Frederick S. Cozzens, author of the "Sparrow Grass Papers" published in *Putnam's Monthly*, made his home there, and among present-day humorists the town lays claim to John Kendrick Bangs. Others distinguished in letters, though not humorists, were Mrs. E. D. E. N. Southworth and Dr. Dio Lewis.

From Yonkers the old Sawmill River Road leads you northward toward Ardsley, and just beyond this you come upon the historic house known as the Rochambeau headquarters. It is now the residence of the Odell family and is in excellent preservation. Here, not far from Dobbs Ferry which is so closely associated with his name, that distinguished Count, Jean Baptiste Donatien de Vimeur, made a brief home during the stressful times in which he aided our country. It was in 1780 that he came to America with a strong force, assisted in the capture of

Cornwallis at Yorktown, and remained several months in America, returning home to be raised to the rank of field-marshal by Louis XVI.

Still farther up the road we come to the picturesque old town of Elmsford, formerly known by the names of Greenburgh and Hall's Corners. On one of the old maps the spot appears to be indicated by the word "Tavern," and a mile or two to the north we find another "Tavern." The latter was probably the Four Corners, a place which figured to a considerable extent in Revolutionary doings.

Col. J. C. L. Hamilton, great-grandson of Alexander Hamilton, is a resident of Elmsford and has in his possession many relics of the war period in that vicinity. Cornelius Van Tassel was his great-grandfather on the maternal side, and he still preserves the andirons brought from the old Dutch home of the Van Tassels. He has, too, the pewter basin which has figured in so many tales of the capture of André. Some say that the young British officer ate his bread and milk from it on the day of his capture; Colonel Hamilton's opinion, however, is that he had but slight appetite for bread and milk.

Down the country road below the Hamilton residence stood the home of Cornelius Van Tassel. It was here he lived at the time that he was captured by the British and taken to the old Sugar House Prison. The British and Tories had already been making much disturbance thereabouts and Van Tassel's dwelling, being a very good one for that period, caught their fancy for destruction. But although that building perished, there was soon a new one to replace it on the same site, and the second, now ancient in its turn, stands to-day. It is in good preservation and is an excellent example of the architecture of the Sleepy Hollow school.

After the original house had been burned, and Van Tassel carried off prisoner, his wife hid in an earth cellar. It was a few nights after the disaster that she heard the sound of hoofs, and thought the British were coming again. But suddenly she recognized a familiar whinny, and peered out to see, silhouetted in the night, her pet horse which had been driven off by the enemy and was now returning to his beloved home. It is said that she ran out from the cellar, threw her arms around his neck, and kissed him. His comradeship became a great comfort in her loneliness; for eleven months and eleven days Van Tassel remained a prisoner.

Back in the center of Elmsford you will find a small bridge where the river intersects the main street—the Sawmill River. This modern structure is at the very spot where the old Storm's Bridge used to stand. Washington, coming south down the Sawmill Road with Rochambeau, was met at this bridge upon one occasion by his quartermaster. "You cannot go further," was the message which halted him. "The British are coming just below." This was a surprise to the Chief who had laid plans that did not harmonize with a British encampment in the neighborhood, and thereupon he and Rochambeau rode on to the "Featherstone House," as it is now called, to hold conference. This house was much used by Washington when in the neighborhood, and you will find it little changed to-day.

It stands a short distance down the road which leads off southeast from the main street opposite the Roman Catholic Church. The present owner apologizes for not having rebuilt it, his intentions being to put up a new porch and a mansard, "bring it up to date"; fortunately we have this relic almost intact. Preserved in its cellar are some interesting old rafters of solid black walnut. Roof, windows, and doors and weatherbeaten walls are delightfully ancient, but a thorough system of electric lighting throughout the house leads one to reflect upon what Washington would say to this substitute for his candle.

There is a well in the yard whose age is not vouched for, but the probability is that it is very old, possibly a relic of the Revolutionary period. The owner of the house says that the late Mr. Jacob Iselin of New Rochelle was particularly fond of its waters, and had never ridden

Elmsford-way for fifty years without stopping for a drink. It is quite likely that Washington and Rochambeau tested its moss-covered bucket.

It was in the currant bushes then surrounding this house that Jim Husted, the British guide, hid in 1777. The Americans had been having a little skirmish with the British near by, and the latter had been well trounced—Barrymore, the leader, and all his men being taken, it was supposed. Not for a long time was it discovered that Husted had escaped, saving himself in the depths of these currant bushes.

Returning to the main street, you will find the old church barely a block below it, to the south, near the railroad track. Next to it stands the pastor's house in which is kept the ancient key, which opens the church by grinding and groaning rheumatically in the ancient lock.

In 1788 the church is supposed to have been built, although the loss of its records leaves a cloud hanging about its earliest history. Within and without it is typical of the severity of that period, when American settlers built their houses of worship for worship alone. The old-time gallery and bare walls are as they have always been. The church-going of the seventeen-hundreds cost an effort. The Rev. Thomas Smith traveled all the way from Sleepy Hollow to hold regular services here, and the farmers flocked from long distances to pray. Thus this parish was linked with that famous Dutch Church above Tarrytown, which calls up all the Irving tradition by its mere name.

Many an old record may be read on the crumbling stones. Here are seen such familiar names as "Van Tassel," "Romer," and "Van Wart." Among the modern stones is a monument erected to the memory of Isaac Van Wart by the County of Westchester. The inscription reminds you that in September, 1780, "Isaac Van Wart, accompanied by John Paulding and David Williams, all farmers in the county, intercepted Major André on his return from the American lines in the character of a spy, and, notwithstanding the large bribes offered them for his release, nobly disdained to sacrifice their country for gold, secured and carried him to the commander of the district whereby the dangerous and traitorous conspiracy of André was brought to light, the insidious designs of the enemy baffled, the American army saved, and our beloved country, now free and independent, rescued from most imminent peril." Fenced in with Van Wart's monument is a little slab snuggling quaintly at its base. It marks the grave of his wife, Rachel Storm Van Wart.

Fronting on the main street of the village stands the Ledger House, considerably changed since the days when Abraham Storm, the originator of Storm's Bridge, built it, but nevertheless the same fundamentally. Storm was a captain, and an active American from the beginning of the Revolution. He built his house on this site, saw it burned by the British, except a part which he saved, and rebuilt upon what was left so that the present hostelry is made up of both buildings.

On past the Ledger House, the road leads eastward to White Plains. It is not the same as the original White Plains Road, though near it. It was up the old road, parallel to this, that the quartermaster found the French had marched when he went back to the bridge at Washington's command to stop them, and order them to camp here for the night. There is a theory that they may not have understood the command in English, at any rate they marched on eastward while Washington and Rochambeau, in the Featherstone house, were laying other plans for them. The heat was such as they had never before endured, and four hundred of them were overcome. They were taken to the French hospital, a building now standing, somewhat south of the trolley line leading to White Plains.

To the north of Elmsford was the old Four Corners, lying on the road that led from Sleepy Hollow to what is now North White Plains, at the point where this road intersected the Sawmill River Road. At present there is not a landmark left except for the old schoolhouse on the site where Paulding went to school in the original building. The Paulding farm adjoined it.

But a century and more ago this was a most active locality. At the Four Corners stood the home of Joseph Young, and the American troops found his dwelling a convenient place to make headquarters. Accordingly they came there and remained there, the commanders living in the house and the soldiers occupying the many outbuildings as barracks. Military stores and provisions were hoarded there.

From August of 1776 to February of 1780 the Americans were quartered here much of the time, and many were the skirmishes in and about the old Four Corners. At one time Captain Williams of the American army and his forty men were attacked by British refugees. The Captain, a party of soldiers, and Joseph Young himself, were taken prisoners. For a year Young was confined in New York City, while his barn up at the Four Corners was burned by the British and a large stock of his cattle stolen. Later, a petition of Martha, Samuel, and Thomas Young recorded the fact that in February, 1780, there was an attack on the post by one thousand British troops and refugees, and "all the clothing, bedding and furniture of said Joseph Young destroyed at that inclement season of the year."

This region is closely associated in tradition with Fenimore Cooper and his "Westchester

The Philipse Manor at Yonkers.

Washington's Headquarters during Battle of White Plains. At North White Plains.

A Mortar Used at the Battle of White Plains.

The Old Inn at Scarsdale, where Drovers Used to Stop in Revolutionary Days. This Was also the Stopping-Place for the Old Mail Coach.

Spy." Here the tale was laid, the site of the hamlet of the Four Corners was the stage of the drama. According to Bolton, a little west of the Van Wart residence stood the "Hotel Flanagan, a place of refuge for man and beast." The sign "Elizabeth Flanagan, Her Hotel," hung before it. Betty Flanagan lived, after her soldier husband had fallen for his country, by driving a cart to various military encampments and serving refreshments. At this time the Virginia Cavalry happened to be making the Four Corners their headquarters, so Betty had brought her cart hither, and here she was stationed when the lawless Skinners dragged in the peddler Spy.

Perhaps the most interesting item recorded in the history of Betty is that "she is said to have invented the well-known beverage vulgarly called 'cocktail.' "

CHAPTER XIX

WITH THE POST TO WHITE PLAINS

LEADING into the heart of Westchester County was the old White Plains Road. Along this route the mail was carried, at its inns the stagecoach stopped, its dust was raised by the tramp of Howe's army. Perhaps children crept forth, half hiding, from some wayside farmhouse to watch the redcoats pass; perhaps a frightened calf flung up its heels and galloped off into the fields; perhaps a farmer warned his wife to hide her fresh-baked loaves.

This road is still a highway, and may be followed to-day. From Bronxdale it passes north through Olinville, Wakefield, and Mount Vernon. For a space it unites with the old Boston Road; McTeague's Corners was the name of the point where the two met. They continued as one from Williamsbridge north, until, at the head of Black Dog Brook, the Boston Road asserted its independence and made toward Eastchester.

White Plains Avenue of the present is equivalent in a general way to the old highway, although it is inclined to keep a trifle to the west of the original line. At some places it follows exactly in the earlier path. Beyond Bronxville, we shall find the Post Road marked, and a mile-stone at Scarsdale bears witness to the present road's integrity.

On the west of the road lies the town of Tuckahoe. Bolton tells the story of an early driver of a market wagon who used to come down this valley, famous for its wild turkeys, shouting "Turkey, ho!" as he reached the village. The name of the place was really formed from an Algonquin word meaning "the bread," but there were formerly many jokes in circulation, playing upon the resemblance of "Tuckahoe" to "Turkey Hollow."

Here before you are the Tuckahoe Heights where Washington's advance corps lay during that throbbing week which culminated in the Battle of White Plains. Two thousand men under General Scott waited here.

Scarsdale is beyond. Beautiful Scarsdale of to-day is connected in our minds with suburban ease; but it had a yesterday, and at times a strenuous one. Settling America once upon a time was no easy task. The Heathcote and the Tompkins families were among those who created the town.

Several very old buildings are to be seen hereabouts, well-preserved types of former days.

One of these fronts directly on the Post Road: a long, low brown house, flanked by a broad lawn, quaintly gabled and touched with moss. This was the wayside inn of pre-Revolutionary days, the well-known and much-patronized hostelry where the drovers stopped for refreshment on their way from the West—meaning Ohio—into New York. The mail coach, too, stopped here regularly. There is a story connected with the place: it is said that the man who owned it at the time of the Revolution, upon hearing that the British approached, hurried to hide in the cellar his two most precious possessions, namely his Bible and his cow. He himself hid in the secret chamber. The old doors still show marks supposed to have been made by the enemy's sabres, for the house was besieged, but the Bible and the cow came through the siege safely.

Near this building stands one of the original milestones, carefully preserved by a bowlder which protects it from wind and weather. Already the inscription on the old red stone is all but erased by time. The date given is 1771.

The Saxon origin of the town's name, from the word "scarrs," meaning "crags," is a "dale enclosed with rocks." The Heathcote family brought the name from their own Derbyshire. The town has boasted many distinguished inhabitants in its time: Daniel D. Tompkins,

Vice-President of the United States, was born here in 1774. Fenimore Cooper lived in a "château" here once upon a time, a building which has unfortunately been demolished. In *The Spy* Cooper treated of this locality. It was included in the "Neutral Ground" which formed the stage setting of the many "Cowboy" and "Skinner" dramas.

Scarsdale was well populated with Tories during the Revolutionary period—indeed it has been said that only three families of patriots lived here, although this may have been an exaggeration of the Toryism of the place. However, its sympathies were chiefly with the British, and Judge Caleb Tompkins, one of the patriots, suffered great discomfort from a situation into which his loyalty to the American cause forced him. In fact, it became necessary for him to leave his own house, and flee for his life from the British, probably doubting whether he should ever see Scarsdale again. He loaded an ox-cart with all the household goods he could gather together for speedy departure, and fled. Just northeast of White Plains was a swamp; upon reaching this, he found the enemy in such close pursuit that there was no use fleeing farther. He therefore abandoned his cattle and sent them into the woods near Kensico. He next hid himself by entering the swamp and walking out in it to such a depth that only his head remained above the water. The result was that he made his escape, and returned happily to his Scarsdale home.

The tract of land which included Scarsdale was ceded by its owners, the Mohicans, to John Richbell, in the year 1660. Richbell is supposed to have been the first white man to settle in the town. The Indian district called "Quaroppas" lay hereabouts, and the tract was a portion of it. The land was finely wooded, and the eastern angle of the town later on came to be known as the "Saxon Forest," which name came from William Saxon, the proprietor of a saw-mill. Gradually the forest was cleared, but even in the time of Bolton's writing, it "abounded with foxes, rabbits and other wild game, and retained much of its ancient grandeur."

To the northwest of the Post Road lies a high ridge. Along this ridge the two British generals, Clinton and De Heister, led their men on the eventful twenty-eighth of October in 1776. Now we are in the thick of preliminaries; approaching White Plains, we picture the various approaches of the soldiers along different paths, all converging toward the historic town.

Hartsdale, on our way, known to the present as an attractive residence town, was one of twin villages—Hartsdale and Hart's Corners. Across the Bronx from its peaceful boundaries one of the Revolutionary skirmishes took place. This happened only a few hours before the Battle of White Plains, when the troops of both sides were on their way to the greater conflict which took place on Chatterton's Hill.

Its Methodist Episcopal Church had the distinction of being organized, and the building erected, "in 1832, during the first cholera season." Into this organization was absorbed a small church which stood to the north, at the Rocks of Scilly.

White Plains, the county seat after 1759, was the destination of the old road. Well in the center of town is the site of the first court-house. Follow Railroad Avenue to South Broadway, turn to the right along the latter street, and at the intersection of Mitchell Place you will find the site. The present building is the town's armory; in front of this stands a monument surmounted by a broad-winged eagle, and bearing this inscription:

"Site of the County Court House where, on July 10, 1776, the Provincial Congress proclaimed the passing of the dependent colony and the birth of the independent State of New York."

The first court-house was erected here in 1759, upon the removal of the courts from Westchester. In 1760 the first Court of Common Pleas assembled here, on May 27th. The building was burned, but the second and third were erected on the site of the first. It was here that the Whigs of the county of Westchester appointed to meet the committees of the several towns, that they might elect deputies to the Continental Congress, who were to assemble on the first of September, 1774, in Philadelphia.

General Nathaniel Woodhull, the same brave soldier whose capture we traced at Hollis, on Long Island, was at the head of the Provincial Congress and highly honored as its President. So not only in that old tavern where De Lancey's major attacked him for refusing to say, "God save the King!" but here in old Westchester County, we are reminded of his services to his country.

Dr. Robert Graham, a young physician who came to White Plains from Connecticut, was a most public-spirited man and ambitious for his adopted town. It was largely through his efforts that the court-house was built here, and the courts removed from Westchester. The land upon which the building was erected was his gift to the county.

No sooner had this change taken place than White Plains became a bustling center of business. Two hotels sprang into being, with almost the haste displayed in a mushroom town of the West. Visitors came to town, in great numbers for those days, and the hotels drove a brisk trade. A country store was needed, and Dr.

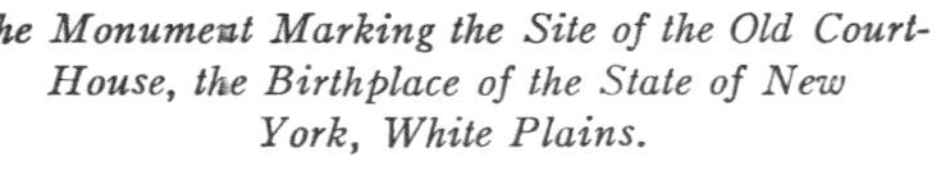

The Monument Marking the Site of the Old Court-House, the Birthplace of the State of New York, White Plains.

Old St. Paul's Church, at Eastchester, Used as a Military Hospital during the Revolution.

The Disbrow Chimney at Mamaroneck, where Cooper's "Spy" is Said to have Hidden.

The Monument to Early Huguenots, at their Landing Place, Bonnefoi Point, New Rochelle.

Graham himself built one. It stood opposite the court-house, and came to be the sort of social center which the country store has always been from that day to this—the men's club of the hamlet, the headquarters in which gossip and spicy tales may be exchanged, business deals discussed and consummated, woes poured forth into sympathetic ears, and congratulations offered on such occasions as a good trade in live stock, the news of a fat legacy, or the arrival of a pair of plump and lively twins.

White Plains (so named from the white balsam which grew all over the region in early days) is associated in every mind with one of the British and American struggles which preceded the fall of Fort Washington. To trace the history of the battle one must go to North White Plains, a distance of about a mile from the original town. One can go by train, but the walk is delightful, along Broadway with its sweeps of green lawn and fine old residences standing far back from the street. About half-way between the two towns is the old mortar, preserved from the days of 1776.

The situation in September of that year was like this. The Americans were strongly entrenched upon Harlem Heights, and Howe decided that his only means of making trouble would be to get in their rear and hem them in upon the head of the island of Manhattan.

Leaving some of his army under Lord Percy, he took the rest, embarked them upon ninety flatboats, and contrived to get through the dangerous passing of Hell Gate, landing upon Throg's Neck.

"A few days afterward," says Lossing, "other troops from Montressor's Island and Flushing landed there; and on the twenty-second, Knyphausen, with the second division of German hirelings, just arrived at New York, landed upon Myers' Point, now Davenport's Neck, near New Rochelle."

The British now had a good position along the shore. Washington, perceiving the movement, sent General Heath with strong detachments to oppose the enemy's landing and occupy lower Westchester. A redoubt was thrown up near Williamsbridge; all passes to Kingsbridge were well guarded, and now entrenchments were made at White Plains by a detachment there. Colonel Hand and his riflemen guarded the causeways to Throg's Neck and Pell's Neck. Howe landed, and on the same night he found himself upon an island, the bridge having been removed.

He first laid the blame upon some Tories who were acting as guides, but ascertained the truth later and realized that his best course was to decamp, Colonel Hand having driven him back from the causeway with the assistance of Prescott and Lieutenant Bryant. Returning to his boats, he made his way to Pell's Point, later to New Rochelle, and finally took a position near Knyphausen. This, then, was the position of the British that Washington looked forth upon: they were established upon the mainland; and with his army weak in training, and cold weather approaching, he had little to reinforce his hopes. "A powerful enemy, well provided, was crouched as a tiger within cannon-voice, ready to spring upon its prey."

Washington called a council of war at General Lee's headquarters, and it was decided to abandon the island of Manhattan. The main part of the American army was now sent forward, marching in four divisions up the west side of the Bronx River and forming a series of entrenched camps up to White Plains, all the way from Fordham.

Parallel to them farther east, the British forces also moved north. Frequent skirmishes now took place. The fact that the Americans came out triumphant in most of these miniature frays, gave them, no doubt, greater heart for the days ahead. The four generals, Lee, Sullivan, Lincoln, and Heath were in command of the marching Americans.

To the west of the town of White Plains you will see a slope rising. This is Chatterton's Hill, still known by the name of those old days. Here the Americans made a hasty breastwork,

Colonel Haslet, with about sixteen hundred men, occupying this eminence. M'Dougal reënforced Haslet and took general command there the next morning. Both armies were now close to White Plains; on the morning of the twenty-ninth of October the British army, thirteen thousand strong, moved toward the village.

After a council, the British general caused a bridge to be erected over the Bronx, and he attempted to cross by this and dislodge the Americans from Chatterton's Hill. But the enemy was forced to recoil in the face of the American guns, in charge of Captain Alexander Hamilton, and they fell back to join another division a quarter-mile below.

The combined force now pushed up the south-western side of Chatterton's Hill. M'Dougal put up a brave fight, holding his position with only six hundred men for an hour, but at last an attack upon his flank compelled him to give way. He retreated in good order down the southeastern side of the hill, under cover of troops led by Putnam. The victors remained in possession of only the breastworks on the hill; M'Dougal was able to carry off his wounded men and his artillery.

"The British troops rested upon their arms all night after the battle," Lossing tells us, "and the next day, after a skirmish with Glover's brigade, they encamped within long cannon shot of the front of the American lines. Awed by the apparent strength of Washington's entrenchments, Howe dared not attack him, but awaited the arrival of Lord Percy, with four battalions from New York and two from Mamaroneck. The loss of the Americans, from the twenty-sixth to the twenty-ninth, did not exceed probably three hundred men, in killed, wounded, and prisoners; that of the British was about the same. Earl Percy arrived on the evening of the thirtieth, and preparations were made to storm the American works the next morning. A tempest of wind and rain arose at midnight, and continued for twenty hours. All operations were delayed, and on the night of the thirty-first, while the storm clouds were breaking and the British host were slumbering, Washington withdrew and encamped upon the heights of North Castle, toward the Croton River, where he had erected strong breastworks along the hills which loom up a hundred feet above the waters of the Bronx. Howe was afraid to attack him there, and on the night of the fourth of November he retreated toward the junction of the Hudson and Harlem Rivers, and encamped upon the heights of Fordham."

If you are walking north on Broadway you will come to the historic mortar just after passing Crane Avenue. It stands on the west side of the street upon a heavy base which is a remnant of the Revolutionary entrenchments of October, 1776, and they "mark the final stand by General Washington at the end of his long retreat; the abandonment by General Howe of his purpose to capture the American army; and the revival of the hopes for national independence."

All the eagles and soldierly figures of the ordinary monument sink to insignificance beside the simple emphasis of this old mortar, a genuine relic of the engagement.

The end of your long walk to North White Plains is one of our most delightful historic houses —delightful largely because of its picturesque remoteness and shabbiness—Washington's headquarters. It is the little old farmhouse that sheltered him during his stay in White Plains. The ridge where Washington presented so formidable an appearance as to alarm the British army confronts you; to the left is the little village store and post office in one: the general dispensary of mail, cough syrups, breakfast foods, and lemon soda. Straight ahead past the store, the branch of the main road leads to the old house.

You must pass into the deeply dusty road of the woodsy country, and plunge into the midst of trees, where a dense tangle grows at the base of the ridge. To the left you will hear the hoot of engines from the track below; to the right lies solitude. And then, all of a sudden emerging from the thick green growth with its deep shadows, a glimpse of a weather-beaten gray wooden building finally meets your eye.

Bolton describes it as "situated amid a deep solitude of woods, surrounded by hills and wild romantic scenery," and then he quotes the following description. It was written by a New York newspaper correspondent in 1845, and is an interesting example of the newspaper style of more than a half-century ago.

"When we entered the little room of Mr. Miller's farmhouse, where that great and good man had resided, and where he resolved to try the hazard of a battle, with a flushed and successful foe, we could not repress the enthusiasm which the place and the moment and the memory inspired. We looked around with eagerness at each portion of the room on which his eye must have rested, we gazed through the small window panes, through which he must have so often and so anxiously looked toward the enemy, and at the old-fashioned buffets, where his table service was deposited for his accommodation. But little change has taken place in the building."

But little change has taken place now, except for the wear and tear of time. In 1851 Lossing visited it and found Miss Jemima Miller, a maiden ninety-three years of age, and her sister, somewhat younger, living there in what had been their childhood's home. They were then carefully preserving a chair and table used by the Chief. Abraham Miller owned the property at that time, but with the change of occupants the treasured pieces of furniture have been taken away and are now preserved in other dwellings. A German family occupy the place and it is in a state of sad dilapidation.

CHAPTER XX

ALONG THE OLD BOSTON POST ROAD

MADAME SARAH KNIGHT of Charlestown, Mass., traveled from Boston to New York in the year 1704. Riding horseback herself, she was guided by the post-rider, following his way to New Haven, Rye, New Rochelle, and New York. In these words she summed up her journey:

Through many toils and many frights
I have returned, poor Sarah Knights
Over great rocks and many stones
God has preserved from fractured bones.

To-day the same route, or approximately the same, is covered by a rapid railroad, by smooth-running trolleys, and by an excellent automobile road. Along it lies much of the greatest historic interest of Westchester County.

The old road started from the fort at the foot of Broadway, opposite the Bowling Green, where the Custom House now stands; pursued its way along Park Row, the Bowery, across Spuyten

Duyvil Creek, and so on through Westchester County until it brought up at Washington Street in Boston.

Beyond Spuyten Duyvil Creek, the road passed near the Fort Independence known to early American patriotism; the Negro Fort; crossed Rattlesnake Brook; and entered the town of Eastchester, now included within the boundaries of Mount Vernon.

Eastchester dates back to 1664, when the first settlement was made near the Hutchinson River, named for Anne Hutchinson. The little stream is still picturesque in spots, where buildings have not crowded and where trees flank it and wild flowers gather along its banks. Upon this stream, saw- and grist-mills were established in early days, those of John Tompkins and Stephen Anderson having been noted in their day. Houses gathered gradually, and the church reared its steeple in their midst. In 1692 the first church was built, and a tablet on the present building gives its history in brief:

"This church stands on the ancient village green of Eastchester, a general training ground and election place in Colonial days and enlisting headquarters for Revolutionary soldiers. The first meeting house, erected on the green north of this church, 1692–1699, adopted the worship of the Church of England, 1702. This church, erected 1761–65, was used as a military hospital during the American Revolution; converted into a Court House 1787."

The stone and brick work are sound to-day, the building and grounds being finely preserved. In the churchyard six thousand lie sleeping.

Directly across the street stands an old white house on whose doorplate we read the name "Fay." This is the only one left of the early Eastchester homesteads. The Fays, from Vermont, settled here in 1732. During the Revolution the house was used as a tavern and was much favored by British officers. The most thrilling event in its history was the hanging of a British deserter to the signpost which stood before the door.

One Billy Crawford was conducting it during these days, but after the war the Fay family returned to it. One of the distinguished members of the family once living here was Theodore Sedgwick Fay, for nearly twenty years minister to Switzerland.

At Sixth Street in Mount Vernon the road crosses the Hutchinson River, continues past Pelham, an old manor, and enters New Rochelle.

In 1913 the people of New Rochelle celebrated the two-hundred-and-twenty-fifth anniversary of the event which gave birth to that town. In the year 1688 the French Huguenots set foot upon Bonnefoi Point, now Davenport's Neck, a group of jutting rocks which thrust themselves out into the waters of Long Island Sound. A small playground which New Rochelle preserves for the public and calls Hudson Park to-day encloses the spot, marked by a monument, where the first Huguenot foot is supposed to have been set.

It was after the revocation of the Edict of Nantes that these French Protestants found refuge here. They had made attempts to colonize in our Southern States during their earlier persecutions, but when the edict issued by Henry IV in 1598 secured them full toleration, both civil and religious, they returned to their own country. The death of Cardinal Mazarin in 1661 marked the beginning of renewed persecutions, and in 1685 Louis XIV revoked the edict. That act caused the exodus of at least 400,000 people—some historians place the number as high as 500,000. France was said to have lost the riches that flowed from skill, sobriety, and industry.

The silk weavers moved their art to England. Thrifty farmers laid out farms in America. The refugees who came to our shores scattered to Massachusetts, Rhode Island, Virginia, and New York, and here on the shore of the Sound they chose a home and named it for their own La Rochelle in France.

They settled on land which Jacob Leisler, a German resident of New York, had obtained

The Municipal Building at Rye, once Haviland's Tavern, on the Old Post Road.

The Fay House at Eastchester, formerly a Tavern, where a British Deserter was Hung to a Sign-Post.

The Holly House, Cos Cob.

from John Pell, the lord of Pelham Manor. The Pell name is to be traced to-day throughout this region. As for Jacob Leisler, the fact that he was hung for high treason has, if anything, added to the high esteem in which he was held, and a monument by the sculptor Solon Borglum stands on North Avenue, perpetuating Leisler's name.

Pioneering brought hardships. At the end of the Seventeenth Century "ye inhabitants of New Rochelle" were "humbly petitioning" thus:

". . . Wherefore they were invited to come and buy lands in the province, to the end that they might by their labour help the necessityes off their familyes, and did spend therein all their smale store, with the help of their friends, whereof they did borrow great sums of money. They are poor and needy, reduced to a lamentable condition. Wherefore your petitioners humbly pray that your Excellency may be pleased to take the case in serious consideration and out of charity and pity to grant them what help and privileges your Excellency shall think convenient."

They pulled through. They were of the stuff that always does pull through. They have proved among the finest stock of early American settlers. Among the names familiar in their lists are Jay, de Peyster, Luquer, Boudinot, and Marquand. Here and there in the town an ancient Huguenot home is to be seen. On Main Street, opposite the Presbyterian Church, is the old Pintard house, where Walter Marvin now lives. On Upper Main Street, out toward the Mamaroneck line, stands the old Flandreau home. On North Avenue, near the station of the electric railroad, is a little old stone building smeared with white; its roof sags, its shingles are weather-beaten, there are sections of its walls which are on the verge of crumbling to dust. Trees and a tangle of grass surround it, and a carpenter's sign hangs across its street face. It is as unchanged and as typical an early Huguenot farmhouse as you will find.

On the old Boston Post Road stood the Huguenots' first church. Previous to building this, they had walked all the way to New York and back, twenty-three miles by the road, for the sake of partaking of the Lord's supper. A little group of the homesick refugees used to gather on the shore at sunset every day, face their beloved France, and raise their voices in hymns.

But it was not long before they had their own house of worship. When John Pell deeded the 6000 acres to Jacob Leisler for the Huguenot use, he threw in an extra hundred acres for good measure, that the church of these new Americans might be erected thereon.

That famous deed is to be seen, along with

other treasures, in the Huguenot Museum on North Avenue. An old bookcase brought from Holland by one of these settlers is in the collection; and a group of Indian relics, gathered over a period of years on the ground where New Rochelle now stands, is the gift of Mr. Henry Lester, a representative of one of the early families.

But the most interesting thing about the museum is the museum itself. It is the old home of "Tom Paine"; a romantic-looking cottage covered with shingles, shaded by green blinds of the old pattern, having a vine-covered porch and a flower-bed where sweet-william and English daisies grow. The place leads you from the period of pioneering into the years of the Revolution, with which Thomas Paine was associated in America's history.

The house stands in a hollow beside the road. Above it is the monument to his memory erected by public contribution in 1839. It was repaired and re-dedicated in 1881, and a bronze bust was placed upon it in 1899. Paine's bones no longer rest here. He died in 1809, and was buried on what was then his New Rochelle farm, but in 1819 William Cobbett took his remains to England.

Nevertheless this Westchester County town preserves every memory of the crratic patriot. He was strongly identified with the place, for it was here that the State of New York selected a farm of three hundred acres to bestow upon him. It was the confiscated estate of Frederic Davoc, Loyalist, and it was given to Paine in 1786, at the same time that Congress gave him three thousand dollars for his services during the Revolutionary War.

He sailed for Europe soon after, where he was royally entertained by many admirers in England and France. Later he was indicted for sedition in London, and finally outlawed. In France, while a prisoner of the Jacobins, he barely escaped the guillotine. At this period he wrote much of his *Age of Reason*. In 1802 he returned to America and spent his time in New York and New Rochelle.

The Quaker staymaker, which Paine had once been in England, was refused burial by the Quakers of the United States. Ingersoll wrote of his funeral cortège:

"In a carriage, a woman and her son who had lived on the bounty of the dead—on horseback, a Quaker, the humanity of whose heart dominated the creed of his head—and following on foot, two negroes, filled with gratitude."

The body was laid in its New Rochelle grave, and for a time there was no great honor paid to the man whose burning pamphlet, *Common Sense*, had touched the fuse, firing a continent to declare its independence.

From this town the old Post Road strikes out toward the Sound, and is much of the way within sight of the water. Mamaroneck is the next historical village which it passes—one of the oldest in the entire county, laid out in 1660. Madame Knight wrote, "From New Rochelle we traveled through Merrinack, a neat tho little place, with a navigable river before it, the pleasantest I ever see."

It is to-day a neat, though hardly a little place, at least not little in her sense of the word. It is full of ancient history and modern prosperity; gasolene whiffs from suburban motors blow across Heathcote Hill, where the Americans of 1776 surprised the Queen's Rangers.

The town's most picturesque relic is the Disbrow chimney—a mere pile of stones, standing in the lawn of what is known as the old Stringer residence. This chimney is the oldest historic relic in all of Westchester County. A few years ago the great fireplaces and closets on each side of the stone work could be distinguished, but so rapidly is the masonry crumbling that now it appears almost shapeless, smothered in vines and sumac boughs. In one of the large closets beside it, tradition has it that Harvey Birch, hero of Cooper's novel *The Spy*, hid when he was being pursued. This pile of stones is all that remains of the Disbrow house, built in 1677. The house was burned.

In the early part of the Eighteenth Century Indians came to the Disbrow family and demanded the property; the residents showed title deeds on which the aborigines made out their own signatures, and they marched off, defeated. Thus the place was held by the original family, who lived to the extent of eight generations upon the property. Almost a century ago a new house was erected upon the land, and the entire property, old and new house, chimney and all, passed into the hands of Mr. Stringer. That "new" house is now venerable but excellently preserved.

The Disbrows were related to that Major General John Disbrow of England who married Anna Cromwell, sister of the Protector.

On the edge of this same land is the rock known as "Washington's Rock" from the likeness which it bears to the austere profile of the Father of his Country.

Just beyond this place is a road house, its new porch adorned by the titles of familiar and popular beverages. This was, once upon a time, the De Lancey house of Heathcote Hill. It is said that it was auctioned off to the highest bidder, who, for some dozen of dollars, became possessor, uprooted the old house, and moved it down the hill to face the road at a convenient nearness. One daughter of old Captain De Lancey married Fenimore Cooper.

It was on October 21, 1776, that Colonel Haslet, leading American forces, surprised the Queen's Rangers upon the very Heathcote Hill which lies before you. Lieutenant-Colonel Rogers, who was a renegade American, commanded these, and our forces bore off a number of prisoners and goodly spoil as well.

A little farther along, on the shore, is an interesting sea-and-land playground for children, maintained by the Village Improvement Association. Swings and croquet are close beside an enclosed bathing beach where a regularly-employed playground worker has an eye out for safety.

Between Mamaroneck and Rye on the Post Road stands the Jay house, which was built by the father of John Jay, the property having been acquired in 1745. John Jay spent his boyhood days here. Jenkins tells us that the original house was "but one room deep and eighty feet long, having attained this size by repeated additions to meet the wants of a numerous family."

"From hence we hasted towards Rye . . . and there arrived and took up our Lodgings," wrote Madame Knight. "Here being very hungry I desired a fricasee wch the Frenchman undertaking managed so contrary to my notions of Cookery that I hastned to Bed superless."

The Rye of to-day can do better. It can

refresh the hungry and thirsty traveler. But its most interesting building is one of the old taverns of the Eighteenth Century, now the municipal building, standing where the Post Road crosses Purchase Street. It was known as "Haviland's Inn" and kept open by Dame Tamar Haviland after her husband and the war were both buried. You can see now the old fireplace where travelers gathered with mug, pipe, and story. One room has been preserved as a museum. Here both Washington and Lafayette have tarried; "a very neat and decent inn" wrote Washington.

In this building, May, 1796, the Episcopalian parish of Rye was reorganized. The Boston stages made a practise of stopping here. John Adams stopped here in 1774 when he was going to attend the Continental Congress. And so on, item by item, one gathers the associations which make "Haviland's" one of the typical inns of the best rank along the old road—a public gathering place, used by both travelers and townspeople.

The land jutting into the Sound, now occupied by the village of Rye, was called Peningo by the Indians, and the island just beyond was Manussing in their language. The white settlement was made on land purchased by New Englanders from the aborigines. The Mohicans lived between the Hudson and Byram rivers. The first purchase did not include Manussing. But it was acquired later, about 1660, in a treaty which stipulated that the purchasers were to be "without molestation from us or other Indians" and that they might feed their cattle upon the mainland, and take "timbers or trees." It is of interest to property owners in this smart suburban region to-day to note that the consideration paid for this entire land was "Eight Cotes and Seven Shirts and fifteen fathom of wompome."

Log cabins soon sprang up, the homes of the settlers from Greenwich who arrived by boat —wives, babies, family cats, and all—rowing down the Sound. They built up a village which came to be noted for its thrift and virtue. So righteous were its ways that the magistrate was given full power to apprehend "such as were overtaken with drinke, swearing, Sabboath breaking." Before the Revolution, however, Rye came to be known as a pleasure seekers' resort, and Rye Flats was famous for its horse racing.

Port Chester to-day, the Saw Pit yesterday, is the village next beyond Rye; the Byram River is crossed; and now the old Boston Post Road finds itself within the State of Connecticut. Greenwich and Cos Cob, closely associated with the name of General Israel Putnam, are just beyond.

The borderline between New York and Connecticut always saw more or less stirring times, beginning with a bottle of fire water in the sixteen-hundreds. The bottle passed from the hands of a Dutch trader of New York into the welcoming hands of a Fairfield County chief, and the peace to which he had bound himself while sober suddenly became exceedingly uninteresting. The Dutch trader found a tribe of customers ready for his goods, and raids soon stirred the territory of the staid Greenwich settlers. From Indian raids the borderline passed into the agitation of the Revolutionary period.

The Holly house, as the old residence is known in Cos Cob, contains the first chapter of the most picturesque historic tale of this vicinity. This ample frame house was built by Captain Bush, a New York merchant, in days before the Revolution. Bush was a friend of General Putnam, and his house was frequently used by the General as headquarters during the throbbing days when Fairfield County was his field of action. Tradition credits Miss Bush, a daughter of the Captain, with at least part of the General's interest in the spot. At any rate, the tradition is a pleasing one, whether true or not, for no stage setting could present a prettier background for romance than the rambling old building swathed in vines and half-hidden by lilacs.

Here, says the story, Putnam was merry-making on the night before his famous ride. He was the distinguished guest at the party. A few hours later he was riding for his life, the dancers scattered and forgotten, the British pursuing.

Putnam's Hill Park, in Greenwich itself, is near the scene of the ride. A tablet marks the spot where on February 26, 1779, General Israel Putnam, "cut off from his soldiers, pursued by British cavalry, galloped down this rocky steep and escaped, daring to lead where not one of many hundred foes dared to follow."

The story has many variations in the annals, but it is a popular belief that Putnam, mounted, rode directly down the seventy-four stone steps which were then standing, despite the fact that his horse was undertaking the feat under a weight of 240 pounds. Putnam was visiting his outposts at West Greenwich when Governor Tryon with a corps of fifteen hundred men was on his march against it. Putnam had 150 men with him, and two pieces of artillery; with only this support he took his station on the brow of the hill, near where the old meeting house stood. From this point he greeted the advancing British with a prompt, sharp fire from his artillery.

But upon seeing that the dragoons were about to charge, Putnam ordered his men to retire to the swamp below where the cavalry of the British could not reach them. The enemy was now upon him; he had one chance, and that was to force his horse directly down the precipice. His pursuers suddenly brought up in astonishment as they saw the steep down which he had fled. Heavy, they could not follow. They took the curve which led gradually to the road below, but long before they could reach it Putnam was far on the road toward Stamford. Here he found militia ready, and, adding these to his former band, he pursued Tryon and reported the taking of fifty prisoners in spite of his small numbers. The British had managed to destroy the salt works at Greenwich, but they had failed to overcome the resourceful American general. Authorities state that the actual steps down which Putnam rode were at some distance south of the roadway. The steps now leading down from the park to the street are sometimes mistakenly called "Putnam's Steps."

A museum of colonial and Revolutionary relics is to be seen opposite the Episcopal church in Greenwich. The building was once the tavern of Captain Israel Knapp, and it is now known as the Putnam Cottage.

Beyond, at Cos Cob, an old settlers' burying ground lies beside the curved road that leads off from the main road, toward the Holly house. The sunken headstones are smothered in grass,

The Tom Paine Monument at New Rochelle.

The Old Huguenot House at New Rochelle.

The Lighthouse at Fort Schuyler.

their names and dates almost obliterated. Here, says tradition, the ancient chieftains Cos Cob and Mianus lie buried. The spot is uncared for, and furnishes to the village merely a field for a cross-cut.

The Holly house is a finely preserved example of pre-Revolutionary building. The colonial entrance, narrow white staircase, and huge fireplaces are intact. The furniture did not belong to Captain Bush, having come later with the Holly family, but it is of the period of the house itself. An old and valuable print of Putnam's ride hangs in the hall.

North and northwest of Cos Cob the land was called "Strickland's Plain," and it was here that Captain Underhill, sent by the Dutch Governor of New York, made his terrific attack upon the troublesome Indians long before the Revolution. The settlers of Greenwich had appealed to the Governor for aid, since Greenwich was then under the jurisdiction of New York. He finally sent Underhill with 130 men, and the captain reached the Mianus River and rested there in the evening until moonrise. As the light slowly came, showing him the way, he led his men across the river at the town of Mianus. He climbed the high bank on the west side, looked over Strickland's Plain, and thereupon made his onslaught. Wigwams perished in the fires he lighted, Indian lives were sacrificed right and left, a wholesale destruction of the enemy was made, and peace achieved for the settlers.

The road between New York and Boston was not the only means of communication for these early villages along the Sound. Hurd tells us that in 1767 Nathaniel Close petitioned to "the benevolent inhabitants of the town of Greenwich," for permission to build a storehouse at the dock at Cos Cob, as "his performing a weekly Pauquet or stage boat to New York" required.

Moreover, there were crossings to the Long Island shore. At Port Chester (or possibly Rye) there was a ferry established as early as 1739, to the island of Nassau at Oyster Bay. This was by royal letters patent of King George. "Which ferry our loving subjects John Budd, Hachaliah Brown and Jonathan Brown, Esqs., propose to undertake . . . and to have free liberty to ask the several fees hereinafter mentioned, viz., for every person 1 shilling and sixpence, for every man and horse 3 shillings, for all horned cattle from 2 years old and upwards each 2 shillings . . . for every full barrel 1 shilling, for every empty barrel 4 pence . . . for every gammon, flitch of bacon or piece of smoked beef 1 penny . . . for every chair 2 pence, for every case with bottles 9 pence, for every frying pan or warming pan 2 pence."

CHAPTER XXI

TO THROG'S NECK AND CITY ISLAND

STRETCHING out into the East River, like stiff-jointed fingers on an ungainly hand, are several peninsulas, to the several tips of which old roads led yesterday along practically the same line of the better roads of to-day. Passing northeast beyond Hell Gate, beyond Ward's and Randall's and North and South Brother Island, we come to Barretto Point and Hunt's Point; Clason Point lies just beyond them, across the mouth of the Bronx River at the end of Cornell's Neck; this in turn is separated from the next by Westchester Creek, and across that stream lie Old Ferry Point and Throg's Neck; still farther along, to the east of Eastchester Bay, we reach Rodman's Neck with its postscript of City Island, almost a part of one peninsula. All of these are within the boundaries of greater New York, being included in the Bronx.

Hunt's Point is generally understood as including Barretto Point, the latter having been named for a New York merchant, Francis Barretto, who did not settle upon it until the middle of the last century. The former name, which included the whole double peninsula, was given in honor of the proprietor of 1688. Previous to this, the Indian name, "Quinnahung," had identified this "long, high place."

The chief object of interest on Hunt's Point is the Joseph Rodman Drake Park, opened in 1910. Two and a half acres are laid out for this, and within its boundaries are included the old burial ground of the Hunt family, and the grave of Drake, whose poem, *To the Bronx*, has immortalized this part of our great city. Drake found poetry in that which was near and familiar, found romance where we are too much inclined to see only commercialism and modern hurry and bustle.

> Yet I will look upon thy face again,
> My own romantic Bronx, and it will be
> A face more pleasant than the face of men.
> Thy waves are old companions; I shall see
> A well-remembered form in each old tree,
> And hear a voice long loved in thy wild minstrelsy.

Nevertheless, in apology for ourselves of this generation, it is only fair to remember that the Bronx River of a century ago was far more romantic than it is to-day, with the pressure of building and business encroaching upon its banks.

The road leads straight down to the end of the point. The land was once known as the "great planting field," and for many years it was rich in meadows and farms. Drake's home was at Hunt's Point, in the original Hunt house known as the Grange. This building, or a portion of it, was erected possibly as early as 1669, by Thomas Hunt. The building has more recently been known as "the Pilot House" because of the curious octagonal tower rising from one end of it and serving as a beacon to pilots on the East River beyond. The dilapidated house was once an ample and fine farmhouse, built of stone, and following the lines of the ancient Dutch homesteads.

Other familiar names associated with Hunt's Point are Willett, Leggett, and Tippett. Members of these families are buried in the old cemetery. Out on Barretto Point is the cemetery where the Hunt and Leggett families buried their slaves.

Cornell's Neck received its name for Thomas Cornell who was one of Throckmorton's colonists. He occupied the land in the year 1643, having bought it from the Indians, according to his statement. The Dutch authorities were satisfied with his proof of the fact, but the Indians drove him out and burned his house, claiming that he had never paid them. However, Governor Kieft issued to him a *grond brief* in

1646, and in 1667 Colonel Nicolls confirmed by patent this land to Cornell's grandson, William Willett—"a certaine Parcell of Land, contained within a neck, commonly called and knowne by ye name of Cornell's Neck."

The road runs down the middle of the Neck and winds up at Clason's Point, named for an owner later than Cornell. The old road used to lead, as does the new one, to the Cornell house. To-day only the kitchen of this edifice remains, this being included in what is now the Clason's Point Inn. Another portion of the inn is what remains of the Willett and Clason mansion. The smokehouse of the original building is still standing, being a small structure of stone not far from the inn.

Castle Hill Neck is a minor point jutting into East River just beyond Clason's, at the mouth of Pugsley's Creek. The Weckquaesgeek Indians formerly built a large castle, which amounted to a stockade, on high land at this place, hence the name which has never changed. From Castle Hill, the spot on which the palisaded stockade stood, the Indians (who belonged to the Mohican tribe) made a trail reaching to Paparinemo, and this was called "the Westchester Path" in Doughty's patent to Archer. Thus an Indian trail came to be a broader path, followed by white settlers, and this eventually became a real road, wide enough for wagons, which is the history of so many of our present roads.

The Ferris family early settled on that neck of land which lies to the east of Westchester Creek, and which finds its conclusion in Old Ferry Point. John Ferris was one of the original patentees of Westchester. One of the earliest ferries in the neighborhood of New York ran from the point of this neck across to Whitestone, Long Island. This point is coupled with Throg's Neck, both having roads which run back inland to the same starting point.

Ferris Avenue, sometimes called Ferry Lane, is the street which leads from Eastern Boulevard down toward both of these necks. To the right of it, a large house stands, once the home of the old owner of this land and known as Ferris Grange. It was built in 1687, has been rebuilt since that period, and was once run down, gone to seed and weed, but is still recognizable as a "handsome residence" of an early period. At the Country Club is another Ferris house; James, who occupied this home in 1776, was at breakfast with his family on the twelfth of October of that year, when a gun from the direction of the water apprised him of the landing of Sir William Howe and his army. Ferris was taken later on by the Queen's Rangers and suffered imprisonment in the "Provost" prison of New York City.

And next, still moving toward the east, we come to the extremely interesting Throg's Neck. To begin with, its very name is interesting. It is a remarkable example of how few generations it takes to corrupt a good old name. Some spell it with a double "g," the average native calls it "Frog's Neck," and a very large percentage of New Yorkers have not the faintest idea of its origin.

That origin is the excellent old surname of John Throgmorton, or Throckmorton, who came here as long ago as 1643. Roger Williams was leading a group of Baptists to the place, they having emigrated from Rhode Island and the Providence Plantations. The land was under the control of the Dutch, and from them Throckmorton took a grant. The land had been called Quinshung in the Indian language, but was destined from that time on to bear his name, or a form of it.

The trolley running down the Neck goes no farther than Eastern Boulevard, leaving the last three miles in undisturbed peace. For a quiet walk, there is no more beautiful road within the limits of greater New York. It is comparatively unfrequented, so that the pedestrian has full opportunity to enjoy it. Beyond the road, on either side, country estates stretch away, and beyond these lies the blue river which, at this point, is widening into the Sound.

The Tom Paine House, New Rochelle.

The Arch Leading through the old Fortifications at Fort Schuyler.

The Hulk of the "Macedonia."

The Old Marshall Residence.

On the day I walked those still, restful miles there was haymaking going on within the estates, and the smell of hot, fresh-cut grass was abroad.

At the first marked turn of the road one confronts a gate leading into the grounds of Mrs. Collis P. Huntington. The turn to the left leads down to the point. Beyond this, the general trend is toward the left.

The Havemeyer estate is just beyond. All of this vicinity is closely associated with Cooper's novel, *Satanstoe*. In the story, the Littlepage family were made owners of much property hereabouts. Corney Littlepage and his friend Dirck Follock stopped at a tavern at Kingsbridge when passing between Westchester and New York City. The author made use of the Indian legend which gave rise to the name of "The Stepping Stones," this being applied to the group of small islands lying to the northeast of Throg's Neck. The tops of these are bare and visible at low tide.

It seems, according to the legend, that the archfiend whom the Indians most feared was at one time baffled by their attacks and retreated to the narrow part of Throg's Neck and looked about to see what his best method of escape would be. His eye lighted upon the little islands, the tide being low. They were bare; so he stepped upon their tops and crossed in safety over to Long

Island. But he left a souvenir of his visit in the print of his big toe as he stepped off the point; hence, "Satanstoe."

By making a short detour along a branch road to the right, you will come to the famous Cedar of Lebanon on the Huntington estate. It is visible at some distance from the road; unfortunately, no nearer to the general public in these days, unless a permit has been obtained from the superintendent. This is the direct and dire result of the work of souvenir maniacs who chipped away bits of the precious wood until it became necessary, for the life of the tree, to refuse all visitors permission to inspect it at close range. It is one of the unfortunate cases where the innocent must suffer for the guilty.

This tree is the finest cedar of Lebanon in the United States, being thirteen feet in girth, forty feet in height, and having a spread of branches reaching beyond fifty feet. It is also very beautiful in outline. It was planted about a century and a quarter ago by Philip Livingston, and has seen a good deal of American history ebb and flow not far from its branches.

Turning back to the main neck road you will come to a big, whole-souled house on the Havemeyer estate where little folks are given a summer outing close to a private bathing beach, with swings and a benign cow to add to their pleasures. Just where the swings hang at the top of the high bank above the bathing beach, a tiny, shaded path runs toward the point. If you will follow this instead of the main road, you will be following in the footsteps of aborigines who used to delight in this green neck of land—no doubt the same aborigines who routed the arch-fiend. This little path, sneaking through a line of trees, is known as an old Indian trail, and it leads to a sloping meadow through which one can cross to the main road and to Fort Schuyler.

To-day this United States post stands as a mere relic of the past. Changing conditions and our national peacefulness have brought it to the point where it hardly seems to find reason for being—unless its immortality be considered to lie in its usefulness to the "movies." Many a motion-picture film is made on these picturesque grounds, many a thrilling scene enacted for the camera, where once a goodly garrison of our bravest troops paraded.

The building of this fort was begun in 1833. Its object was to accommodate 1250 men and to mount 318 cannon. The granite of which the old fortifications were built was brought from Greenwich; an austere gray stone, making a formidable front to any enemy who might dare approach from the water, as you can see for yourself to-day.

By the year 1851, when the cost was looked over, it was found that the construction and repairs of this now almost useless fort had reached $873,013.

Walking out to the giant gray walls which face upon the water, you pass through the old barracks, prison-like in appearance. Here is a green stretch shaded by old trees, once the parade ground; beyond, concave in line upon the parade ground, are the original fortifications. Their sternness, their somberness, their loneliness, have to be seen to be appreciated. They are immensely impressive, intensely melancholy.

On the high point above stands the well-known lighthouse which has guided many a boat at this gate of the Sound. At some distance back from the point are the old guns, now only a landmark. There are modern ones besides, built-up guns, with modern electric harnessing in control of them. But the entire fort is in charge of only a handful of men. A non-commissioned officer and his eight or ten privates take the place of that early 1250.

This point has been the scene of important military operations and was, for a very short time, in possession of the British during the Revolution. For five consecutive days Sir William Howe held Throg's Neck before advancing in the direction of New Rochelle.

Opposite, on Long Island, stands Fort Totten, and it is there that the active military life for both goes on. It is on Willett's Point, a short distance from Whitestone, and there is a boat connecting the three points and available for visitors.

These sister forts across the water from one another together command the eastern entrance to the East River, which is narrow just here. Their nearness and the height of the Throg's Neck cliffs give them a most advantageous position.

General Philip S. Schuyler was the officer who bequeathed his name to the fort. He it was who commanded the Northern army in 1777. He managed his campaign in such wise that Burgoyne's defeat and capture were made possible to the American commander who succeeded, namely Horatio Gates.

It was in 1911 that the garrison was finally withdrawn, although the fort had been gradually slipping into slumber. It was realized that the defenses at Fisher's Island had rendered the Schuyler defenses of no use. So the acres of the Government reservation which were purchased in 1826, several years before the building of the granite fort began, are to-day mainly of use to the motion-picture companies.

On beyond Throg's Neck we come to Rodman's Neck and that long island attached thereto by a bridge and almost one with it. This is City Island, "the village that dreamed of greatness." Within the actual limits of New York City you wake to a sense of being on the coast of

Maine. The smell of the sea is in the air, doddering old fishermen with a truly down-East look are around you, half-wrecked boats lie beached on a still shore, and the snores of a slumbering village are in your ears.

City Island is a curious relic of a proud ambition which swelled some century and a half ago to a point where it dreamed the fair dream of becoming the American metropolis and leaving New York to jog mournfully in its meteoric wake. But the dream spent itself. The quaint, ambitious little town slipped back into quiet after the revolution which had stirred it. That was before the end of the Eighteenth Century, and since then no stone has been thrown heavy enough to cause a splash. The inhabitants took up their semi-nautical life, settled down to fishing and sailing and boat-mending, and have remained thus ever since.

The only monorail of the United States used to be operated on the Pelham Park Railroad running from Bartow out to the bridge. It was installed in 1910 and ever contended with an unlucky star. On its first day a bad accident occurred, a number of persons were killed, and the unpopularity of the road afterwards warranted the use of only one car. When a strong wind was blowing even this one might fail the traveler, so there was many an enforced walk out to the end of Rodman's Neck. The weather-beaten car, however, with its loyal charioteer who sang its praises, was one of the picturesque features of this vicinity.

From the end of the monorail line, two horse-cars operated across the bridge and out to the end of the island. They were as weather-beaten as the monorail car, and one of the drivers would have been an excellent painter's model for an ideal pirate, adding another nautical touch to this curious land.

A trolley has now replaced these old means of conveyance.

The bridge is a well-built, modern structure, replacing a dismal and narrow one which used to stand. Before 1868 only a ferry spanned this distance.

Beyond it, a strip of land covering 230 acres and shaped like a string bean, extends into the water. All the way along you feel sea life in the air; launches are to hire, fishermen stroll, there rises a large sail factory, and, most important of all, you will find a great group of yachts laid up for repair—yachts of the wealthy, famous for their pleasure trips, yachts for racing, often a cup defender. For years this beach has been the repairing headquarters of such boats. The ship-building industry in this region began in 1676 or perhaps earlier, and ever since that time the shores of and near City Island have sheltered a long line of famous boats.

The most unique historical building on the island is the Macedonian Hotel—Smith's Hotel, to the native thereabouts. A portion of the building is the "remains of the English frigate *Macedonia*, captured Friday, October 25, 1812, by the United States frigate *United States*, commanded by Captain Stephen Decatur, U. S. N. The action was fought in Latitude 24° N., Longitude 29° 30′ W., that is 600 miles N.W. of the Cape De Verde Islands off the west coast of Africa. Towed to Cowbay in 1874."

This curious building is to be found by turning east at Ditmars Street. The old hotel is at the water's edge. Inside the hulk of the ship are the great hooks where the sailors of old used to hang their hammocks, and the iron rings for the cannon. Jenkins tells us that the hulk here displayed is not that of the original vessel which Decatur took, but its successor, a second ship of the same name, built immediately after the first *Macedonia* had been taken, launched in 1836, and broken up in Cow Bay, Long Island, which was a graveyard of condemned vessels.

City Island was once known as Minnewits Island, with several explanations given by as many different historians. Probably the theory that the name came from Peter Minuits, the Dutch governor and purchaser of Manhattan Island, is acceptable. It was not until the boom of the seventeen-sixties that the name City

Island was bestowed, with the idea that it could be better promoted thus. That boom was much like those which animate mushroom towns of the West to-day. The place was advertised, pushed, promoted, and the information given out broadcast that this was soon to be the great city of the Atlantic coast. A regular ferry must be established, to connect it with the mainland; bids were made for the lease of this ferry, and the winner was one Mrs. Deborah Hicks, "the best and fairest bidder."

The boom was short-lived and the settlers went back to their oyster culture, fishing, and piloting. It is claimed that oyster culture in America began at this place, and it is known that an Algonquin village, subsisting on the bivalve, used to occupy this strip of land. Fishing now goes on at Belden Point, since the new bridge has spoiled it at the north end.

There is a bit of tradition recorded to the effect that the first case of witchcraft tried in New York was connected with City Island. Ralph Hall and Mary, his wife, were tried for this crime and they escaped, fleeing to the island and taking refuge there in a hut where they lived for three years. They were finally acquitted. Unfortunately the hut has vanished, leaving us no tangible memorial.

Strolling back from the point of the island and crossing the bridge, you will find yourself at Marshall's Corners, at the end of Rodman's Neck. This point is marked by a fine old colonial house of Southern type, built by the Marshall family about the Revolutionary period. The house is now used as an inn.

To the east of this, along the shore, is Orchard Bay colony—a great city of three hundred tents under the régime of the Park Commission of the City of New York, a vast playground and summer resort for the people. Streets are lined with the little canvas homes, grass is kept cut, order prevails. For ten dollars any family can obtain the water privileges for a season, no charge being put upon the land; this means that for only ten dollars any New Yorker can pick up his tent, family, bathing suit, turkish towels, and rocking chair, and betake himself to an excellent bathing beach, having all the comforts of home within city limits. The lone bachelor is debarred.

The three hundred camps represent a thousand persons, and it is estimated that seventy or eighty thousand bathers disport themselves here in a season. A volunteer life-saving corps is stationed on the beach, and constant watch is kept of bathers.

Returning to the main portion of Rodman's Neck, you can trace history by walking up to the Split Rock Road. You will find Glover's Rock, memorial of American courage in the Revolution.

One of the Old Guns at Fort Schuyler.

The Old Fortifications, Fort Schuyler.

The Old Shot Tower, Built in 1821 to Replace One of Revolutionary Days.

An Old Block House, a Relic of the War of 1812, in Morningside Park.

Its tablet reads, "In memory of five hundred and fifty patriots who, led by Col. John Glover, held General Howe's army in check at the Battle of Pell's Point, October 18, 1776, thus aiding Washington in his retreat to White Plains." Glover's Rock, as it was afterwards called, was the point at which the battle began. Howe had been crossing from Throg's Neck, his men disposed in several boats, and he landed at what was known as the Bowne house and proceeded to march toward Bartow. Here, at the rock, he met Glover. The outcome was victorious for the British commander, but he met with such losses that he was crippled as to numbers, and time was gained for Washington in his retreat. Glover, overcome, retreated by way of Split Rock Road. He had had an advance guard of only forty to hold the British in check until his men could be disposed to advantage behind the trees and walls round about, and, with so great disadvantages, he had met defeat almost as if it were conquest.

Split Rock Road won its name from the peculiar formation of a rock standing on either side of a tree as if the tree had forced its way up, dividing the stone.

Not only was the mainland at this point stirred by the Revolution, but City Island awoke. On the day of the Battle of Long Island, August 27, 1776, two ships and a brig came to anchor a little above Throg's Neck, and Colonel Graham's regiment was ordered immediately to the spot by General Heath to prevent the British landing to plunder and burn. Before the regulars arrived several barges from the ships, full of armed men, landed on City Island and a great killing of cattle was the result. Two companies of Americans were carried by ferry—the only means of reaching the island then—and they promptly compelled the British to withdraw.

This region was a great headquarters for Tories, whom Colonel De Lancey led under the name of the "Tory Westchester Light Horse." They fought along the banks of Westchester Creek.

BACK TO THE HEART OF NEW YORK

CHAPTER XXII

OLD MANHATTAN

BACK within the heart of New York, on old Manhattan Island itself, the traveler finds a network of historic streets, some exactly in the line of early paths, others more or less altered to suit the convenience of a vast and growing city. Here, when summer is drawing to a close and green stretches no longer tempt, the history-devotee can enjoy many a brisk walk tracing the varied lore of old localities.

In his *Historical Guide to the City of New York*, Frank Bergen Kelley traces twenty-eight such little journeys all within the borough of Manhattan. Some of these are unfamiliar to even the native New Yorker. If a record were taken, showing how many residents of this island know old Horn's Hook, for instance, or ever heard of the Smuggler's Cave, or could tell the story of the Shot Tower, it is a safe guess that the hands-up would be oases in a desert of ignorance.

A little tour on the upper East Side begins at 53rd Street. Turning east on this street, you find yourself approaching a ferry slip, the route to Blackwell's Island. The Indians called it Minnahanonck which meant "Long Island." In the year 1664 it was granted to the Sheriff of New York County, Captain John Manning. Nine years later he disgraced himself in public opinion by surrendering the city to the Dutch, and he was obliged to retire to his residence, or "castle," on the island, his sword having been broken. His step-daughter inherited the island, and her marriage to Robert Blackwell gave it its permanent name. It was not until 1828 that the city of New York bought the strip of land, paying fifty thousand dollars for it.

You may make the trip to the island, where the penitentiary, charity hospital, and other city institutions now stand, by obtaining a pass; but whether you cross in this ferry or not, do not fail to notice the curious old brick tower which rises at your left near the ferry slip. It is surrounded by squatty buildings, lumber-yard piles, disorder, and rubbish.

The tower was erected in 1821, almost a century ago, by Youle. It was built to replace one still older, the original having been used as far back as Revolutionary days. In its day, the tower looked down upon the cultivated ground which surrounded the "Spring Valley Farmhouse." Sleek patches of vegetables, cow-cropped grass, flanked the substantial old Dutch house which was called the oldest building on Manhattan Island. Its land ran down to the river's edge. David Duffore was probably the builder. It was one and a half stories high, low and stalwart, its cross-beams hewn from the heaviest oak.

Turning back to Avenue A and going north, under Queensboro Bridge, you turn east again into 61st Street. A huge gas tank looms; close beside it, on an elevation of ground, you will see a quaint house with two wings, and a receding entrance between them. Rough, stoutly laid stones indicate ancient masonry. This place has been known since New York was young as Smith's Folly, and thereby hangs a tale.

Colonel William S. Smith was fortunate enough to lead to the altar no less distinguished a bride than Miss Adams, the daughter of the President of the United States. This event, of so great social importance, took place not a great while after the Revolution, wherefore the bridal roses are faded, the echoes of the bridal music vanished, this many a day. Nevertheless this memorial to Colonel Smith's joy stands; he set out to build for his bride the finest house possible, he spared his purse not at all (having been most successful in trade, he could afford to indulge the fair lady's tastes), and a proud residence was erected, its date, 1799, being wrought in the rear wall of the barn.

But the roof was no more than on the building, when Colonel Smith's bubble burst, he failed completely in business, and the name of "Smith's Folly" was fixed upon the house and barn for all time.

The mansion was burned, and the fine stable became a dwelling-place. Later, Monmouth C. Hart acquired it, and turned it into a tavern. It was used in this way until 1830, when it was bought by Jeremiah Towle, who had visited it in its road-house days, was interested in its quaint charm, and at last turned it into a residence, carefully preserving all its old-fashioned features—the tiny panes in the hall windows, the ancient staircase, the slim old balusters. It is one of the very few Manhattan residences now standing which date back of 1800; those left are fast slipping away.

Only in 1914, one landmark of this vicinity succumbed to progress—progress, heralded by pick and shovel and crane. The old Schermerhorn farmhouse stood until the summer of that year at the foot of East 64th Street, on the grounds of the Rockefeller Institute. It was famed as having been the summer home of Governor George Clinton. It was razed in a week, and excavations were begun for a new building.

Following First Avenue north to 68th Street and turning west a few doors, you come upon the German Reformed Church, 156 years old, where John Jacob Astor served as elder more than a century ago. The original church was far down-town, but when it was moved north its famous monument was carried along, and you will find it to-day, yellowed with years, set in the wall above the staircase. Its inscription runs:

"Sacred to the memory of Fred^{k} Willm Aug^{s} Baron Steuben, a German, Knight of the Order of Fidelity; aid-de-camp to Frederick the Great King of Prussia; Major General and Inspector General in the Revolutionary War. Esteemed, respected and supported by Washington, he gave military skill and discipline to the citizen-soldiers; who (fulfilling the Decrees of Heaven) achieved the independence of the United States. The highly polished manners of the Baron were graced by the most noble feelings of the heart. His hand, 'open as day for melting charity,' closed only in the strong grasp of Death. This memorial is inscribed by an American who had the honor to be his aid-de-camp, the happiness to be his friend. Ob. 1795."

As you continue north in your walk, you are passing through Jones' Wood of early days. It is a forest of buildings now, but once upon a time the farm of the Provoost family occupied this vicinity, and the well-known wood was a part of the farm. It covered the East River shore, from what is now 70th Street, for some distance north. "Dead Man's Rock" was the high point at which the wood began. The name "Jones" was attached to it after the Provoosts' time; but the most picturesque part of its history was connected with those earlier settlers.

Two remarkable cousins, Samuel and David Provoost, have passed into history. The former was the first bishop of New York, and the president of Columbia College. But David was famed in a widely different way. He was one of the most dare-devil smugglers known, and a rocky hole once existing on the shore of this wood was known as "The Smuggler's Cave." Here, and in another cave across the river at Hallett's Point, he hid his treasure, and the boys of the early eighteen-hundreds used to shiver and tell delicious, creepy stories of the old rascal whose ghost haunted these two black caverns. Not until he was ninety years old did David yield up his law-defying, rollicking, money-scattering career.

Walking north to 88th Street, you reach Horn's Hook. It is a hook of land jutting out from East River Park, marked on present-day maps as Harris Hook. Surmounting it stands the once magnificent residence of Archibald Gracie, built about 1813, now sadly out of repair.

Siebert Classen came from Holland in days

The Jumel Mansion.

The Gracie Mansion, at old Horn's Hook.

Looking down the "Hollow Way" of the Revolution, "Widow Davids's Meadow" of Dutch Days, now Manhattan St.

before the Revolution, made this crook of land his own, and named it for Hoorn, in Holland, which had been his home. During both wars with England it served as a fine station for batteries, commanding the entrance below Hell Gate.

And the house which later rose upon this spot! Tread its broad halls to-day and conjure up the visitors it has entertained! Washington Irving, who wrote *Astoria* while visiting his friend Astor next door, used often to come here. Tom Moore, John Quincy Adams, Louis Philippe, and Josiah Quincy were other guests. To-day the building is decaying and will soon be beyond repair. A sewing class for girls and a carpenter shop for boys occupy a small portion of its spaciousness.

If you will cross to St. Joseph's Orphan Asylum on 89th Street, the sisters will lead you into the inner court where you can see the old home of Nathaniel Prime, who, like Gracie, was a merchant prince of old New York. It was built in 1800 and is included within the present asylum grounds. Prime was first a coachman, later the wealthy head of a banking-house, and later still the tragic victim of a poverty-mania, in which he ended his own life.

Gracie, on the other hand, led an even life of steady success, and his fleet of clippers, with their red and white signals, were a well-known sight on every sea.

Another little history-tour on Manhattan traces the Battle of Harlem Heights. Summon your memories. . . .

The fox chase bugle notes of the British sounded across the Hollow Way. At once the gallant Americans took up the challenge; sharp orders pelted, muskets clattered, the flutter of a flag retorted. . . .

But that was almost a century and a half ago. To-day, the honking of many motors sounds instead of the bugle, and the Hollow Way of Revolutionary days is Manhattan Street of 1915, and there are trolley cars and coal and milk wagons that clatter.

That is to say, unless you can blot out sights and sounds of the Twentieth Century and step back to 1776. It was just after the Battle of Long Island, you will recall, that the conflict on Harlem Heights took place. Mrs. Lindley Murray of Murray Hill, smiling and gracious, had received Howe and his officers in her home, had lavishly regaled them with cake and wine, and made herself so agreeable that it was more than two hours before they could tear themselves away. With a loyal Whig smile up her graceful silken sleeve Mrs. Murray reflected that General Putnam was surely taking advantage of the opportunity she was thus giving him.

Records have not yet been found to show that "Old Put" ever missed any opportunity for a shrewd military move. While Howe was thus occupied with the charming lady's entertainment, Putnam was able to march his four thousand men up the shore of the Hudson, until he touched the right wing of the main army. Thus the Americans were gathered, Washington in his headquarters at what was later called the Jumel Mansion.

110th Street marks the southern boundary of that district formerly called Harlem Heights. On Broadway, north of 113th Street, stands St. Luke's Home for Aged Women; here is a memorial of the battle. This height which stretches about you at this point, sloping down toward the river on the west, is the land occupied by the British just before the conflict. The memorial window is on the staircase landing of the Home.

North along Broadway, you come to the tablet at 118th Street, on the Engineering Building of Columbia University. "To commemorate the Battle of Harlem Heights, won by Washington's troops on this site, September 16, 1776," runs the inscription. The flags, swords, muskets, and smoke of battle, and heroic figures, are depicted.

On that autumn day of '76 which this square of bronze pictures, the British forces were round about here. They had made their camp on this side of 125th Street, and were filled with overweening confidence. It did not disturb them in the least that two detachments of American Rangers had been sent out that morning from the Point of Rocks at the corner of 126th Street and Columbus Avenue, under the command of Knowlton and Leitch, with the aim of getting in the rear of the British on Vanderwater's Heights, now the grounds of Columbia University. Nor were they disturbed by a frontal attack; this, in fact, was so unsuccessful that the British became overbold, and one of their buglers advanced to the height near the river, now Claremont, and sounded the fox chase. The insolence of the challenge roused all the fire that slumbered under American coats.

The upshot was the battle in the Buckwheat Field. Where Barnard College rises, where its athletic field fronts its doors of learning, there waved the grain in '76. It was to this point, near 119th Street, that the Americans pushed their way; here for two hours raged one of the sharpest conflicts of the Revolution. Shepherd says:

"The field, snowy with the blossoms of coming harvest, an hour before peacefully smiling under the rays of a September sun, was now ruthlessly trampled by the hurrying feet of the combatants, its sunlight obscured by a pall of dust and smoke. Still, though the harvest of grain might be destroyed, a harvest of hope was to be garnered. Another impetuous charge, and the British were driven headlong from the field."

Before continuing in the path of this battle-story, it is convenient to cross to Amsterdam Avenue, where you can see the remains of the old blockhouse with its flying flag at the head of Morningside Park. It is associated with the War of 1812. Fort Horn was the height of rocks just to the south of it, partially cut out by a park path to-day, but still high and rugged. This point took its name from Major Joseph Horn, who supervised the erection of the works at McGown's Pass. Another memorial of the War of 1812 is to be seen near by, in the tablet on Fayerweather Hall, at 117th Street and Amsterdam Avenue.

Back to Broadway and the Revolution. As you go north you will find yourself descending into a little valley, reaching its lowest line at Manhattan Street. This valley was the boundary line between the British and American camps; you have been walking through the district of the former, you are now confronted by the latter, on the rising ground beyond. The Americans had the advantage of a higher position.

In pre-Revolutionary days, when Dutch names abounded, this depression of land, reaching west to Fort Lee Ferry, had been known as Matje David's Vly, or the Widow David's Meadow. In Revolutionary days it came to be known as the Hollow Way. It was across the

Hollow Way that the insolent bugle sounded the fox chase, from Claremont to the American camp north of the valley. At the western end of the valley was a little ferry even then; at the eastern end was the Point of Rocks from which the Americans could watch the movements of their enemies. This was at Columbus Avenue, and has been blasted away.

Continuing north on Broadway to 162d Street and turning east for more than a block, you reach the Roger Morris or Jumel Mansion where Washington made his headquarters from September 16th to October 21st of 1776. The American camp reached upward from the Hollow Way to this building, and commanded the situation. Here, in the north room known as the Council Chamber, the General discussed his plans and gave commands, to a most successful issue.

Familiar as the house is, with its quaintly furnished rooms, its stately chairs and cabinets of past days, its four-posters and other specimens of mellow mahogany, there are additions made from time to time which give it a refreshed interest. It is rather recently that the attic of the old house has been opened to the public, and here are displayed some of the most delightful treasures of the whole building. The quilting room has an ancient frame set up, a quilt in the making stretched upon it. The spinning room has a fine collection of old wheels. Tucked away under the eaves is the candle room, with all the dips in a row, hanging by their wicks and suggesting a line of Bluebeard's wives.

In the yard is an ancient fireplace and the floor of a hut used by a military officer at Fort Washington. The curious fire irons of 1776 are in place, and the floor has been relaid as it was originally.

The first streets on Manhattan grew from cowpaths and footpaths which wound deviously and wandered at their own sweet will. In the lower part of the island to-day, the streets have the same habit of twisting and tangling, following about the same lines as the original paths. The fort, standing where the present Custom House stands, was the heart of old New York; it furnished the center of defense, and, during days of peace, it furnished in its open space (Bowling Green) a gathering spot where Maypole dances were held and soldiers paraded.

Naturally, roads led from this fort; one in the direction of the Brooklyn ferry, practically equivalent to the line of Stone Street and Pearl Street of to-day, winding up at Peck Slip. The other set out toward the north, through the heart of the island, and so on into the uninhabited land beyond the town. In Broadway of the present we see the traces of this. Later on, Wall Street followed the line of a wooden wall. Albert Ulmann says:

"The wooden wall that was erected along the line to which the name still clings was built in 1653 to protect the town against a threatened invasion of New Englanders, 'a lithe, slippery, aggressive race,' whom the Dutch looked upon half in fear and half in scorn. The invasion never took place, but the wall remained for nearly half a century and succeeded nobly in keeping the town from growing beyond its useless barrier."

More and more roads developed as time advanced. One of these was the Greenwich Road, about the same as Greenwich Street of the present. It came to be a fashionable driveway when weather permitted; during violent rains it was unpopular, because of its crossing of Lispenard's Meadows and Minetta Water.

The most of New York's early growth tended toward the northeast, hence the streets in that direction developed earlier than Broadway and the west side. The Bouwerie Lane, later the Bowery, was important among these.

There are various origins alleged for the name of Maiden Lane, which to the Dutch was "The Maiden's Path." It followed a stream, and some claim that here the maidens gathered on wash-day, hence the name. Others more romantically say that it was a lover's lane where the most beautiful maidens abounded.

But no street is so filled with pulsing New York life, both in the present and in tradition, as Broadway. Stephen Jenkins has summed it up as "The Greatest Street in the World." It deserves its own chapter as the main artery from the heart of New York. It throbs with the very life-blood of Manhattan, which Charles Hanson Towne has described in verse:

Man's greatest miracle is accomplished here.
Steeple and dome he hurls high in the air,
Until, like dreams in marble and in stone,
They lift their wonder to a world amazed.

So here, when visions of new beauty rise,
Behind them float the dreams of cities old
Fallen now to silence, with the dust of kings.
Who wrought these granite ghosts, saw more than we
May ever see. He saw pale, tenuous lines
On some age-mellowed shore where cities rose
Proudly as Corinth or imperial Rome;
He saw, through mists of vision, Baghdad leap
To immaterial being, and he sought
To snatch one curve from her elusive domes;
He saw lost Nineveh and Babylon,
And Tyre, and all the golden dreams of Greece,
Columns and fanes that cannot be rebuilt,
Ev'n as Shakespearian lines can never sing
Again on any poet's resplendent page.
But the vague Source of these most lovely things
Were his for one high instant; and he caught
Their spirit and their glory for all time.

CHAPTER XXIII

THE GREAT ARTERY—BROADWAY

BROADWAY does indeed represent, as no other street can represent, the very heart of New York. As Jenkins says, "it is the epitome of the life of the great metropolis, with its various activities, mercantile, social, political and theatrical." To the Manhattanite himself, and to the stranger within his gates, Broadway *is* New York.

As the preceding chapter has shown, its development was not as early as that of some other streets, although its actual beginning dates back to the days of the old fort at Bowling Green. But the northwestern part of the town grew more slowly than the northeastern, and for a time Broadway blazed its solitary trail through the wilderness in its upper portion.

The Heere Straat was the old Dutch name for Broadway. From the fort, it went north as far as Park Row in early days, following the course of Ann Street. Orchards and gardens, with their accompanying homesteads, flanked it in the

Seventeenth Century, and in fact it did not cease to be a residence street until well into the Nineteenth.

The first building, geographically speaking, on Broadway, is Number 1—the Washington Building. This in itself is modern, but it bears a tablet which marks it as the site of the Kennedy house, an old landmark which stood until the latter part of the last century. Archibald Kennedy was a captain in the British navy, later becoming Earl of Cassilis, and he built his mansion on this spot, connecting it by a bridge with his father-in-law's house at Number 3, so that on the occasions of his balls the belles of old New York were to be seen passing back and forth across this rialto above the river and garden.

When General Israel Putnam came to New York during the Revolution he took up his headquarters in this house and remained here until the American forces were driven from the city. It was in April, 1776, that he came to take command of New York until the arrival of Washington. Later on, it was for a time the residence of Nathaniel Prime, the wealthy merchant, whose up-town dwelling we visited in the preceding chapter.

Bowling Green, adjoining the ancient fort, was the center of life in early days, when soldiers and merrymakers gathered there. In the following century, when the days of the Revolution approached, it saw stirring events. The gilded equestrian statue of George III, which had been set up in 1770, was torn down by a riotous mob six years later, and the lead of which it was made was converted into bullets for the American army. It is said that 42,000 bullets were made from the statue, by the wife and daughter of Oliver Wolcott of Connecticut. The tail and bridle of the horse, together with a portion of the pedestal, have been preserved in the museum of the New York Historical Society.

Where Wall Street meets Broadway stands Trinity Church, the parish dating from 1696. The plot of land now occupied by the church and graveyard was set aside in early days as a garden for the Dutch Company. The old Dutch burying-ground was closed about 1676, and this plot has been used as a burying-ground since that time. Many famous Americans have been laid to rest here; the sarcophagus of Captain James Lawrence is one of the most widely known tombs within the old yard. His words, "Don't give up the ship!" have passed into history.

The original church was burned in 1776, rebuilt after the Revolution and the present building was erected in 1839. The bronze doors were designed by St. Gaudens, and the reredos was the gift of J. J. and William Astor.

Just above, where a modern skyscraper stands,

"Smith's Folly," Built for a Bridal Gift to the Daughter of President Adams.

The Old Home of Nathaniel Prime, the Merchant Prince of Early Days.

The Van Cortlandt Mansion.

was the fine house of the Van Cortlandt family, and the sugar-house was behind it. Before leaving Broadway, we shall come to another Van Cortlandt home, which, happily, is well preserved.

St. Paul's Church, near Fulton Street, was one of Trinity's many children, but the building itself is older than the present Trinity building, dating back to 1764. The pew occupied by Washington is preserved. General Richard Montgomery was buried here; his remains having been brought from Quebec where he fell. Upon leaving his wife for the expedition against Quebec it is said that he told her, "My honor is engaged, and you shall never blush for your Montgomery."

So ended an ideally romantic love-story, for the two were never to meet again. The funeral-boat bearing his remains came slowly down the river, and, looking from her house, she saw it approach. "The pomp with which it was conducted added to my woe," she wrote. He was buried with the honors of war.

Across the way from St. Paul's the old Astor House was opened in 1836, and the names of its early patrons include almost all the famous persons who visited New York in those days. Irving, Dickens, Jenny Lind, Hawthorne, Daniel Webster, Abraham Lincoln, and Henry Clay are some of the names picked up at random.

Broadway continues past City Hall Park, which was the Commons of earlier days, and played a vital rôle in the city's history. It came to be a meeting-place on public occasions, when speeches were to be made and the voice of the people heard. The first popular assembly in opposition to the Stamp Act was held here November 1, 1765. Over and over similar meetings were held here during the months before its repeal. In rum and ale and a roasted ox the people celebrated their victory the following year—on the Commons, also.

Early government was conducted on and about the Commons. The poor-house was erected where the county court-house now stands, and near it the jail. Stocks, cage, pillory, and whipping-post were added to the gloomy gathering. Not far away, near the corner of Chatham and Chambers streets, the gallows was erected, having been removed from the neighborhood of the old fort. The famous old Bridewell was built near Broadway in 1775, and served as a patriot prison, along with the jail, during the Revolution.

To-day our own modern City Hall stands on the site of these early buildings, in the thick of their history. Among the interesting spots now to be seen is the "Governors' Room," containing portraits of almost the complete line of New York State governors, beginning with George Clinton.

The statue of Nathan Hale, by Macmonnies, stands near by, opposite the post office and facing Broadway. Jenkins relates the story of pointing out this statue to an Englishman who looked long at the bronze face, then said:

"If that is a correct picture of Hale, surely no man was less fitted to be a spy than he."

The old theatrical district began on Broadway not far above the Commons. The Broadway Theater was between Pearl and Worth streets—Edwin Forrest and young Lester Wallack are among the names associated with its halcyon days. The first Wallack's Theater was at the corner of Broome Street, the second at 13th Street, and many a famous production saw its first night in these two houses. Henry Irving and Ellen Terry made their first American appearance in the upper house, which had been named the Star; Booth and Barrett, Bernhardt and Modjeska, added to its glory.

A walk along all these blocks of lower Broadway is a passing among ghosts, for not a stone is left of most of the buildings once famous. The birthplace of Julia Ward Howe, for instance, used to stand at the corner of Bond Street; one of the homes of Fenimore Cooper was a house near Prince Street; but these, along with the other homes of distinguished Americans, old hotels, theaters, and famous business centers, have vanished. Only some half-century ago

Pfaff's beer-cellar near Bleecker Street was the chosen resort for such bohemians as Walt Whitman, Artemus Ward (C. F. Browne), Henry Clapp, and many more. Wilson says, "Lounging into Pfaff's place one day in 1856, in company with Fitz-James O'Brien, he [Clapp] was so delighted with the beer served him that he straightway sounded its praises among his comrades, who thereupon made Pfaff's their favorite resort."

Jenny Danforth and Ada Clare were two of the brilliant members of this group. The latter was both actress and author, as well as beauty, "and the embodiment of female bohemianism. She parried thrusts of wit as deftly as a swordsman would a foil, and her laugh rang the clearest when an unfortunate one was unhorsed in the shock of intellect."

Niblo's Gardens—the old National Academy of Design—the farm of Andrew Elliott at Fourth Street—they are among the procession of memories. Grace Church at the corner of 10th Street dates back to 1846, a comparatively early year when one looks down the line of modern buildings leading up to it.

A century ago and more, the Bowery and Broadway were the two important thoroughfares of the island. In 1807 the commissioners laid out a plan to make these two roads meet at the "Tulip Tree" which stood in what is now

Union Square. Above Union Square was the Bloomingdale Road in those years. Broadway had bent at 10th Street, just below, to preserve the Brevoort homestead, and at Union Square it met the Bloomingdale Road which started on its course by making a diagonal line across the Square.

In the center of Union Square a large fountain was placed in 1842, to mark the introduction of Croton water into the city. It has remained ever since, surrounded by tulips and pansies each spring.

A statue of Lincoln stands in Broadway near the Square. The story is told that while a Lincoln's Birthday celebration was taking place all around the statue, nobody remembered to decorate the bronze. Late in the day a policeman passed and observed the neglect; he hied him to the nearest florist, purchased a small bouquet of carnations, laid it on the bronze arm, and for many days the withered little offering clung to the great sculptured figure.

Madison Square is on the site of the old Potter's Field. It was laid out for a parade ground, to extend as far north as 34th Street. Gradually its outline contracted, but it still remains a refreshing spot of green in the midst of a seething city. Opposite, on the west side of Broadway, stood the famous old Hoffman House, in the bar-room of which the paintings attracted visitors from all over the country. *Nymphs and Satyr* by Bougereau was particularly admired, among works by the greatest artists of two continents.

From this point on came to be the chief hotel district, the Gilsey, the Grand, and the Albemarle being among the list. It is not many years, indeed, since the hotels moved up ten to twenty blocks, and left this district to its traditions.

Passing on up through the many blocks now given over to new theaters and hotels, we arrive at Long Acre Square, or Times Square as it is now known, where the New York Times building rears its many stories. Jenkins gives the following account of its Revolutionary history:

"On the fifteenth of September, 1776, the British landed at Kip's Bay from Long Island with the intention of cutting off the American Army, then in full retreat. The greater part of the army was well up on the Bloomingdale Road, but Putnam with four thousand troops was still in the city. Washington despairingly attempted to prevent the landing of the British on the shore of the East River, but his troops fled almost before a shot was fired. Word had been sent to Putnam to join the chief, and he hurried his troops out of the city. Guided by Aaron Burr over the Middle Road from the fortifications above Canal Street, he managed to escape the cordon of British troops being thrown across the island and joined the chief on the Bloomingdale Road at this point, barely getting through in the nick of time. A tablet to commemorate this joyful meeting of the two generals was erected on the west side of the square by the Sons of the Revolution."

Country seats of wealthy New York merchants occupied the bank of the Hudson in colonial days, reaching along near the Bloomingdale Road. Lorillard, Livingston, and Clarkson were among the well-known property owners below 96th Street. Some of the estates were confiscated during the Revolution because of the Loyalist tendency of their owners.

At 68th Street you will find the Bloomingdale Reformed Dutch Church, lineal descendant of the old church built close by in 1805. Yellow fever had broken out in the city below, and many inhabitants desired to hold service in this safer locality; hence the establishment of the church.

Broadway uptown passes over Harlem Heights of the battle story, and through the property of Columbia University, once King's College. Changes have taken place in the course of the old street, and the present Broadway does not coincide in all parts with the old road; but if you will turn east at Manhattan Street, for about half an ordinary block, then go north to Lawrence Street, you will come upon a short street marked "Old Broadway." This follows for its brief course the actual line of the old Bloomingdale Road. Near it is St. Mary's Church on Lawrence Street; it is only a few years ago that the original building, more than a century old, gave way to the new. It is said that the early parishioners who lived farther down-town used to come to church by boat, up the North River.

On the old road, at 140th Street, Alexander Hamilton erected his country residence which he named "The Grange," after his ancestral home in Scotland. The building has been moved, and now stands on the east side of Convent Avenue, used for the parish house of St. Luke's church. Hamilton always drove back and forth from this house to his city office. On the day when he was to meet Aaron Burr, in response to the duel challenge, he set out to drive to town as usual, without letting his wife know that he might never return.

The Jumel Mansion has been mentioned in the preceding chapter. It was built by Roger Morris for his bride, Mary Philipse of Yonkers. The legend of Mary's suitors has been told in Chapter XVIII. Later it came into the possession of John Jacob Astor, and about a century ago he sold it to Stephen Jumel, whose brilliant widow lived to become the reluctant bride of old Aaron Burr, who won her by bringing a clergyman along as his lieutenant, and demanding that the wedding take place then and there.

Above here, at 168th Street, Broadway and the Kingsbridge Road become one, and continue under the name of the former. It leads us past Fort Washington, that sister fort of Lee on the Palisades, whose plans were drawn by Washington's engineer, Major Rufus Putnam. It is the highest point of land on Manhattan Island, and offered a remarkable situation for a defense; this fact was appreciated by the British, who took it and re-named it Fort Knyphausen. A marble seat and tablet, the gift of James Gordon Bennett, mark the site of the fort.

The King's Bridge of old days stood about twenty yards east of where the bridge of to-day stands. It was built in 1693 and was established by Royal Grant of William and Mary to Frederick Philipse of the Manor of Philipsburgh. Its successor, built in 1713, saw the retreat of Washington's troops in October of '76, and was broken down, but repaired. After the Revolution a new and good bridge was built.

Among the old homes to be found along Broadway is the Dyckman house, at the corner of 209th Street. Another is the Macomb mansion facing the Broadway bridge. In the Seventeenth Century this was a public house; at the time of the Revolution it was "Cox's Tavern"; and in 1797 it was bought by Alexander Macomb. From Fordham, Edgar Allan Poe often came to visit at the house. The old inn is referred to by Cooper; in *Satanstoe* he shows us his hero, Corney Littlepage, and Dirck, Corney's friend, often stopping at this hostelry, which, in the tale, was kept by Mrs. Lighte.

General Macomb built a dam and mill near by. About the middle of the last century the house was sold to J. H. Godwin.

Above here our way leads to Van Cortlandt Park, named for the owner of the mansion still preserved within its boundaries. The house was built in 1748, and is now in the charge of the Colonial Dames, who have established a museum within its walls. Frederick Van Cortlandt was the builder.

In Revolutionary days the building served as headquarters for the Hessian Jaegers. One of the traditions of the house is that therein expired, in the arms of his betrothed, one Captain Rowe of the Jaegers, who had received a mortal wound while battling with some American troops not far away.

Many famous guests were entertained at the house, Washington having spent a night there, just before he left for Yorktown in 1781. Again, in 1783, he found lodging there, just before entering New York by way of King's Bridge. Rochambeau, and King William IV (then the Duke of Clarence) were entertained there.

Frederick Van Cortlandt died the year after erecting the building, but his eldest son, Jacobus, fell heir to it and maintained it with all the ambition which his father had shown.

Near the house is preserved a window of the old sugar house in Duane Street. Another point of interest is the set of old Dutch keystones above the windows of the house.

Broadway now proceeds to Yonkers. We have already followed it to Sleepy Hollow.

ITINERARIES

CHAPTER XXIV

EASY ROUTES FOR THE TRAVELER OF TO-DAY

IN setting out to make the little pilgrimages around Manhattan which have been sketched in the foregoing chapters, the traveler in automobile or carriage, or the doughty pedestrian, will probably find sufficient directions within the chapters themselves. For him who travels by ferry, trolley, or railroad, the following brief itineraries may prove convenient.

LONG ISLAND

1. *To Jericho.* (Chapter II.)

Take L. I. R. R. to Jamaica; or go from Brooklyn Bridge by Elevated Road (Lexington Avenue and Cypress Hills train) to terminus at Cypress Hills. Take Jamaica trolley to King's Park. See other landmarks on Fulton St.

Take trolley to Hollis.

Take electric car to Hempstead. Runs every half-hour.

Take trolley to Mineola, then to Hicksville.

By leaving the car en route, and walking to the north, a detour may be made to Old Westbury.

From Hicksville, walk or procure a conveyance for Jericho (about two miles).

2. *To Astoria and Flushing.* (Chapter III.)

Take Second Avenue trolley or Elevated Road to 92d St.

Walk east to the river, and take Astoria ferry.

Take Broadway trolley; at Woodside, transfer to Flushing trolley. Leave the car at St. George's Church, Main St. Other landmarks within short walking distance; Quaker Church near the Playground, Bowne House on Bowne Ave., etc.

3. *To Flatlands.* (Chapter IV.)

Take Brooklyn subway to Atlantic Avenue.

Take Flatbush Ave. trolley to Lefferts Homestead, 563 Flatbush Avenue. Walk to points named near by.

Continue on Flatbush Ave. trolley to Flatlands Church, King's Highway.

Return to trolley, continue to point of transfer, take Bergen Beach car.

4. *Over the Battleground of Long Island.* (Chapter V.)

Take Myrtle or De Kalb Ave. car at Brooklyn Bridge, ride to Fort Greene Park.

Take Myrtle Ave. car, transferring to Vanderbilt Ave. car, to Prospect Park.

Walk up Eastern Drive to Battle Pass Tablet, thence to Lookout Hill.

From Ninth St. entrance of Park take car to Greenwood Cemetery.

(Side trips may be made to Navy Yard, entrance at Sands St., and to Battle Tablet at corner of Flatbush Ave. and Fulton St.)

New York Harbor and Sandy Hook Region

5. *The Highlands.* (Chapter VI.)

At foot of West 42d St. take Sandy Hook route steamer to Atlantic Highlands, or C. R. R. of N. J.

Take Leonardo trolley to Chapel Hill Road. Walk to Chapel Hill, about a mile. Various points to be seen close together.

Start along highway toward the coast. Short detour to Lighthouse.

Continue to Water Witch. Return by boat or train. It is possible to return from the Highlands to New York by trolley, by way of South Amboy. This requires several hours.

Staten Island and Beyond

6. *To Oude Dorp.* (Chapter VII.)

Take ferry to St. George, Staten Island, at South Ferry. Walk to Lighthouse Reservation, then to Public Museum.

Returning to Bay St., take trolley to Grant, "Planters' Hotel."

Continue on Bay St. to Clinton, walk up Pavilion Hill. Return to Bay St. and walk to other points named. Detour at Chestnut Ave. to Garibaldi House.

South Beach car to Fort Wadsworth and Arrŏchar Park.

7. *To Richmond.* (Chapter VIII.)

St. George ferry and Richmond car to Emerson Hill.

Continue on Richmond car, stopping at Perrine house, to New Dorp. Leave car at Moravian Church. Walk to Black Horse Tavern and Fountain House.

Continue on car to its terminus at Richmond.

8. *Tottenville and Perth Amboy.* (Chapter IX.)

St. George ferry, Staten Island Railroad to Tottenville. The ferryboats which leave on the hour connect with the trains.

Walk to Billopp House, then cross by ferry to Perth Amboy.

Return by C. R. R. of N. J.

New Jersey

9. *Newark.* (Chapter X.)

Take Cortlandt or Desbrosses St. ferry to Jersey City, then trolley to Newark. Or take Tube directly to Newark.

Visit points near Market and Broad sts., going north to State and Broad, the old Plume Homestead.

Take Clinton Ave. car to Gouverneur St., walk to Mt. Pleasant Ave., see Cockloft Hall.

Take Main Line trolley to Old Lyons Farms, leaving car at Chancellor St.

10. *Elizabeth and Beyond.* (Chapter XI.)

Take Penn. R. R. to Elizabeth; or, Tube to Newark, thence Main Line trolley, leaving car at East Jersey St.

Continue to Rahway by Penn. R. R., thence to Woodbridge, by branch railroad.

Or, continue on main line of Penn. R. R. through Rahway to New Brunswick.

New Brunswick can be reached by trolley from Elizabeth by way of Bound Brook. Main Line trolley.

11. *Plainfield and Bound Brook.* (Chapter XII.)

Take C. R. R. of N. J. to Plainfield.

Take trolley to Dunellen, and make side trip to Washington Rock.

Continue by trolley to Bound Brook.

Or, take Tube to Newark, and thence trolley all the way. The running time from Newark to Bound Brook is about two and one-half hours.

12. *To Springfield and Morristown.* (Chapter XIII.)

Take D. L. and W. R. R. to Milburn, thence continue by trolley to Springfield, Chatham, Madison, and Morristown. Return by D. L. and W. R. R.

Or, take Tube to Newark, thence trolley all the way, stopping at above-named towns. This trolley goes all the way to Lake Hopatcong. At Newark, take Springfield Ave. line to Maplewood, changing there for Springfield car.

13. *To Passaic and Paterson.* (Chapter XIV.)

Take Erie R. R. to Passaic.

Continue on same railroad to Paterson. (Or go by trolley.)

Upon returning, detour by trolley may be made, from the Erie R. R. on the New Jersey side, to Weehawken, to see Hamilton monument.

Or, take Broadway subway to Manhattan St. station, go west, and take Fort Lee ferry, at its terminus take trolley for Paterson, and return by way of Passaic. It is possible to trolley from Paterson to Passaic, to Hoboken, to Weehawken.

In Paterson, take Singac car for Falls.

14. *To Alpine, Fort Lee, and Hackensack.* (Chapter XV.)

Take N. Y. C. and H. R. R. R. to Yonkers.

(Or Broadway subway to terminus, then trolley to Getty Square, Yonkers.)

Take ferry to Alpine.

Walk south along shore to Fort Lee (about 7 miles).

Take trolley to Hackensack.

Return by trolley to Fort Lee ferry, cross, and take subway.

Or, return by Erie R. R. from Hackensack to New York.

Rockland County, New York

15. *Sneden's Landing and Tappan.* (Chapter XVI.)

Go to Dobbs Ferry by N. Y. C. and H. R. R.R. (Or, trolley to Hastings as in 16, then take railroad to Dobbs Ferry.)

Take ferry to Sneden's Landing.

Walk up Palisades and on to Tappan.

Westchester County, New York, and into Connecticut

16. *Along the Hudson to Sleepy Hollow.* (Chapter XVII.)

It is possible to trolley to Hastings, going by Broadway subway to terminus, then trolley to Getty Square, then taking Warburton Ave. car to Hastings.

Or, take N. Y. C. and H. R. R. R. to Hastings.

Continue by same railroad to Dobbs Ferry, Irvington, Tarrytown and Sleepy Hollow. (Philipse Manor is the station for the last-named point.)

17. *On the Sawmill River Road.* (Chapter XVIII.)

Go to Yonkers by N. Y. C. and H. R. R.R. or by trolley. (See 14.)

Take same railroad (Putnam Div.) to Ardsley.

Walk to Rochambeau house.

Continue on same railroad, or walk, to Elmsford.

Walk to Four Corners.

18. *To White Plains by way of Scarsdale.* (Chapter XIX.)

Take N. Y. C. and H. R. R. R. (Harlem Div.) to Tuckahoe, Scarsdale, Hartsdale, White Plains, and North White Plains.

Or, take Bronx Park subway to West Farms station, then trolley to Mt. Vernon, and there take White Plains trolley, stopping at other points en route.

Or, take N. Y., W., and B. electric road to White Plains.

Walk from White Plains to North White Plains if you are to see ancient mortar about midway between.

19. *The Boston Post Road.* (Chapter XX.)

Take N. Y., N. H., and H. R. R. to Eastchester (Mt. Vernon), New Rochelle, Mamaroneck, Rye, Greenwich, and Cos Cob.

Or, take Third Avenue Elevated Railroad to 129th St., thence N. Y., W., and B. electric road to Kingsbridge Road station. (This is Eastchester.)

Continue on same railway to New Rochelle.

Take Stamford trolley to all other points.

THE BRONX

20. *Throg's Neck and City Island.* (Chapter XXI.)

Take N. Y., N. H., and H. R. R. (Harlem River Branch) to Hunt's Point, Clason Point, Westchester (Throg's Neck), City Island Station.

By taking Third Ave. Elevated Railroad to 129th St., and there taking the Westchester Ave. trolley, it is possible to trolley all the way to Clason Point and Westchester. Trolley continues part of the way down Throg's Neck, one must walk or drive the rest of the way.

Trolley to end of City Island.

Or, take Government boat directly to Fort Schuyler (Throg's Neck). Pass must be secured in advance from the Commandant at Fort Schuyler. Boat goes Tues., Thurs., and Sat.

MANHATTAN

21. *Old Manhattan.* (Chapter XXII.)

Take Second Ave. Elevated Railroad, walk east on 53d St., continue north to various points, walking or by trolley, to 89th St. (East Side trip.)

Take Broadway subway to Cathedral Parkway station, continue north, walking or by trolley, to various points as far as Manhattan St. There take subway again for Roger Morris Mansion (162d St.). (Trip over battleground of Harlem Heights.)

22. *Broadway.* (Chapter XXIII.)

The Van Cortlandt House, Macomb House, and other points named in the northern part of the city are most conveniently reached by the Broadway subway.

BIBLIOGRAPHY

Allibone, Samuel Austin. *A Critical Dictionary of English Literature and British and American Authors.* Philadelphia, 1872.

Appleton's Cyclopædia of American Biography. Ed. by Jas. Grant Wilson and John Fiske. New York, 1888.

Bacon, Edgar Mayhew. *Chronicles of Tarrytown and Sleepy Hollow.* New York, 1897.

—— *The Hudson River, from Ocean to Source.* New York, 1907.

Baedeker, Karl. *The United States Handbook for Travellers.* Leipsic.

Baird, Henry M. *History of the Rise of the Huguenots of France.* New York, 1883.

Bancroft, George. *History of the United States of America.* New York, 1890.

Bayles, Richard Mather. *History of Richmond County.* New York, 1887.

Bibliographical and Genealogical History of Morris and Sussex Counties, New Jersey. New York and Chicago, 1899.

Bolton, Robert. *The History of the County of Westchester.* New York, 1881.

Brief History of Flushing.

Chambers's Encyclopædia. Philadelphia, 1897 (London and Edinburgh).

CLAYTON, W. WOODFORD. *History of Bergen and Passaic Counties, N. J.* Philadelphia, 1882.

—— editor. *History of Union and Middlesex Counties, New Jersey.* Philadelphia, 1882.

CLUTE, J. J. *Annals of Staten Island.* New York, 1877.

COMFORT, RANDALL (and others). *History of Bronx Borough.* New York, 1906.

COOK, HARRY T., and KAPLAN, N. J. *The Borough of the Bronx, 1639–1913.* New York, 1913.

COOPER, JAMES FENIMORE. *The Spy.*

—— *Satanstoe.*

—— *The Water Witch.*

DAVIS, T. E. *First Houses of Bound Brook.*

DAVIS, WILLIAM T. *Staten Island Names: Ye Olde Names and Nicknames.* New Brighton, New York, 1896.

DOREMUS, HENRY M. *The Growth of Newark, N. J.* Newark, 1903.

DRAKE, JOSEPH RODMAN. *The Culprit Fay and Other Poems.* New York, 1836.

ELLIS, J. FRANKLIN. *History of Monmouth County, New Jersey.* Philadelphia, 1885.

Encyclopædia Britannica, The. New York, 1910 (Cambridge, England).

FIELD, T. W. *Historic and Antiquarian Scenes in Brooklyn and its Vicinity.* Brooklyn, 1868.

FISKE, JOHN. *The American Revolution.* Boston, 1891.

Flatbush Past and Present. Pub. by Flatbush Trust Co.

Flatbush of To-day. Published on the Occasion of the Tri-Centennial Celebration of the Coming of the Dutch to America, Held in All Souls' Church, Flatbush. Brooklyn, 1908.

FOSDICK, LUCIAN J. *The French Blood in America.* New York, 1911.

FURMAN, GABRIEL. *Antiquities of Long Island.* New York, 1875.

"Half-Moon Papers," Second Series (*Historic New York*). New York, 1899.

HAMILTON, J. C. L. *Poverty and Patriotism of the Neutral Grounds.* Elmsford, N. Y., 1900.

Harper's Encyclopædia of United States History. New York, 1905.

HARTE, BRET, *The Poetical Works of.* Boston, 1870.

HATFIELD, EDWIN F. *History of Elizabeth, New Jersey.* New York, 1868.

HINE, C. G. *The New York and Albany Post Road.* New York, 1905.

Historic Buildings Now Standing in New York which Were Erected Prior to 1800. Printed for Bank of the Manhattan Co. New York, 1914.

History of Morris County, New Jersey. New York, 1882.

HONEYMAN, A. VAN DOREN, editor. *Somerset County Historical Quarterly.* Plainfield, N. J., January, 1912.

HULBERT, ARCHER BUTLER. *The Historic Highways of America.* Cleveland, O., 1905.

HURD, D. HAMILTON, compiler. *History of Fairfield Co., Conn.* Phila., 1881.

INGERSOLL, ERNEST. Rand McNally & Co.'s *Illustrated Guide to the Hudson River and Catskill Mts.* New York.

INGERSOLL, ROBERT GREEN, *The Works of.* New York, 1912.

IRVING, WASHINGTON. *History of New York, by Diedrich Knickerbocker.*

—— *Life of George Washington.*

—— *Salmagundi* (With William Irving and James Kirke Paulding).

—— *Sketch-Book.*

IRVING, WASHINGTON. *Stories and Legends from Washington Irving.* New York, 1896.

—— *Wolfert's Roost.*

JENKINS, STEPHEN. *The Greatest Street in the World.* New York, 1911.

—— *The Old Boston Post Road.* New York, 1914.

—— *The Story of the Bronx.* New York, 1912.

JOHNSON, CLIFTON. *The Picturesque Hudson.* New York, 1909.

KELLEY, FRANK BERGEN, compiler. *Historical Guide to the City of New York.* (Auspices of the City History Club.) New York, 1913.

—— (compiler), and DIX, WARREN R. (editor), *Historic Elizabeth.* Elizabeth, N. J., 1914.

KNIGHT, MADAM SARAH. *The Private Journal of a Journey from Boston to New York, in the Year 1704.* New York, 1825; Albany, 1865.

LAMB, MRS. MARTHA J. *History of the City of New York.* New York and Chicago, 1880.

LIVINGSTON, WILLIAM FARRAND. *Israel Putnam: Pioneer, Ranger, and Major-General.* New York, 1901.

Long Island Historical Society, Memoirs of.

LONGWELL, CHARLES PITMAN. *A Little Story of Old Paterson.* 1901.

LOSSING, BENSON J. *The Pictorial Field-Book of the Revolution.* New York, 1860.

MACK, ARTHUR C. *The Palisades of the Hudson.* Edgewater, N. J., 1909.

MANDEVILLE, G. HENRY. *Flushing, Past and Present.* Flushing, 1860.

Maps. Country Thirty Miles around the City of New York, The. By I. H. EDDY. New York, 1828.

—— Hudson River District. Amer. Automobile Ass., 1914.

Maps. Landmark Map of Fort Lee, N. J. By E. HAGAMAN HALL, for the Amer. Scenic and Historic Preservation Society. (In volume by Mack.)

—— New Jersey Traveller. Reduced from T. Gordon's Map by H. S. TANNER. Phila., 1834.

—— Road Map of the Country around New York. C. S. HAMMOND & Co. New York, 1914.

—— Staten Island. By CHARLES W. LENG. (In Davis's volume)

—— Suburban Long Island. Amer. Automobile Ass., 1914.

—— Suburban New Jersey. Amer. Automobile Ass., 1914.

—— Twelve Miles around New York, by SIDNEY. 1840.

—— Westchester Co. Amer. Automobile Ass., 1914.

——(Other maps in various historical volumes named.)

MESSLER, ABRAHAM. *First Things in Old Somerset.* Somerville, N. J., 1899.

MILLS, W. JAY. *Historic Houses of New Jersey.* Philadelphia, 1902.

MORRIS, IRA K. *Memorial History of Staten Island.* Staten Island, 1900.

National Cyclopædia of American Biography. New York, 1898.

NELSON, WILLIAM, editor. *The First Presbyterian Church of Paterson, N. J.* Paterson, 1893.

—— *The Van Houten Manuscripts.* Paterson, 1894.

Newspaper Clippings and Files. In Library of Long Island Historical Society.

—— In Library of New Jersey Historical Society.

—— In Plainfield Public Library.

OSTRANDER, STEPHEN M. *History of the City of Brooklyn and Kings Co.* Brooklyn, 1894.

PAINE, THOMAS, *Life and Writings of.* New York, 1908.

Pamphlets, Circulars, Reports etc., of The First Presbyterian Church, Newark, N. J.
—— Home for Aged Women, Elizabeth, N. J.
—— *Old Home Week.* (MOODY.) Elizabeth, N. J., 1907.
PAPE, WILLIAM J., Compiler with WILLIAM W. SCOTT. *The News History of Passaic.* Passaic, N. J., 1899.
Picture of New-York, The: or the Traveller's Guide through the Commercial Metropolis of the U. S. By a Gentleman residing in this City. New York, 1807.
Picture of New-York, The, and Stranger's Guide to the Commercial Metropolis of the U. S. New York, 1828.
POST, JOHN J. *Old Streets, Roads, Lanes, Piers, and Wharves of New York.* New York, 1882.
PRIME, NATHANIEL S. *History of Long Island.* New York, 1845.
ROMEYN, THEODORE B. *Historical Discourse Delivered at Hackensack, N. J.* New York, 1870.
ROSS, PETER. *History of Long Island.* New York and Chicago, 1903.
SALTER, EDWIN, and GEO. C. BEEKMAN. *Old Times in Old Monmouth.* Freehold, N. J., 1887.
SALTER, EDWIN. *A History of Monmouth and Ocean Counties.* Bayonne, N. J., 1890.
SCHARF, J. THOMAS. *History of Westchester Co., New York.* Philadelphia, 1886.
SHAW, WILLIAM H., compiler. *History of Essex and Hudson Counties, N. J.* Philadelphia, 1884.
SHERMAN, ANDREW M. *Historic Morristown, N. J.* Morristown, 1905.
SHONNARD, FREDERIC, and W. W. SPOONER. *History of Westchester Co., N. Y.* New York, 1900.
SHRINER, CHARLES A. *Paterson, New Jersey.* (Auspices of the Board of Trade.) Paterson, 1890.
SPARKS, JARED, editor. *Library of American Biography.* Boston, 1834, 1844. New York, 1854.

Staten Island and Staten Islanders. Compiled by the Richmond Borough Association of Women Teachers, New York, 1909.

STILES, HENRY R. *History of the City of Brooklyn.* Albany, 1869.

STONE, WILLIAM L. *History of New York City.* New York, 1872.

THOMPSON, BENJAMIN F. *History of Long Island.* New York, 1843.

TOWNE, CHARLES HANSON. *Manhattan.* New York, 1909.

Trolley Exploring, Pub. by the Brooklyn *Daily Eagle.*

TRUMBULL, L. R. *A History of Industrial Paterson.* Paterson, New Jersey, 1882.

ULMANN, ALBERT. *A Landmark History of New York.*

URQUHART, FRANK JOHN, and others. *A History of the City of Newark.* New York and Chicago, 1913.

VALENTINE, DAVID T. *History of the City of New York.* New York, 1853.

VAN RENSSELAER, MRS. SCHUYLER. *History of the City of New York in the Seventeenth Century.* New York, 1909.

VAN VALEN, J. M. *History of Bergen Co., N. J.* N. Y. and N. J., 1900.

WALLER, HENRY D. *History of the Town of Flushing, Long Island.* Flushing, 1899.

WATSON, JOHN F. *Annals and Occurrences of New York City and State.* Philadelphia, 1846.

WHITEHEAD, JOHN. *The Passaic Valley, N. J., in Three Centuries.* New York, 1901.

WHITEHEAD, WILLIAM A. *Contributions to the Early History of Perth Amboy.* New York, 1856.

WILLIS, NATHANIEL PARKER, *The Poems of.* New York, 1861.

WILSON, JAMES GRANT, Ed. *Memorial History of the City of New York.* New York, 1893.

WILSON, RUFUS ROCKWELL. *Historic Long Island.* New York, 1902.

—— "The National Pike and its Memories." *New England Magazine,* 1902.

—— *New York: Old and New.* Phila., 1909.

INDEX

N
LONG
ATLANTIC OCEAN
Explanation

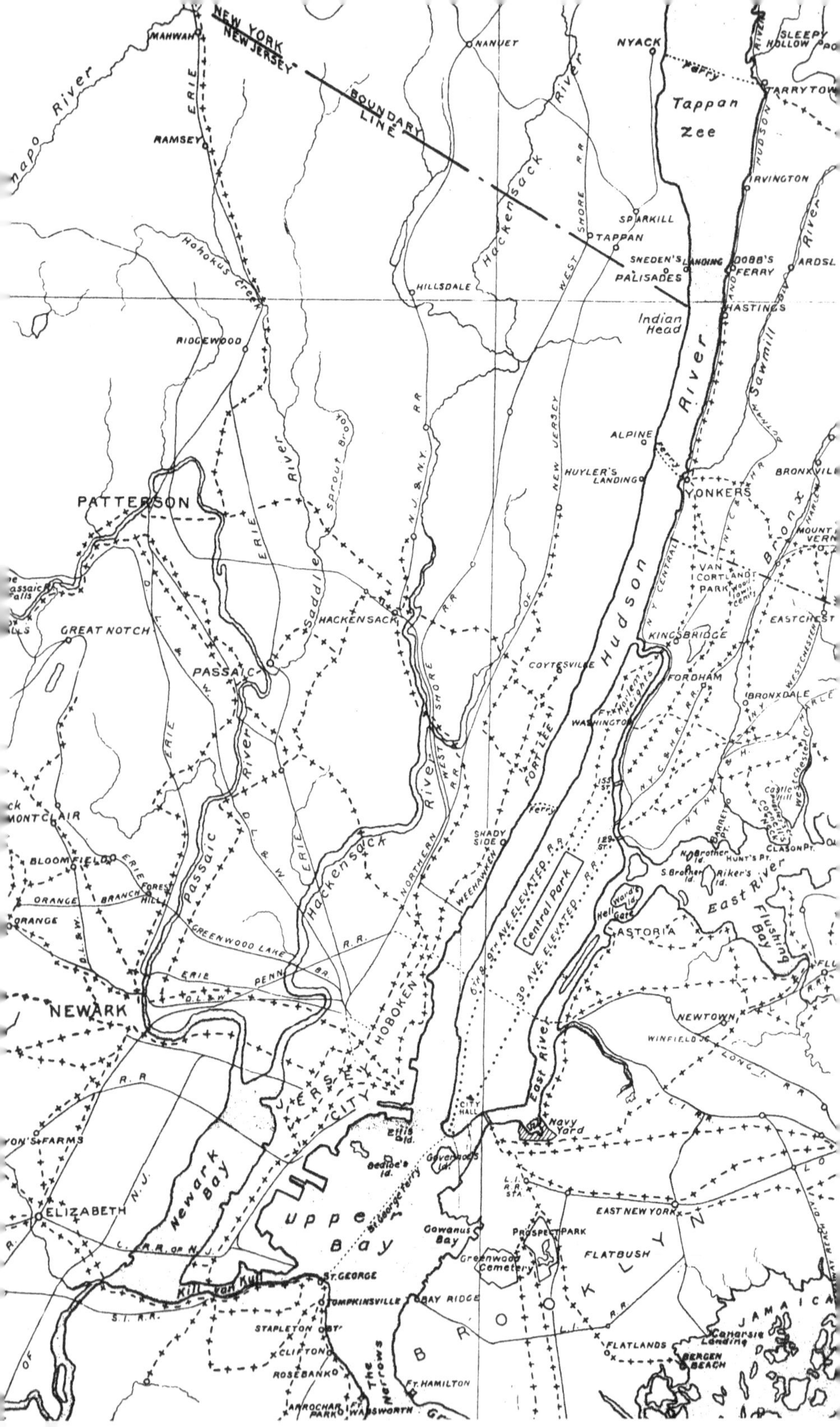

NEW YORK
NEW JERSEY
BOUNDARY LINE
MAHWAH
NANUET
NYACK
SLEEPY HOLLOW
Ferry
TARRYTOWN
Tappan Zee
RAMSEY
ERIE
Hackensack River
WEST SHORE R.R.
HUDSON
IRVINGTON
SPARKILL
TAPPAN
SNEDEN'S LANDING
DOBB'S FERRY
ARDSLEY
PALISADES
Hohokus Creek
HILLSDALE
HASTINGS
Indian Head
RIDGEWOOD
Sprout Brook
River
Sawmill
N.J. & N.Y. R.R.
NEW JERSEY
ALPINE
HUYLER'S LANDING
YONKERS
BRONXVILLE
PATTERSON
Saddle River
Hudson River
N.Y. CENTRAL
VAN CORTLANDT PARK
Woodlawn Cemy.
Bronx
MOUNT VERNON
GREAT NOTCH
HACKENSACK
WEST SHORE
KINGSBRIDGE
EASTCHESTER
PASSAIC
COYTESVILLE
FORDHAM
Ft. Washington
Harlem Heights
BRONXDALE
ERIE
Passaic River
FORT LEE
N.Y.C. & H.R. R.R.
WESTCHESTER
MONTCLAIR
155 ST.
Ferry
Castle Hill
Westchester Cr.
BLOOMFIELD
SHADY SIDE
129 ST.
N. Brother Id.
HUNT'S PT.
CLASON PT.
ORANGE
BRANCH
FOREST HILL
Hackensack River
NORTHERN R.R.
WEEHAWKEN
6th & 9th AVE. ELEVATED R.R.
Central Park
3d AVE. ELEVATED R.R.
S. Brother Id.
Riker's Id.
East River
ORANGE
GREENWOOD LAKE R.R.
Hell Gate
Ward's Id.
ASTORIA
Flushing Bay
ERIE
PENN. R.R.
D.L. & W.
NEWARK
HOBOKEN
NEWTOWN
WINFIELD JC.
LONG I. R.R.
JERSEY CITY
East River
CITY HALL
Navy Yard
Ellis Id.
Bedloe's Id.
Governor's Id.
L.I. R.R. STA.
ELIZABETH
N.J.
Newark Bay
Upper Bay
St. George Ferry
Gowanus Bay
EAST NEW YORK
PROSPECT PARK
Greenwood Cemetery
FLATBUSH
C. R.R. OF N.J.
ST. GEORGE
Kill von Kull
S.I. R.R.
TOMPKINSVILLE
BAY RIDGE
BROOKLYN
JAMAICA
STAPLETON
CLIFTON
The Narrows
FLATLANDS
Canarsie Landing
BERGEN BEACH
ROSEBANK
FT. HAMILTON
ARROCHAR PARK
FT. WADSWORTH

Upper Bay
Lower Bay
Sandy Hook Bay
Newark Bay
Jamaica Bay
Gravesend Bay
Gowanus Bay
Flushing Bay
Coney Island
Rockaway Inlet
Rockaway Beach
The Narrows
Central Park
East River
NEWARK
ELIZABETH
JERSEY CITY
HOBOKEN
BROOKLYN
ASTORIA
FLUSHING
NEWTOWN
EAST NEW YORK
FLATBUSH
FLATLANDS
PROSPECT PARK
Greenwood Cemetery
Navy Yard
CITY HALL
Ellis Id.
Bedloe's Id.
Governor's Id.
Barren Id.
ST. GEORGE
TOMPKINSVILLE
STAPLETON
CLIFTON
ROSEBANK
ARROCHAR PARK
FT. WADSWORTH
SOUTH BEACH
DONGAN HILLS
RICHMOND
NEW DORP
BAY RIDGE
FT. HAMILTON
Canarsie Landing
BERGEN BEACH
Kill Van Kull
STATEN ISLAND R.R.
S.I.R.R.
C. R.R. OF N.J.
SANDY HOOK
PORT MONMOUTH
KEYPORT
ATLANTIC HIGHLANDS
LEONARDO
WATER WITCH
Navesink Highlands
Chapel Hill Light
CHAPEL HILL
MIDDLETOWN
Navesink River
REDBANK
LITTLE SILVER
Shrewsbury R.
SHREWSBURY
EATONTOWN
LONG BRANCH CITY
ATLANTI
COUNTRY
SHOWING
LEADING
"OLD ROA
APPROXIMA
0 1 2 3 4 5 6 7

www.ingramcontent.com/pod-product-compliance
Lightning Source LLC
LaVergne TN
LVHW090544110826
845146LV00001B/15
* 9 7 8 1 4 2 5 5 8 6 1 5 7 *